CHRISTIANITY
AND
CIVIL SOCIETY

The Boston Theological Institute Series

The Boston Theological Institute (BTI) was incorporated in 1968. Its purpose is to further, in and through the constituent schools, theological education that pursues the truth in love, advances the unity of the Church, and brings closer the healing of broken humanity; to create and foster a milieu for dialogue, envisioning, and experimentation in theological inquiry and preparation for ministry; to contribute to the formation of church leaders with strong ecumenical commitment; to strengthen the schools for their respective missions and tasks, and to enhance the particular gifts of each of them; to promote and provide opportunities for faculty, curriculum, and program cooperation among the schools; and to provide resources for schools that are best made available through cooperation and coordination.

The BTI is comprised of Protestant, Roman Catholic, and Orthodox schools. Three of the schools are colleges and universities. The schools are Andover Newton Theological School, Boston College Department of Theology, Boston University School of Theology, Episcopal Divinity School, Gordon-Conwell Theological Seminary, Harvard University Divinity School, Holy Cross Greek Orthodox School of Theology, Saint John's Seminary, and Weston Jesuit School of Theology.

Books Published in the Series

Volume 1   *Human Rights and the Global Mission of the Church*

Volume 2   *One Faith, Many Cultures: Inculturation, Indigenization, and Contextualization*

Volume 3   *Reconciliation: Mission and Ministry in a Changing Social Order*, by Robert J. Schreiter

 Andover Newton
Theological School
Newton Centre, MA

 Episcopal Divinity
School
Cambridge, MA

 Holy Cross
Greek Orthodox
School of Theology
Brookline, MA

 Boston College
Department of Theology
Chestnut Hill, MA

 Gordon-Conwell
Theological Seminary
South Hamilton, MA

 Saint John's Seminary
Brighton, MA

 Boston University
School of Theology
Boston, MA

 Harvard Divinity
School
Cambridge, MA

 Weston Jesuit
School of Theology
Cambridge, MA

The Boston Theological Institute
Volume 4

CHRISTIANITY
AND
CIVIL SOCIETY

Theological Education
for Public Life

Rodney L. Petersen
Editor

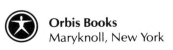
Orbis Books
Maryknoll, New York

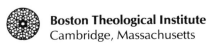
Boston Theological Institute
Cambridge, Massachusetts

BV4030
.C48
1995

Copyright © 1995 by the Boston Theological Institute, 210 Herrick Road, Newton, Massachusetts 02159.

The hymn "Sing Together on Our Journey" by Brian A. Wren was commissioned by the Boston Theological Institute in 1992. Orbis Books is grateful to the publishers for permission to reprint the words of the hymn. Words copyright © 1992 by Hope Publishing Company, Carol Stream, IL 60188. All rights reserved. Used by permission of Hope Publishing Company and Oxford University Press (London).

Published by Orbis Books, Maryknoll, New York 10545, U.S.A., and the Boston Theological Institute.

Manufactured in the United States of America.

Library of Congress Cataloging-in-Publication Data

Christianity and civil society : theological education for public life
 / Rodney L. Petersen, editor.
    p. cm. — (The Boston Theological Institute ; vol. 4)
  Papers presented at a symposium held to celebrate the 25th anniversary of the Boston Theological Institute, 1992-1993.
  Includes bibliographical references.
  ISBN 1-57075-009-2 (pbk.)
  1. Theology — Study and teaching — United States — Congresses. 2. Sociology, Christian — United States — Study and teaching — Congresses. 3. Church and the world — Congresses. I. Petersen, Rodney Lawrence. II. Boston Theological Institute. III. Series: Boston Theological Institute series : vol. 4.
BV4030.C48 1995
207'.73 — dc20
                                      94-43405
                                        CIP

Contents

Preface   *vii*

Foreword   *xiii*

Chapter 1
How to Understand the Church in an Individualistic Society   *1*
Robert N. Bellah

To Whom and How Are We Speaking?   **15**

Chapter 2
Social Theory and Christian Public Morality   **26**
            for the Common Life
Max L. Stackhouse

Chapter 3
A Black Church Challenge to and Perspective on   **42**
            Christianity and Civil Society
Lawrence H. Mamiya

Chapter 4
The Bible in Public Discourse   **62**
Richard Lovelace

What and How Are We Learning?   **77**

Chapter 5
The Foundation of Theological Knowledge   **89**
David Hollenbach

Chapter 6
Formation for Ministry in the Nineties   **99**
Brian O. McDermott

Competing Paradigms for Theological Education   *113*

Chapter 7
Elements for Effective Seminary-Based   *121*
      Urban Theological Education
Eldin Villafañe

Chapter 8
The Global Challenge   *137*
Kwok Pui-lan

Chapter 9
The Classical Challenge   *150*
Robert Cummings Neville

An Afterword
"Coming to Our Senses"   *161*
Robert N. Bellah.

Appendix
"Sing Together on Our Journey"   *166*
A Hymn for the Boston Theological Institute
Brian A. Wren, lyrics
Peter Cutts, music

Preface

Frederick Law Olmstead is credited with having put into place, to-gether with Charles Eliot and others, what has come to be called Boston's "Emerald Necklace." This band of green park and woodland that sur-rounds the Greater Boston area, always menaced by destruction or forfei-ture, provides space for reflection and recreation for the inhabitants of the city. Similarly we might think of the schools of the consortium known as the Boston Theological Institute (BTI), the seminaries, schools of theol-ogy, university divinity schools, and departments of religion in the Boston area, in such a way as offering on their diverse campuses space for the kind of personal and corporate religious or ethical reflection and re-crea-tion that is required to take us into the years that lie ahead.

If anything, relationships such as church and state, mission and iden-tity, or faith and science are more complex at the end of the twentieth century than they were at the beginning. Our societies are experiencing patterns of migration and dislocation that are unprecedented in recent memory. More is being asked of churches and communities of faith at a time when their leadership is coming under closer social scrutiny. The technological change that has reshaped our societies and the way we un-derstand things has had a profound effect upon religion, Christian faith, and theological education. In the face of such change, schools — and seminaries in particular (traditional places for seeding new ideas of indi-vidual and social transformation) — are being asked to bear the added burden of defining anew what it means to be a Christian minister at a time when the consensus of what this means and the constituency whom it serves is no longer self-evident for many.[1]

Freestanding seminaries, schools of theology, university divinity schools as well as departments of religion are being confronted by ques-tions of purpose, structure, and relationship.[2] Some churches are reassess-ing these connections and reaffirming them. Others now train their future leadership within their own local ecclesial communities.[3] Faculty and staff struggle with the need to meet the expectations of the university, the church, and the immediate needs of civil society.[4] Nevertheless, despite such uncertainties, seminaries and similar schools of instruction will con-tinue to perform their pedagogical role into the foreseeable future. This relationship between theological education and public life in the United States has a particular history in the Boston environs. As is true elsewhere, this has not always been a story of mutual support or cooperation.

Among the schools of the consortium in Boston, Andover Theological Seminary (now part of Andover Newton Theological School) is arguably the "mother" of all seminaries in the United States (1807), having been birthed in theological controversy out of Harvard College. Harvard, at first founded for the education of ministers and magistrates in the new Puritan colony (1636), yielded up its own Divinity School in 1811-16. In the course of things, Congregationalist Andover later merged with the generally Unitarian or nonsectarian Harvard Divinity School (1908) but, again in controversy, was "refounded" (1931/merged in 1965) with the Newton Theological Institute (1825), the oldest Baptist seminary in the United States, located on its own verdant hill across the Charles River. Both of these latter institutions played central roles in the Protestant mission movement and in the ensuing debate over the forms it should take. Episcopal Theological School (later, "Divinity" School after its merger with the Philadelphia Divinity School in 1974) dates back to 1831-36. Although the Anglican community in North America is considerably older than these dates indicate, the effects of Revolutionary radicalism reached like a long shadow into the nineteenth century so as to undermine perceptions of national loyalty and Anglican affiliation. Boston University's School of Theology, founded as The Seminary at Newbury, Vermont, and Concord, New Hampshire (1839), is the oldest Methodist seminary in the United States, moving to Boston in 1867 as the Boston Theological Seminary. Together with the aforenamed institutions it helped to birth the idea of voluntarism in the United States, setting a pattern of thinking, social organization, and political activity that is accepted as commonplace throughout the world today.

In 1863 Boston College was formed, one of the oldest Jesuit-funded universities in the United States, later to be enhanced through its relationship with Weston School of Theology (1922-32), which in 1994 specifically added the term "Jesuit" to its nomenclature. In 1883 Saint John's Seminary was founded as the Boston Ecclesiastical Seminary to serve the needs of the local Roman Catholic archdiocese. These institutions and their founding dates remind us of older controversies and shifting population patterns in nineteenth-century urban America. Shortly thereafter, evangelical Calvinists, dissatisfied with the current tenor of religious life in Boston, founded The Boston Missionary Training School in 1889, the forerunner of today's Gordon-Conwell Theological Seminary and its Center for Urban Ministerial Education. Eventually Hellenic College and Holy Cross Greek Orthodox School of Theology (founded in 1937 as the Greek

Orthodox Seminary for the Western Hemisphere) would move from Pomfret, Connecticut, to the Boston area (1946/7) and, with its campus nearly abutting the Olmstead Museum, complete our theological "Emerald Necklace."

It has been said that Christian ecumenism and ethical necessity brought the BTI into existence.[5] The significance of this statement is in the history of the churches. The Greek Orthodox and Latin churches separated in the eleventh century over issues of theology and culture. Division between the schools of Protestant and Roman Catholic derivation reaches back to debates over theology and ethics in the sixteenth century. Some of the aforenamed Protestant schools were founded explicitly to refute other schools that are now recognized as sister institutions. The very years of this century that have raised deepened questions of the churches have also seen the emergence of an ecumenical spirit that gained a new visibility and vocal constituency after Vatican II (1962-1965). This reassessment of Christian division has offered new opportunities for dialogue among the churches and common academic work among the faculties staffing their schools. Advances in biblical studies, theological expression, and liturgical perception made such ecumenism possible.[6] The social crises that have buffeted the human community over the past century have made an ethical mandate for such cooperation necessary. However, they have also made achieving such cooperation more elusive.[7] Nevertheless, the vision of a reconciled community and the need for a higher moral law in society have called for the joining together of theology and social theory. The purpose behind the coming together of the consortium in Boston, then, has been to envision and to work toward a healthy moral ecology of church and society but without compromise to issues of truth, understanding, or embodiment as such are recognized by the different communities of faith and understanding in this consortium.[8]

The articles in this book are a part of this vision. They grow out of a symposium held to celebrate the twenty-fifth anniversary of the BTI in 1992-1993. The date of their publication falls in the middle of a process to reassess the standards of accreditation among the schools of the Association of Theological Schools in the United States and Canada, the accrediting body of seminaries and schools of theology.[9] These anniversary articles offer in this context a renewed opportunity for conversation between the worlds of religion and sociology as such pertain to theological education. It is hoped that this volume might be both an acknowledgment of that anniversary as well as a contribution to discussion in the schools. Whether it is the schools of the BTI, other consortia, or freestanding theological seminaries, institutions like these strive to promote not only what is right, but also what is good.

In our litigious society many believe they understand what is right. Our sense of individuality encourages us to strive for it. Yet what is right needs always to be placed within the context of the good, particularly as we move beyond ourselves.[10] It is the very purpose of our theological communities, churches, and the voluntary societies that are derivative of such, to promote the common good. As such these communities and the schools that serve them are caught in a unique position between the claims of individuality and civil society. Along with families, churches, levels of political government, and other voluntary institutions we struggle to embody the good society. The BTI is a place to deal with the tensions involved in coming to know and to do the right in the context of the good. Known for its faculty and resources, this theological consortium is the only one to include as full members schools representing all of the major Christian traditions. In a world riven by social conflict, this is a good thing. The consortium in Boston has been graced as a community in profound ways. Together with its member universities, the schools of this consortium not only have access to the best of human learning and reflection, but also reach into communities of widely differing religious belief and practice. It is a microcosm of the learned world. Like the one who held the pearl of great price (Matt. 13:45) or the seer who beheld the gates to the apocalyptic Jerusalem (Rev. 21:21), the schools of the BTI have been blessed with a goodly heritage that may be fostered or dissipated (Matt. 7:6). Both in the agreement as well as in the disagreements of the constituencies of the schools, to wrestle like Jacob of old (Gen. 32:22-32) with what it means to participate in the reign of God on the cusp of the age is a good thing.

There are many for whom a word of thanks is in order for a volume like this. First are the members of the faculties of the BTI and its trustees, the students and staffs of the schools, most of whom have offered their continuing encouragement and support for the development of this educational endeavor. Next, I would like to give thanks to Brian Boisen, BTI Operations Manager, whose editorial assistance helped to pull this volume together. Finally, I wish to thank Fred L. Hofheinz and the Lilly Endowment, Inc., for assistance in helping to make our twenty-fifth anniversary possible. All of these and others have helped the schools of the BTI to remain ecumenical in conception and publicly engaged.

Rodney L. Petersen

Notes

1. Glenn T. Miller, "Professionals and Pedagogues: A Survey of Theological Education," in David Lotz, ed., *Altered Landscapes: Christianity in America, 1935-1985* (Grand Rapids: Eerdmans, 1989), pp. 189-208; and Barbara G. Wheeler and Edward Farley, eds., *Shifting Boundaries: Contextual Approaches to the Structure of Theological Education* (Louisville: W/JKP, 1991).

2. George M. Marsden documents the role of Christianity in American universities in *The Soul of the American University* (New York: Oxford University Press, 1994); cp. Jaroslav Pelikan, *The Idea of the University: A Reexamination* (New Haven: Yale University Press, 1991) and Marsden's review of it, "Christian Schooling: Beyond the Multiversity," *Christian Century* (7 October 1992): 873-75. Such discussion is a part of similar debate surrounding education today; see Michael B. Katz, *Reconstructing American Education* (Cambridge: Harvard University Press, 1987). In a now classic booklet on church and university, George H. Williams outlines five ministries to be performed by Christians to universities that can be applied to seminaries: (1) a recovery of the Christian legacy behind university education, (2) an emphasis upon those dimensions of natural theology which remind us of God's care for the natural order to mitigate loneliness and alienation, (3) the tightening of bonds of love and understanding in the human community, (4) an accent upon the ministry of the critic, or prophet, and (5) a continual arousal of the university of its judicial and critical role as a third force between church and state. See *The Word, the Church, and the University* (Cambridge: The Student Christian Movement in New England, 1964).

3. Earlier studies include those by Robert Kelly (1924), Niebuhr, Williams, and Gustafson (1957) and Welch (1971). See, e.g., Terrance W. Klein, "U.S. Culture and College Seminaries," *America* (18 June 1994): 16-21; Bruce L. Shelley, "The Seminaries' Identity Crisis," and an interview with David Allen Hubbard, "The Twenty-First Century Seminary," in *Christianity Today* (17 May 1993): 42-44, 45-46. Important ecclesiological considerations behind seminary education are offered by Judo Poerwowidagdo, *Towards the 21st Century: Challenges and Opportunities for Theological Education* (Geneva: WCC, 1994).

4. This tension is illustrated in ongoing analyses of theological education. See in the years of the founding of the BTI, Jesse H. Ziegler, "Future Trends in Theological Education," *N.E.X.U.S.*, vol. XII, no. 3 (Spring 1969). Successive volumes of *Theological Education*, published by the Association of Theological Schools in the United States and Canada, document and illustrate the issues that have preoccupied the theological schools in North America. See vol. XXX, no. 2 (Spring 1994) for issues of quality and accreditation under discussion and a bibliography of recent works on theological education.

5. Walter D. Wagoner, "The Boston Theological Institute: A Brook Farm Experiment?" *N.E.X.U.S., A Journal of the Boston University School of Theology*, vol. XII, no. 3 (1969): 17-20, 55. Wagoner, first executive director of the BTI, presents his hope in this article that the BTI might become the model seminary or graduate school of religion as he envisioned it earlier in "A Model for Theological Education," *N.E.X.U.S.* (1964): 31-36, 47. See on the relation between churches and seminary education, idem, "Seminary Clustering: The Way the Wind Blows," *American Ecclesiastical Review*, vol. CLIX, no. 6 (December 1968): 378-390.

6. Ruth Rouse and Stephen Neill, eds., *A History of the Ecumenical Movement, 1517-1948*, vol. 1 (Geneva: WCC, 1954; 1986 edition); and Harold E. Fey, ed., *The Ecumenical Advance: A History of the Ecumenical Movement, 1948-1968*, vol. 2 (Geneva: WCC, 1970/1986 edition).

7. Meredith Handspicker, "Faith and Order 1948-1968," in Harold E. Fey, ed., *The Ecumenical Advance: A History of the Ecumenical Movement, 1948-1968*, vol. 2 (Geneva: WCC, 1986, 2nd ed.), p. 147; the problems of social agenda alluded to by Handspicker, encountered in the World Council of Churches and ecumenical movement, are reflected upon in relation to the larger purposes of the ecumenical movement by Konrad Raiser, *Ecumenism in Transition: A Paradigm Shift in the Ecumenical Movement?* (Geneva: WCC, 1991) and Institute for Ecumenical Research, *Crisis and Challenge of the Ecumenical Movement: Integrity and Indivisibility* (Geneva: WCC, 1994).

8. Brian Boisen, "A Brief History of the First Twenty-Five Years of The Boston Theological Institute," submitted in partial fulfillment for the M.A. degree, Gordon-Conwell Theological Seminary (typescript, BTI, 1994). The Mission Statement of the BTI and important constitutive documents are summarized here, particularly manuscripts by John B. Coburn, "Theological Education: One Perspective and Two Proposals" (20 April 1966); and Walter G. Muelder, "The Boston Theological Institute and the Religious Leadership of Boston" (5 May 1968).

9. At the 39th biennial meeting of The Association of Theological Schools in the United States and Canada in June 1994, the theme was "The Good Theological School." The agenda for this meeting began a process of reassessing the standards for accreditation of member schools.

10. The need for a philosophical and moral framework in which to locate human rights in order to guarantee individual freedom and a common civic life is defended from a legal perspective by Mary Ann Glendon, *Rights Talk: The Impoverishment of Political Discourse* (New York: The Free Press, 1991), pp. 171-183. Harold J. Berman argues that our legal crisis is derivative of foundational philosophical issues, often related substantively to religion, that reflect contemporary social, economic, and political global transformations. See his study, *Law and Revolution: The Formation of the Western Legal Tradition* (Cambridge, MA: Harvard University Press, 1983).

Foreword

With the image of "the emerald necklace" in mind we can turn to the questions implied in the title of this book. First, what is, or has been, the place of Christianity in civil society in the United States? Second, what is, or should be, the nature of theological education in relation to this society? The issues are as controverted as they are related. The Constitution of the United States rejects the establishment of a religion in this country, yet charges that nothing be done to hinder the free exercise of it. Since the foundation of the Republic it has been held that stable republics and a virtuous people presuppose each other. Virtue, a term of classical origin meaning strength or power, came to imply ethical preeminence.

Whether through national origin or our history of religious revivals, a bond of mutual support was forged between the Christian movement, its people and churches, and definitions of private and public virtue in the nascent United States.[1] This role for Christian faith and the churches in promoting social virtue continues as educators seek support for theological education by affirming the distinctive contribution such schools make to society's cultural values and public policy.[2] However, with the fabric of religious life more complex than it has ever been, it is both less clear what this contribution is and more necessary that we discover what it can be.[3]

Divided by theology and polity, the denominational idea that different churches could be a part of one whole arose in this country. Denominationalism, reflected by the churches in their schools, promoted the conception that religion and American society stand together as fostered by this ideal of federated plurality. This permitted the existence of different ways of organizing religion under a broadly Christian conception of life. This organizational idea made possible social tolerance as fostered by the Enlightenment. There now developed a way to envision how plurality might be wed to the idea of a common conception of virtue with Christian lineaments in civil society. The questions that grew out of defining what is Christian, virtuous, and proper to the order of civil society have only deepened in our own time.

The early colleges and seminaries of this country were understood to be the nurseries of piety for the sake of the churches that stand within but also transcend civil society. These schools would help to define, clarify, and nurture the virtues that were needed to sustain the Republic. Many of the schools of the BTI date from this formative period of institutional develop-ment. In their diversity they represent different perspectives on the questions of who is to be involved in establishing that virtue, what is to be taught, and how such instruction is to occur. Each of these three issues — who, what, and how — is central to debate in the churches, in our universities, and in society generally. The schools of this consortium have had a considerable influence on these three sectors of American life. Yet it would be a miscon-strued task to see here either a misplaced exemplarism or a call to return to some form of Christian identity in the past. We are all called not to identities locked in the past, but to a process of continual conversion.[4]

It is the task of this volume to remind us that our national social agenda, whatever it may be, cannot be pursued apart from the virtues that make common life possible. It is to remind us as churches that questions of ecclesiology (the theory of the nature of the church) relate not only to the church's transcendent self-understanding but also to civil society. If churches are to continue to be seen as "ideal forms" of social organization, then it is mandatory that instruction in the seminaries be commensurate with that vision. Finally, this task of education is profoundly related to the canons of truth and demonstration as fostered by our universities. Never-theless, Christian truth, as grounded in Jesus Christ as the *logos* of God, is not different from general truth. Understanding this statement is the work of theological education. This work calls for our best efforts in apologetics and in philosophical correlation both in thought as well as in the manner in which we lead our lives.

How can we be the church today? More particularly, how can we be a church in a culture that appears to be founded upon and to celebrate individuality? This question lies behind those which began this forward. These are questions faced not only by churches that stand within and beyond the civil order, but also by every voluntary association.[5] Such issues have added weight given Adam Smith's argument that free-market systems, central to our social order, require for their own existence viable social safety nets. The Lockean ideal of individuality in the eighteenth century was, arguably, embedded in such a moral context. Churches and similar communities of faith, families, and voluntaristic societies provided for this social stability.[6] However, the way in which they are to be the context for and not become subsumed by that economic system is a di-lemma for us today and of concern to the papers in this volume.

In addressing the topic of what it means to be a church in an individual-istic culture, Robert N. Bellah draws our attention to an issue that is central to this problem and that lies behind that of the title of this book, questions of individuality and community. They are embedded in the three divisions that follow his paper: Who is to be involved in establishing that virtue? What is to be taught? How should such instruction occur? Or, "To Whom and How Are We Speaking?" "What and How Are We Learning?" and "Competing Paradigms for Theological Education." These three areas — who, what, and how — are three ways of addressing the question of the way in which virtue is promoted in the nation. In this sense the papers and structured remarks given in the context of the symposium that lies behind this volume are a vignette of a larger discussion in society today over the formation of national virtue and the nature of theological education.[7]

Bellah's address reminds us that this society was founded in an age that placed a new emphasis upon the individual. Such may be seen in the Declaration of Independence (1776), the public act by which the Second Continental Congress not only declared the thirteen North American colonies to be free and independent of Great Britain, but did so in a way that appealed to the individual conscience. Like the French Declaration of the Rights of Man (1789), modeled on the American Declaration, social forces and a philosophical tradition that reached back in the Western classical tradition and to the Renaissance were summarized in these documents. The argument of the American Declaration took on special significance in a land generally unfettered by European custom and open to the challenges of new frontiers. The formation of individuality in relation to community is briefly traced by Bellah: political theory in the Greek *polis*, its transmutation by the idea of the *ecclesia* in early Christianity, an institution separate from the cultic life of the *polis*, and in relation to the separate sphere granted religion and eventually the individual conscience in Europe since the Peace of Westphalia (1648). Religion, holistic in conception but now relegated to a private sphere in civil society, provides the basis for social conflict and cooperation.

We stand at the far end of the age opened up by Westphalia. What this may mean is not yet clear. Christianity as we have known it for almost five hundred years and ideas of individuality have been mutually supportive philosophies. This can be traced in Puritan debate, revivalist fire, and in pedagogy in the schools. Individualism and Christianity were virtually equated by the early years of the twentieth century.[8] Several of the schools presently in this consortium were part of that story. William James and Charles Eliot at Harvard University promoted the philosophical and institutional development of religiously suffused conceptions of individualism.[9] Across the river, at Boston University, Daniel Dorchester championed the freedom of the will while Bordon Parker Bowne promoted personalism, the identification of Christian theology with the autonomous experiences of the individual. Whether at Harvard, Boston University, or among the Andover liberals, various conceptions of individuality also promoted a social gospel seen to be key to the highest form of human community, God's immanent kingdom on earth.[10]

Individualism, heralded for its power of emancipation or expressive liberation, challenges our ability to live together in community. Yet it offers a way toward deeper communal authenticity. For communities of Christian expression, and particularly forms of Protestant reform since Martin Luther's Petrine appeal (Acts 5:29) to obey God rather than man, individualism has often been the only doctrine left when others have fallen away.[11] Thus, individuality, while promoting personal responsibility, can undermine community. A philosophy of individualism may, out of a spirit of liberality, allow each to do what seems right yet permit thereby communal disaster, which undermines the very possibility of meaningful individualism. Luther's appeal was for reform in community.[12] He believed that the church (if not all of society) was called to exhibit that community seen in the Trinity (John 17: 21). For Luther's heirs, together with other Christians, the church is the body of Christ in the world (Eph. 1:22-23), called to be a "chosen people," "royal priesthood," and "holy nation" (I Pet. 2:9; cf. Exod. 19:5).[13] It is a body not living for itself but in service to others. The question of the extent to which this church is to encompass all of society marks Christian debate from Luther's day to ours.[14] It is one that lies behind our political parties and process.[15]

This body represents the good society, the ideal form of civil expression. It is the church. As Bellah points out, the emergence of the idea of the *ecclesia* as separate from the *polis* underscored individuality in a new way, but thereby created a problem for civil society. Was the church to be one with society as in the Constantinian state? Or was it to be separated from the state as a prophetic voice, tolerated or persecuted, ignored or followed depending upon the politics of the day? In either case a prophetic role could be opened up for the individual, one granting heightened autonomy, but through the terms of a covenant, or contract, as laid out in Christian theology. The "good society" is that society shaped by the church, heir of God's covenantal promise to Abraham (Gen. 12:1-3) and David (II Sam. 7), envisioned prophetically by Daniel (Dan. 7:27), implied in the Apocalypse (13, 18-21) and conjoined with classical overtones in European political theory.

In his collaborative study, *Habits of the Heart*, Bellah and his coauthors explore a means for recovering a vision of the good through recourse to that "second language" beyond and prior to contemporary psychological and managerial expression, the deeper language derivative of republican virtue and biblical insight.[16] In his subsequent book, *The Good Society*,[17] Bellah seeks to talk about the "good" by recognizing the ways that we live through institutions, families, churches, and other economic or political arrangements. By impoverishing these corporate entities, we impoverish ourselves. We live in a society in need of a new covenant or social contract.[18] Accepted patterns of individuality and community appear increasingly dysfunctional. The role of religion to define the "good" and to legitimize the quest for what is "right" is presently misconstrued, misunderstood, or in sectarian retrenchment.

Bellah offers three approaches to this tension. First is the positive value placed upon individualism, understood as autonomy, illustrated in the work of Jürgen Habermas.[19] Here religion, formerly of value but now conceived of as socially regressive, interferes with the autonomy of individuality. Churches represent cultural eddies frozen out of the mainstream of critical social development. The individual, responding to reason alone, participates in the construction of the humane civil order. Bellah questions this approach, both its implied philosophical anthropology and its conception of rationality. In his opinion it may contribute to patterns of social conformity that misplace or overlook the human need for orientation, which religion alone provides.[20]

A second way to understand the church in an individualistic culture offers a more critical analysis of individualism and provides a more positive place for the church in society. Here individualism offers not only the means toward narrow self-interest, but also a path toward self-authenticity. Drawing this nuanced understanding of individualism from the work of philosopher and political scientist Charles Taylor,[21] Bellah illustrates the interdependence in which this conception of individuality stands with respect to others. Individualism, a pervasive element recognized in our culture by Alexis de Tocqueville,[22] has as its darker side a consumerist attitude that, as seen in religion, implies as Bellah writes "the idea that each individual chooses his or her religious affiliation without any external influence, religion being quintessentially a private matter." This attitude contradicts the existence of religious communities. However, the perception of its accuracy supports legal scholar Stephen Carter's argument that the "trivialization" of religion in contemporary American public life is detrimental to our civil society.[23]

The third approach rejects the assumptions of modernity and turns to the self-defined Christian community as offering its own self-authenticating reason for being apart from a civic or social justification. Since its inception the church has understood its being to transcend this world and whatever society in which it is found. In fact, it is the shape of a more real social order than that in which it resides. To describe this relationship G. K. Chesterton coined the phrase, "a nation with the soul of a church."[24] It is a perspective that may be found in the narrative theologies of George Lindbeck, Stanley Hauerwas, and John Milbank. Rationality, as defined by the Enlightenment, is qualified by the narrative of scripture. Rather than describing Chistianity from the world's point of view, the world is described from a Christian perspective. Christians themselves may come to feel as if they are "resident aliens," those who are in this world, but not of it.

While sympathetic, Bellah scores the narrativist for failing to show how one gains entry to the self-defined story, a point raised in this volume by ethicist David Hollenbach, S.J., and his commentator Ronald F. Thiemann. Second, the narrativist fails to deal fully with the totality of one's context, compromising any pure interpretation of a text. Third, since Westphalia and the consequent end of the Constantinian state with its privileged place for religion, we cannot be said to be "resident aliens" in the true sense of the term. Our problem is not with a powerful religious establishment, but with the privatization and subsequent trivialization of religion in society. Drawing upon elements of the narrativist perspective, Bellah brings its positive assessment of the church to bear in argument upon the consumerist approach to religion in his second perspective on the nature of the church in an individualistic culture: By applying the market metaphor to all of life, objective morality and patterns of personal interdependence are broken down. This cultural disengagement and its implicit anomie, or loss of norms, represent an elevation of autonomy as almost the only good.

This heightened conception of autonomy is not, Bellah writes, "a fully adult virtue." Locating individuality in a stage of development analogous to the maturation of personal identity, Bellah turns the Enlightenment on its head by arguing that Kant's "coming of age" is not the end of adulthood, but the end of adolescence and the beginning of the life of a responsible adult. The significance for the church is that "we cannot just declare ourselves to be resident aliens" and make an end of social engagement. Rather, by drawing upon the wellsprings of Christian thought, we must become engaged in a critique of a culture "that is incapable of offering even its own professed goods of authenticity and autonomy." This call to engagement is more than a call to Christian "identity," a term laden with restorationist and nativist overtones. It is a call to a deep conversion that is individually conceived and socially committed.[25] It is one that encapsulates within it all of the tensions with which we are confronted by the multiplicity of Christian narratives.[26] Can one understanding of Christian truth express the fullness of its larger narrative? Can churches capably embody it?[27] Such are the questions of a new "Christian Realism" at the near opening of the twenty-first century.

Modernity and individuality have posed special problems for theological education. Ironically, both principles have come from, or at least grown up together with, the development of Protestantism and are accorded validity at some level by most Christian communities. In the United States, with its separation of church and state, the place of theological education will remain one of tension as its disciplines are susceptible to redefinition and absorption in other academic curricula or to marginalization as its own curriculum fails to be perceived as contributing centrally to public life. To the extent that the church is problematic for civil society, so too will be theological education. The effect of a diminished moral voice upon values in society is a part of the debate on religion and values in public life today.[28] The effect of the weakening of intermediate structures, like the church in and alongside of civil society, is not only a cultural crisis but poses a central challenge to political theory and traditional patterns of legitimacy in the United States.[29] Churches bearing an ecclesiology that understands the church to be coterminous with society will see little continuing purpose in a distinctive theological education.

The place of theological education in society is derivative of questions of church and state. This can be traced through the history of theological education.[30] However, it is more particularly shaped by an understanding of the church. To the extent that ecclesiology becomes more defined and particular, so too will theological education. The idea of the *ecclesia* as "an assembly which has come into existence through a call" might also be applied to theological education.[31] The nature of that "call" has been heard differently in sectors of contemporary Protestantism,[32] Roman Catholicism,[33] and among the Orthodox churches.[34] The shape of theological education varies with the tonality of the call. Issues of particularity and universality, determinism and freedom of the will, an apophatic (the unknowability of God, cf. Matt. 11:27) or kataphatic (God who is clearly seen) theology were embedded in the Great Schism between the Greek and Latin churches (1054).[35] Such issues have been made real again in light of the globalization of theological education.[36] We continue to live with the rupture of the Latin Church in the sixteenth century, the consequent Protestant and Catholic reforms and subsequent divisions over theological and moral issues as they are seen to be constitutive of the church.[37] As consortia like the BTI have emerged, opportunities exist for healing the brokenness of the church.[38] To the extent that churches are the "good societies" that they seek to be, that healing will extend into public life. However, consortia of theological schools are also easily marginalized by the traditions themselves and their schools, or marginalize themselves to the extent that consortia or their constituencies fail to take into consideration the depth and subtlety of the issues that divide the churches.[39]

Theological education is also related to contemporary crises in the general academic community. This should not surprise us given the history of the relationship between higher education, once so dependent upon the church, and theological education.[40] While their differences are grounded in questions of professional development and appropriate curriculum, it was seldom conceived of by seminaries, schools of theology, university divinity schools, or even early departments of religion, that their ethos or even philosophy would be at odds with that of the university. To discover that such is often the case today is to discover a position that ranges from distrust to open hostility. However, clarification and constructive activity are possible. There are important areas in which consortia in particular can provide space for conversation to occur. These areas include questions of comparative theology, or interreligious dialogue, and matters of faith and science.[41] Together with questions of ecumenical reception and social tensions derivative of contemporary civil society, these issues constitute an agenda for theological consortia.

How will theological education continue to evolve in the future? It is, of course, the point of this volume to raise up a chorus of voices to help answer this question. Consortia have developed in the last years of the twentieth century to help shape that future.[42] In line with what has already been sketched out, consortia can promote the idea of a "principled pluralism" in society in dealing with the civil, ecclesial, and pedagogical issues with which we are confronted.[43] By the way in which they model the pursuit of theological and religious understanding, they promote or impede attitudes that make for social peace or conflict. Through consortia, schools once grounded in division can lead the way toward a multiculturalism grounded in principled dialogue.[44] Perhaps this is the institutional answer to Bellah's conclusion that all three of the answers to the question of the church in an individualistic culture are required as we move from adolescent self-preoccupation to adult responsibility.

Rodney L. Petersen

Notes

1. William Lee Miller, "The Moral Project of the American Founders," in James Davison Hunter and Os Guinness, eds., *Articles of Faith, Articles of Peace: The Religious Liberty Clauses and the American Public Philosophy* (Washington, DC: The Brookings Institution, 1990), pp. 17-39; and Harold J. Berman, *Faith and Order: The Reconciliation of Law and Religion* (Atlanta: Scholars Press, 1993), pp. 1-20, on the religious dimensions of law; cp. Martin Marty, "Religion and the Constitution: The Triumph of Practical Politics," *Christian Century* (23-30 March 1994): 316-327.

2. See the *Corporate Case Resource Document: Making the Case of Investment in Theological Education*, published by the Association of Theological Schools in the

United States and Canada with funding from Lilly Endowment, Inc., June 1994. A definition of virtue with enduring significance in the West and for Christian moral theology was outlined by Cicero for his son, Marcus, in *De Officiis* [Concerning Moral Duties], a handbook on Stoic morality. See vol. XXI, translated by Walter Miller (Cambridge, MA: Harvard University Press, 1975), I.iv-viii.

3. The mark of this change in religious identity can be traced from a largely Protestant heritage at the nation's founding to the mid-twentieth century with the appearance of the sociological study by Will Herberg, *Protestant, Catholic, Jew* (Garden City: Doubleday, 1955), equating these three faiths with establishment status. The work of Diana L. Eck and the Pluralism Project at Harvard University and similar programs in the Boston University School of Theology illustrate the further extension of this religious pluralism in the United States. See her book, *Encountering God: A Spiritual Journey from Bozeman to Banaras* (Boston: Beacon Press, 1993), pp. 22-44, 166-231; and *World Religions in Boston: A Guide to Communities and Resources*, ed. with introductions by Diana L. Eck (Cambridge, MA: Harvard University Press, 1974). Phillip E. Hammond contends that recent social revolutions have yielded an increased emphasis on personal autonomy and have removed the churches from their traditional role as institutions mediating accepted values in American life; see his *Religion and Personal Autonomy: The Third Disestablishment* (Columbia: University of South Carolina Press, 1992). Whatever the validity of Hammond's argument, a growing complexity in religious demography is found across the American landscape, which makes a common moral voice more difficult to discern.

4. The challenges of ethnic, racial, and other tribal integralisms face us today. See *Religious Resurgence in the Modern World: Social, Economic and Political Implications*, of the *Journal of Interdisciplinary Studies*, vol. IV, no. 1/2, 1994. The point is well made for the Protestant and Catholic churches by the French Reformed-Catholic study group known as *Groupe des Dombes*, in *For the Conversion of the Churches* (Geneva: WCC, 1993).

5. James Luther Adams as edited by J. Ronald Engel, *Voluntary Associations: Sociocultural Analyses and Theological Interpretation* (Chicago: Exposition Press, 1986); see "Voluntary Associations in Search of Identity," and "The Voluntary Principle in the Forming of American Religion," pp. 160-170 and 171-200, respectively. Such issues are especially pertinent given the recently reemphasized interest in the private sector. See Peter Drucker, *The New Realities* (San Francisco: Harper and Row, 1989), p. 195.

6. Herbert Wallace Schneider, ed., *Adam Smith's Moral and Political Philosophy* (New York: Harper and Row, 1970). Discussions on the nature of community and economic organization are legion; see Donald Meyer, *The Protestant Search for Political Realism, 1919-1941* (Middletown, CT: Wesleyan University Press, 2nd ed., 1988); and Oliver Williams, C.S.C., and John Houck, eds., *The Judeo-Christian Vision and the Modern Corporation* (Notre Dame: University of Notre Dame Press, 1982).

7. The Association of Theological Schools in the United States and Canada, in beginning the process of a reconsideration of the nature of seminary accreditation, sketched four areas of study, outlined by articles appearing in *Theological Education*, vol. XXX, no. 2 (Spring 1994). These are: Donald Senior and Timothy Weber, "What Is the Character of Curriculum Formation and Cultivation of Ministerial Leadership in the Good Theological School?" (pp. 17-33); Philip S. Keane and Melanie A. May, "What Is the Character of Teaching, Learning, and the Scholarly Task in the Good

Theological School?" (pp. 35-44); James H. Evans, Jr., and Jane I. Smith, "What Is the Character of the Institutional Resources Needed for the Good Theological School?" (pp. 45-59); and Robert E. Cooley and David L. Tiede, "What Is the Character of Administration and Governance in the Good Theological School?" (pp. 61-69). Additional issues and a helpful bibliography are included in the volume.

8. George M. Marsden illustrates this with specific focus in the thought of William Rainey Harper, in *The Soul of the American University*, pp. 249-250.

9. Marsden, *Soul of the American University*, pp. 181-195. Additional examples may be seen in such persons as Octavius B. Frothingham (1822-95) in William R. Hutchison, *The Modernist Impulse in American Protestantism* (Durham: Duke University Press, 1992), pp. 33-39. On the history of HDS, see George H. Williams, ed., *The Harvard Divinity School: Its Place in Harvard University and in American Culture* (Boston: Beacon Press, 1954), and idem, *Divinings* (forthcoming, Pilgrim Press, 1995). On personalism and its place at Boston University, see Paul Deats, Jr., ed., *Toward a Discipline of Social Ethics: Essays in Honor of Walter George Muelder* (Boston: Boston University Press, 1972).

10. In this theological context ideas about the relationship between individuality and community were driven by Immanuel Kant's work. In *Religion within the Limits of Reason Alone*, Kant argues that the individual has a duty to elevate himself or herself as much as possible but qualifies this to some extent by his idea of the ethical commonwealth. To the extent that this qualification remains that which is made for the "weaker brother," the way is opened toward egocentric autonomy. See James M. Gustafson's discussion in *Ethics from a Theocentric Perspective*, vol. 2, *Ethics and Theology* (Chicago: University of Chicago Press, 1984), pp. 121-125. The significance of this is seen in Gustafson's discussion of Martin Luther King, Jr., pp. 124-125.

11. Karl Holl, *What Did Luther Understand by Religion?* ed. by James Luther Adams and Walter F. Bense (Philadelphia: Fortress Press, 1977).

12. Martin Luther, "The Right and Power of a Christian Congregation [*Gemeinde*] or Community [*Versammlung*] To Judge all Teaching and To Call, Appoint, and Dismiss Teachers," *WA* 11, 4011-16; *Works*, ed. by H. E. Jacobs and Adolph Spaeth (Philadelphia: Westminster Press), vol. 4, pp. 75-85; see in George H. Williams, *The Radical Reformation*, vol. XV, *Sixteenth Century Essays and Studies* (Kirksville, MO: Sixteenth Century Journal Press, 1992), pp. 144-148.

13. Classic expressions on the models of the church are seen in Paul S. Minear, *Images of the Church in the New Testament* (Philadelphia: Westminster Press, 1960) and in Avery Dulles, S.J., *Models of the Church* (New York: Doubleday, 1974).

14. Rodney L. Petersen, *Preaching in the Last Days: The Theme of "Two Witnesses" in the Sixteenth and Seventeenth Centuries* (New York: Oxford University Press, 1993), pp. 120-261.

15. Michael Walzer, *The Revolution of the Saints: A Study in the Origins of Radical Politics* (Cambridge: Harvard University Press, 1966).

16. Robert N. Bellah et al., *Habits of the Heart* (Berkeley: University of California Press, 1985).

17. Robert N. Bellah with Richard Madsen, William M. Sullivan, Ann Swidler, and Steven M. Tipton, *The Good Society* (New York: Alfred A. Knopf, 1991).

18. Idem, *The Broken Covenant: American Civil Religion in Time of Trial* (New York: Seabury Press, 1975/1992); on the background to the theological idea of the covenant, Charles S. McCoy and J. Wayne Baker, *Fountainhead of Federalism: Hein-*

rich Bullinger and the Covenantal Tradition (Louisville: W/JKP, 1991).

19. Jürgen Habermas, *Habermas, Modernity, and Public Theology* (New York: Crossroad, 1992).

20. The nature of such conformity is studied by Martin Marty, *A Nation of Behavers* (Chicago: University of Chicago Press, 1976); cp. William Whyte, *The Organization Man* (1956) and Chris Argyris, *Personality and Organization* (1957). See Hans Küng, *Freud and the Problem of God* (New Haven: Yale University Press, 1990). The author argues that the search for meaning, rather than constituting a neurosis, is central to our understanding of what it means to be human (pp. 127-158).

21. Charles Taylor, *Sources of the Self: The Making of the Modern Identity* (Cambridge: Harvard University, 1989), pp. 495-521; and idem, *The Ethics of Authenticity* (Cambridge: Harvard University Press, 1992).

22. Alexis de Tocqueville, *Democracy in America*, ed. by R. D. Heffner (New York: New American Library, 1956), Book II, sec. 27-28.

23. Stephen L. Carter, *The Culture of Disbelief: How American Law and Politics Trivialize Religious Devotion* (New York: Basic Books, 1993), p. 36; cf. Hannah Arendt, *Crises of the Republic* (New York: Harcourt Brace Jovanovich, 1969).

24. Sidney E. Mead has picked up this phrase and developed it in "The Nation with the Soul of a Church," in *American Civil Religion*, ed. by Russell E. Richey and Donald G. Jones (New York: Harper & Row, 1974), pp. 45-75.

25. Paths of *koinonia*, *marturia*, and *diakonia* are sketched by Judo Poerwowidagdo in relation to contemporary challenges, in "Global Phenomena and the Local Imperatives," in *Towards the 21st Century: Challenges and Opportunities for Theological Education*, pp. 24-49; see the essays in George Papademetriou, ed., *Essays in Honor of the 100th Anniversary of Father Georges Florovsky* (Brookline: Holy Cross Greek Orthodox Press, 1995).

26. Commenting on the traditional four marks of the church, the authors who call themselves *Groupe des Dombes* write about the way in which the church might be reconceived: "The Christian confessions must give up the idea of *unity* as uniformity or as a federation; of *holiness* as a canonization of devotion to the ecclesial *res publica* or contrariwise as praise of virtues that are only private; of *catholicity* as a universalism conquering or holding on to conquered territories; of *apostolicity* as a literal return to origins or repetition of beginnings." See *For the Conversion of the Churches*, p. 79.

27. Christian Realism in the mid-twentieth century foreshadowed aspects of this problem as against a theological adaptation of Christian theology to modernism, explicit immanentism, and religiously-based progressivism. See Reinhold Neibuhr, *Moral Man and Immoral Society: A Study in Ethics and Politics* (New York: C. Scribner's, 1932) and the wider critique by Neo-Orthodoxy.

28. Glenn Tinder asks the question, "Can We Be Good without God?" *The Atlantic Monthly* (December 1989): 69-85. He summarizes current literature, arguing the need for transcendence. The relation of "religion and values in public life" is the focus of current endeavor at Harvard Divinity School. See the journal of that title, vol. 2, no. 2 (Winter 1994) and note the conversation between Michael Walzer and Ronald Thiemann.

29. Apart from such structures, Hannah Arendt warns of the rise of totalitarianism through the creation of an "atomistic mass" directly dependent upon central government, in *The Origins of Totalitarianism* (New York: Harcourt Brace, 1951); Carter, *Culture of Disbelief*, p. 36.

30. Patrick Henry, ed., *Schools of Thought in the Christian Tradition* (Philadelphia: Fortress Press, 1984). A political dimension to this can be seen in Petersen, *Preaching in the Last Days*, pp. 30-40, 200-226.

31. Karl Barth, *Credo* (New York: Charles Scribner's, 1962), p. 137 as cited by Judo Poerwowidagdo in *Towards the 21st Century: Challenges and Opportunities for Theological Education*, p. 9.

32. Examples include Edward Farley, *Theologia: The Fragmentation and Unity of Theological Education* (Philadelphia: Fortress Press, 1983), John C. Fletcher, *The Futures of Protestant Seminaries* (Washington, DC: The Alban Institute, 1983), and Joseph C. Hough, Jr., and John B. Cobb, *Christian Identity and Theological Education* (Chico, CA: Scholars Press, 1985). On historical change, see George H. Williams, "Translatio Studii: The Puritans' Conception of Their First University in New England, 1636," in *Archiv für Reformationsgeschichte*, vol. LVII, no. 1/2 (1966): 152-181; and C. C. Goen, "Changing Conceptions of Protestant Theological Education in America," *Foundations*, vol. IV (October 1963).

33. Examples include the authoritative apostolic exhortation, *Pastores Dabo Vobis* (Rome, 25 March 1992); *Developments of Pastoral Care for Vocations in the Local Churches: Experiences of the Past and Programmes for the Future*, by the International Congress of Bishops and Others with Responsibilities for Ecclesiastical Vocations (Vatican, 10-16 May 1981); and Katarina Schuth, O.S.F., *Reason for Hope: The Futures of Roman Catholic Theologates* (Wilmington: Michael Glazier, 1989).

34. Examples include Alkiviadis C. Calivas, "Orthodox Theology and Theologians: Reflections on the Nature, Task, and Mission of the Theological Enterprise," *The Greek Orthodox Theological Review*, vol. 37, nos. 3-4 (1992): 275-307; Metropolitan Damaskinos of Switzerland, "La Mission actuelle de l'Orthodoxie," *Episkepsis*, 23.480 (30 June 1992): 7-18; and Daniel Ciobotea, "Spiritual Theological Formation through the Liturgical Life of the Church," in *Ministerial Formation*, no. 47 (Geneva: WCC, 1989): 12-20.

35. Such issues are touched upon in Kallistos [Timothy] Ware, *The Orthodox Church* (New York: Penguin, 1963), pp. 58-61.

36. The term *globalization* is one that has been of focused study in theological education since at least 1980. See Robert J. Schreiter, "The ATS Globalization and Theological Education Project: Contextualization from a World Perspective," *Theological Education*, vol. XXX, no. 2 (1994): 81-88. Additional reference might be made to *Theological Education*, vol. XXIX, no. 2 (Spring 1993), "Globalization and Theological Education"; *International Review of Mission*, vol. LXXXI, no. 321 (January 1992), "Education in Mission"; James M. Phillips and Robert T. Coote, eds., *Toward the 21st Century in Christian Mission* (Grand Rapids: Eerdmans, 1993); Lamin Sanneh, *Translating the Message: The Missionary Impact on Culture* (Maryknoll: Orbis, 1989); and Ruy O. Costa, ed., *One Faith, Many Cultures: Inculturation, Indigenization, and Contextualization* (Maryknoll: Orbis/Cambridge: BTI, 1988). On the relation of the term "globalization" in theological education to Christian mission, see Dana L. Robert, "From Missions to Mission to Beyond Missions: The Historiography of American Protestant Foreign Missions since World War II," in *International Bulletin of Missionary Research*, vol. 18, no. 4 (October 1994): 146-162.

37. Ernst Troeltsch, *The Social Teaching of the Christian Churches*, tr. by Olive Wyon (London: Allen and Unwin, 1950).

38. See the nine elements of the contemporary ecumenical crisis as summarized by

the Institute for Ecumenical Research, in *Crisis and Challenge*, pp. 4-22.

39. Walter D. Wagoner, "The Boston Theological Institute: A Brook Farm Experiment?" As cited earlier, Wagoner writes of the importance of four factors: clear ecumenical purpose, sensitivity to different religious traditions, the importance of an independent financial base, and a foundation in faculty alliances (pp. 19-20, 55).

40. George M. Marsden, *The Soul of the American University*, pp. 3-9.

41. Judith A. Berling, "Theological Consortia: The Creative Space between Church and University," in Joseph Mitsuo Kitagawa, ed., *Religious Studies, Theological Studies, and the University Divinity School* (Atlanta: Scholars Press, 1992): 171-181.

42. James W. Fraser, Monica Ellen Friar, Barbara Anne Radtke, Thomas J. Savage, S.J., and Katarina Schuth, O.S.F., *Cooperative Ventures in Theological Education* (New York: University Press of America, 1989); on difficulties cooperative work has faced within the BTI itself, see Brian Boisen, "A Brief History of the First Twenty-Five Years of The Boston Theological Institute."

43. The term "principled pluralism" is taken from Os Guinness, *The American Hour: A Time of Reckoning and the Once and Future Role of Faith* (New York: The Free Press, 1993). His use of this term implies the American policy of giving all religious convictions an equal playing field. It is his conviction that this practice will yield a spiritually healthy society.

44. Marsden, *The Soul of the American University*, pp. 214-15. The idea behind a "principled pluralism" might be traced back to Abraham Kuyper, theologian, philosopher, and politician in the Netherlands at the end of the nineteenth century. Delivering the Stone Lectures at Princeton in 1898, Kuyper argued on behalf of publicly supported multiple school systems on the basis of the idea that Christians might draw different conclusions from science than non-Christians, a view that supported the unity of truth but recognized the signficance of diversity in perspective.

1

How to Understand the Church in an Individualistic Society

Robert N. Bellah

In considering the theme of "Christianity and Civil Society," or more specifically the place of theological education in public life, I will focus on the meaning of the church in an individualistic culture. To do this I wish to suggest that we consider three perspectives on the question, taking each of them seriously if we are to find a viable understanding of the church that will inform both theological education and the role of Christianity in public life.

I would like to start with a contemporary Enlightenment position, that of Jürgen Habermas. Habermas is not unsympathetic to religion — indeed he gives it considerable importance in his notion of social evolution. Religion, in his view, has made a significant contribution to the progressive sequence of enhanced social learning capacities, which is what he means by social evolution. It is just that with the advent of modernity, religion's role has come to an end. Its conception of the sacred and of religious truth is too "frozen," too closed to critical examination, to be viable in the modern world.

Conceptions of the sacred and of religious tradition, according to Habermas, need to be "thawed" or "liquefied" if we are to have a genuinely modern culture based on undistorted communication, which Habermas defines as the open argumentative redemption of validity claims concerning issues of truth, rightness, and authenticity where the best argu-

Robert N. Bellah is Maxine Elliot Professor of Sociology at the University of California, Berkeley.

ment carries the day. From Habermas's perspective the pernicious survival of frozen religious forms blocks free communication and so interferes with the autonomy of individuals. Since the autonomy of the
individual is the highest good of Enlightenment modernity, religion is
clearly a danger.[1]

Without being able to put it so elegantly, many of our friends — particularly in the university but quite broadly in the well-educated middle
class — would argue that if religion confines itself to private life and the
expressive concerns of individuals, eschewing any claim to influence public life and public decisions, then it may have a justifiable and harmless
role to play in contemporary society, for those who continue to be interested in it.

This understanding of religion, commoner than we might think within as
well as without the churches, is not only the result of cultural forces associated with the Enlightenment. It is rooted in critical social changes associated with the emergence of modern society. All the terms that we
confidently use in discussion of the issues raised in this symposium —
such as religion, civil society, and the state — are products of a specifically
European history that it might be useful for us to consider, even if briefly,
before we go on.

Many people know that sociology is a quite recent term, coined by
Auguste Comte in 1837. We are perhaps not so aware of the fact that
society and religion are also, in their current meanings, quite modern
terms. Society is not only a new term but it is only intelligible as a contrast
term to two other relatively new terms: state and economy. I might remind
you that the ancient Greek word *polis* — from which comes a rich variety
of modern words, examples in English being politics, policy, police, and
many others — meant simultaneously city, state, society, and community,
so that we have no modern word that really translates it. Economy is also
Greek in origin, but in ancient Greek it meant household management —
economy in our sense was for them just one more aspect of the *polis*.

It was the rise of the modern Western nation-state, beginning in the
seventeenth century but maturing in the eighteenth and nineteenth centuries, that gave rise to the notion of society as something different from the
state. In early notions of "civil society," society and economy were not
clearly differentiated, but with the rise of industrialization the realms of
society and economy came to be seen as different from each other and
both of them as different from the state. It is interesting to note that
religion is also a term that took on its modern meaning at about the same
time the terms state, society, and economy were differentiating out from
each other.

If we go back to ancient Greece, religion is simply the cultic life of the *polis*, and not conceivable outside it. It is true that Christianity developed the idea of the church, interestingly enough borrowing the word *ecclesia*, the assembly of the citizens, from Greek political life to denominate itself. But the church, though having an independent identity (a concept only barely foreshadowed by earlier Greek religious associations), was nonetheless very much embedded in the whole of society. Religion as a separate sphere was in considerable part itself the product of the rise of the nation-state system, which in turn was in part a reaction to the religious wars between Protestants and Catholics in the early seventeenth century.

From the time of the Peace of Westphalia in 1648 religion was seen as a matter for each state to decide for itself and no longer a valid cause of international warfare.[2] From this idea there developed in the eighteenth century the idea that religion should be separate from the state altogether, being a matter of individual conscience. Thus emerged the idea of religion as something separate from other spheres and rooted in the experience and conscience of individuals, which most of us still take for granted in our modern usage of the term.

Serious conceptual difficulties occur when we take these terms, arising from a specific history, but now common not only to social science but to modern discourse around the world, and apply them as universal categories. When we look at tribal societies that do not have a differentiated state or economy, etc., then we can plainly see that religion cannot be a separate sphere of largely private experience. Rather religion permeates and expresses the whole way of life of the tribal people. When we seek to study their rituals we soon find we are learning about their kinship relations, the exchange of goods, the hierarchies of power and influence (such as they are), and many other things. Indeed singling out something we call "religion" from other things that tribal people do may be convenient for our analysis, but it is reading into their way of life a category that is not separated in that way by the people we are studying.

When we look at what are frequently called the world religions (which I have called the historic religions), we find significant differences from tribal religions in that there are written religious texts, groups of priests or religious teachers, religious associations and schools — all things unlikely to be found in tribal societies. Yet religion is still deeply embedded in the whole way of life of the people. It is certainly not a matter primarily of private experience and conscience and it is not a sphere of life that we take as separate in modern society. Since Judaism and Christianity are themselves "historic" religions, they exist somewhat uncomfortably in modern society. Protestant Christianity, with its strongly individualistic tendencies, has gone farthest in accepting the place to which modern culture assigns religion, but even there we will find more than a little unease.

Religions that believe God created heaven and earth and is the Lord of all do not easily accept being assigned to a delimited sphere.

On the other hand, the very nature of modern life, whatever our beliefs, tends to assign our religion to a highly private sphere. Most modern states guarantee our religious freedom but tend to assume that this freedom will only be used within that private sphere. This assumption does not derive from some arbitrary prejudice against religion: it has a real historical source, namely, early modern wars of religion. The modern nation-state came into existence in part as an effort to calm religious passions and end religious wars. In the twentieth century nation-states have been responsible for the most terrible wars in human history, so we must consider them ambiguous projects at best, but we cannot entirely forget their initial connection to the search for peace. Particularly in religiously pluralistic societies, the salience of a national rather than a religious narrative — and the national solidarity created by such a narrative — has to some degree overcome the possible hostility that could and did divide the nation along the lines of different religious communities. Where such national narratives have failed, as in Northern Ireland, Lebanon, or most recently the lands that were once Yugoslavia, the possibility of religious warfare, so obvious in the seventeenth century, becomes actual again.

I point out these uncomfortable facts to help us understand why some of our Enlightenment friends are so nervous about any role at all for religion in public life, and why they would like religion to remain safely ensconced in the private sphere.

However, there is a further development that I cannot discuss extensively here but that must be mentioned at this point: the nation-state that emerged with the Peace of Westphalia in the middle of the seventeenth century may itself be undergoing a decline in significance. From being the primary unit of international order (or disorder) it may be on the verge of being superseded by supranational and subnational entities that may reduce it to a less dominant (though still significant) role than it has had for over three hundred years. Bryan Hehir recently said we are moving into a post-Westphalian era, though certainly we are not yet in a post-Westphalian world. By a post-Westphalian era we naturally think of a period in which nation-states will, probably mercifully, have less power. But one of the points that Hehir makes is that a post-Westphalian era releases the church from some of the understanding inherent in that era. Exactly what that means for us we will have to think about for quite some time. It opens up enormous opportunities as well as possible dangers.

We have come a long way from Habermas, but I want to return to his argument before taking up the second answer to how we understand the church in an individualistic society. How do we answer Habermas when he says essentially that religion is outmoded in modern culture or can at best be a purely private consolation? I think we can answer by showing that Habermas himself has no adequate answer to the distorted modernization he criticizes, what he sometimes refers to as the depletion of nonrenewable cultural resources. Habermas's response to the distortions of modernity involves controlling the economic and political systems that impinge on what he calls the lifeworld, that part of our life which is steered by language. So far so good, but when we ask how the lifeworld is supposed to provide a moral anchorage to the systems and prevent the systems from, as he puts it, colonizing the lifeworld, then his answer — namely, a further rationalization of the lifeworld itself — seems unconvincing. The lifeworld, as Habermas at times seems to know, involves a balance between the taken-for-granted, the traditional, and that which is open to question.[3] But instead of seeing that relation as a vital and dynamic one, Habermas tends to see it as a zero-sum relationship in which advance lies in the continuous increase of areas of life controlled by voluntary and autonomous action responding to the criteria of reason, and the continuous decline of everything else. I cannot argue the point here, though some of what I will say later bears on it, but I believe Habermas gets himself into an impossible and ultimately self-defeating position because of an inadequate philosophical anthropology and ultimately an inadequate conception of rationality. In short, religion may be more critical in transforming the distortions of modernity that Habermas has so acutely analyzed than he is as yet willing to admit.

The second answer to the question of how we are to understand the church in an individualistic culture starts out with a more critical analysis of individualism than Habermas offers, but still suggests the possibility of an immanent critique of individualism that provides an opening for showing why something like the church is necessary, even from the point of view of individualism itself. Charles Taylor made this case in a most persuasive way.[4] Taylor points to that pervasive element in modern culture which we have come to call, since Alexis de Tocqueville's use of the term in *Democracy in America*, individualism. Whatever our cultural background it is unlikely that by the time we are adolescents we have not imbibed a considerable amount of the culture of individualism. Habermas tends to view individualism through the category of autonomy, a moral good, but Taylor, following a long line of critics going back at least to de Tocqueville, points to its negative side in which individualism tends to emphasize looking out for number one, getting one's own satisfactions without worrying too much about others — in general shutting ourselves up in our own lives where our own ambitions, fears, and desires determine how we act.

But Taylor does recognize a positive side, one closer to Habermas's ideal, in which individualism emphasizes our responsibility to be true to ourselves, to find a worthwhile way of life that is authentic and valuable. In order to combat the negative side, in *The Ethics of Authenticity* Taylor argues that we can use the intuitions contained in the positive side to help people find a richer and more responsible form of life.

I have recently taken music — and I am using music as shorthand for all the arts — as an example to clarify Taylor's argument. Only after making the case with respect to music will I apply Taylor's understanding to the church, something Taylor himself has not done, though he is an avowed theist and active Catholic layman. Music can be a kind of focal practice (to borrow a term from another philosopher, Albert Borgmann) that can bring a coherence that transcends the world of one's own desires and fears.[5] But in spite of our romantic notions of radical personal autonomy, one cannot just pick up an instrument and make whatever sounds one pleases. We are up against the objective possibilities of the instrument, the fact that to make it do what one wants takes much time and skill, and that even the most original music is a variation on traditions of music that must be learned before one can innovate.

The existence of a focal practice requiring discipline and the ability to come to terms with what we might call an objective horizon of musical practice and tradition does not crush our individuality. By learning the focal practice we become free to perform and create in a way that expresses our deeper self, indeed helps us discover what that deeper self really is.

But when we learn to play music we learn another terribly important lesson. We learn that we cannot do it all alone. At a minimum we need a teacher. You will never learn to play the violin by reading a book about playing the violin. That relation between student and teacher is indispensable. Much of what is transmitted cannot even be verbalized. It occurs through the deep interaction of two persons. One can go further. One can say that in an important sense the student must internalize the teacher. The teacher becomes part of the student's self. Indeed, the dialogue with the teacher goes on inside the student even years after the student has left the teacher. The student may move far away from the teacher's ideas, but the argument will continue. The relation to the teacher, as in a much fuller way the relation to a parent, is a defining relationship.

The deeply interpersonal nature of all learning in the arts is another way in which the negative possibilities of our radical individualism can be moderated. We learn that we become our true selves not apart from others but in relationship to them. To push the musical example a bit further, when one learns to play in any kind of ensemble, the importance of relationships becomes all the more evident. I was listening to St. Paul Sunday Morning some time ago when the Marlborough Players were performing the Mendelssohn Octet. After the performance the host of the program commented on how the players looked at each other during the performance, with a kind of immediate understanding that is rare in our interactions with others in our society. If you are playing chamber music you need to know where the other players are at all times. This can become almost intuitive, yet it always involves a deep sensitivity to other human beings.

So learning how to play music, or to dance, or to engage in other forms of art moderates in two ways an individualism that threatens to become radically egoistic: it provides some objective standards that are not completely relative to one's own wishes and desires; and it pulls us into rather deep relations to other people. In neither case is our individuality crushed. Indeed this kind of learning enhances us as individuals, allows us to find the forms and relationships through which we can really be the kind of people we want to be. I would suggest that the lessons learned here have implications for the whole of one's life, and specifically for our religious life.

But before developing the analogy I would like to consider how the negative side of individualism Taylor criticizes actually operates in our religious life in American society today.

What Taylor calls the negative side of individualism has been codified in economics and to some extent in social science generally as what is called rational action theory, the idea that human action is based on the maximization of individual values — usually economic, but not necessarily so. The sociology of religion has not embraced rational action theory with much enthusiasm, but it applies surprisingly well to the actual religious behavior among many in Western, perhaps particularly American, society. By this I mean to indicate what could be called religious consumerism, which has certainly become evident as a social reality.

The religious consumer fits a certain ideological model of religion in American society: namely the idea that each individual chooses his or her religious affiliation without any external influence, religion being quintessentially a private matter. While this could not in fact be the case, for only the existence of religious communities would make it possible for individuals to know they have religious options, and indeed most Americans are still raised in some kind of religious community, the ideology still powerfully affects behavior: the person who has accepted this notion of religion feels no particular loyalty to his or her religious community. If another congregation offers concrete advantages, such as services at more convenient hours, better daycare for children, or whatever, then there is little hesitation in changing allegiance.

If one believes in a conception of religious traditions that are deeply formative of individual and social identity and demand profound loyalty from their adherents, then this kind of behavior is indeed disturbing, but it has to be taken seriously as an empirical reality. My question is whether we can show religious consumers that their way of thinking about religion will not work, just as we might show the romantic individualist who wants to play the violin that he cannot simply pick up the instrument for the first time and express himself. But does the analogy work? The religious consumer may well believe that religion, unlike the arts, requires no horizon of external standards and no deeply engaged community, that indeed one can be religious perfectly spontaneously, that reading Joseph Campbell, or better yet watching him on television, is all one needs to do to set forth on one's spiritual journey.

Although the task of convincing the religious consumer that this view of religion is illusory is more difficult than the task of convincing the aspirant musician, I still think it can be done. Before fully developing the argument, however, I would like to consider the third answer to the question of how we are to understand the church in an individualist culture. This is a stance that rather uncompromisingly rejects the entire set of assumptions of modernity and proclaims the Christian narrative as an adequate and sufficient basis for the organization of our lives. Such a view has been expressed in varying degrees of radicality by George Lindbeck,[6] Stanley Hauerwas,[7] and recently by the English theologian John Milbank.[8]

Just to show how forceful this position can be, let me illustrate it by positions expressed in two recent books by Stanley Hauerwas: *Resident Aliens* (which he wrote together with William H. Willimon) and *After Christendom?* In the first book Hauerwas and Willimon ask Christians to think of themselves as a colony, a colony of heaven, in a foreign land. By speaking of Christians as "resident aliens," they take up a usage, not uncommon in the ancient world, that the Jews in the Diaspora used to think of themselves: strangers in a strange land. The second book continues the strong language in its very title, for, it argues, we now live "after Christendom," that is, in an alien culture that is no longer (if it ever was) Christian in substance. In that book Hauerwas shows the divergence of his position from accepted views in a series of provocative chapter subtitles such as "Why There Is No Salvation Outside the Church," "Why Justice Is a Bad Idea for Christians," and "Why Freedom of Religion Is a Subtle Temptation." John Milbank, in his important book *Theology and Social Theory: Beyond Secular Reason*, would replace current social science with Christian sociology based on "meta-narrative realism," an idea too complex for me to explain briefly, even if I could. All of this is related to George Lindbeck's moderate proposal in *The Nature of Doctrine* that Christians describe the world from a Christian point of view rather than describing Christianity from the world's point of view.

Now, I am more sympathetic to this third answer to the question of how we understand the church in an individualistic culture than you might think. I am not at all ready to dismiss such views as fideist or sectarian (however tired I am of hearing about Christendom and Constantinianism from some of my friends in this quarter). Indeed I think something like this third position is necessary as the basis for developing the Christian analogy to music if we are to persuade religious consumers that their understanding of religion is inherently flawed and will not do for them what they hope it will.

My problem with those who hold some version of this third position is that I do not think they have really explained to us how we get there from here. There are two almost opposite problems that I think they have not adequately faced. One is that none of us educated in modern Western culture, and that includes almost all educated people anywhere in the world today, can simply jump out of our skins, deny that culture, and, by a sheer act of will, imagine that we are radically resident aliens within it. The second problem is that however secular our culture has become, it is still saturated in language and practice with elements of biblical religion, even if those elements are no longer coherently organized. That is, it is a false analogy to imagine ourselves living in something like the pagan culture of the classical world. Again, even for non-Westerners, the Christian substance of Western culture is unavoidable, so that, for example, Japan, which has a church membership of less than one percent of the population, has a higher percentage of college graduates who have read the Bible entire than we do.

So how do I rescue what I think is valuable in this third position from what I think is unhelpful? To begin with, I think it is unhelpful to continue to beat the dead horse of Constantinianism and Christendom. Once the ruling class of a society has been converted, the resident alien model does not work, or at least it has a very reduced utility. It has often been noted that the political triumph of Christianity coincided with the rise of monasticism, a kind of institutionalized resident alien status within the larger Christian body. No matter how allegedly Christian the culture may be, it will surely always need demonstration communities within it to call it more rigorously to follow its professed beliefs, but that does not change the fact that there are a whole series of problems in a society with a Christian ruling class that the resident alien model cannot deal with at all, and for which Ernst Troeltch's church type is still enormously helpful in our understanding.

But that is not the main line I want to pursue, for, though Yoder, Hauerwas, and others do not seem to recognize it, Constantinianism and Christendom died in 1648 at the Peace of Westphalia. If we are in a post era it is post-Westphalia, not post-Christendom. Whatever their language, the animus of their criticism seems to be more on target: it is not the oppressive monolithic church using the state to gain its ends that is the problem today. Rather, as Hauerwas sees quite clearly, it is the Westphalian privatization of religion that creates most of our problems. I don't think Hauerwas believes in the notion that there is no salvation outside the church in a way that even the Vatican discarded well before Vatican II. His point, in the current cultural milieu, is well taken: we are saved together or we are not saved at all. The church is integral to our very identity as Christians and the piety that dreams of being alone in the garden with Jesus is, as Harold Bloom recently pointed out, not Christian at all but gnostic.[9] Similarly when Hauerwas speaks of freedom of religion as a subtle temptation, he is surely not arguing for an establishment of religion and an enforcement of worship. He is objecting to the notion that the state has granted us a special sphere of "freedom" within which we must safely stay if we do not want to get in trouble, more likely with the cultural elite than with the police, though the latter possibility can never be ignored. What happens when we really move into a post-Westphalian world, and the whole religious settlement associated with the Westphalian era no longer makes sense, is a really exciting possibility that most of those in the third position, because they are still fighting old wars, have hardly begun to envision.

Let me turn from a direct encounter with the third position to developing the immanent critique of individualistic, consumerist religion that the second position is concerned to make, using elements of the third position in the process. Such an immanent critique must do more than reassert in strong terms the social reality of the church, important though (as we shall see) that is. For the problems in the area of religion are endemic to the culture as a whole, and are especially clear in the areas of family and marriage and of politics, as well as of religion. In every case the very viability of a coherent form of life is endangered by placing a priority on individual interest-maximizing at the expense of both objective standards and social engagement.

Nowhere is this clearer than in the area of marriage and the family. A graduate student at Berkeley, Karla Hackstaff, is currently writing her dissertation on what she calls "the divorce culture." She argues that a generation or two ago we had a marriage culture and now we have a divorce culture. This is not a matter of the statistical prevalence of divorce but of its cultural meaning and the expectations it creates for everyone: not yet married, married, and divorced alike. She gave a seminar on her thesis topic to Berkeley seniors and discovered that most of them wanted to use the seminar as group therapy rather than as a sociology course. The majority of the students were from families of divorce and they wished to share the anger and pain their parents' actions had caused them. But when Karla asked whether divorce is morally all right, the students could only say, of course, people have to be free to do what they want.

The moral of this is not that we should abolish divorce, though some of the so-called no-fault divorce laws should certainly be reformed, but that we need to reinvigorate a "marriage culture" that will help people understand why, even though they have the option of divorce, they should value marriage as a good in itself, something they want to sustain, not subject to constant monitoring in terms of individual payoff.

Just as, as it has been said, the family is now seen less as something we belong to than as something at the service of the individual, so politics is increasingly seen less as a means of democratic participation than a source of interest maximization. Just as we have consumer Christians, so we have consumer voters. The market as the master metaphor of all aspects of life undermines both any sense of objective morality and any need to think of oneself as deeply involved with other people. But the politics of interest is as healthy for our political life as the divorce culture is healthy for our family life. Here again, the profound dissatisfaction with our national political system, expressed so obviously in recent years, at least provides the opportunity for reasserting a more ethical meaning of democratic citizenship than we have been used to hearing for quite some time. I may say that in my view this means a reinvigoration of political parties. The rise of so-called political independents parallels the rise of religious independents and of divorce. All are symptoms of social and cultural disengagement and anomie; all are symptoms of a sick society, one that has elevated autonomy as almost the only good.

My quarrel with the primacy of autonomy is that it is not really a fully adult virtue. It is the critically important virtue of late adolescence, when an individual needs to be freed from parental and other authority in order to find a form of fidelity to oneself. This is the normal outcome of the adolescent identity crisis. It is a working out of needs for individuation and separation that began as early as the second year of life. But it is a moment that must be included and surpassed in a return in later adulthood to a larger sense of social responsibility and religious sensitivity based on a recognition of dependence and interdependence as forming a polar complementarity to autonomy. Thus Kant's coming of age turns out in its literal meaning to be quite appropriate — it is the attaining of majority by the child. But it is the beginning of adulthood, not the end of it.

The point can be illustrated with the example of social roles. To the adolescent just come of age roles may appear to be oppressive, masks that inhibit the "true self." Above all such persons do not want to be told that they are "too young" to question existing authority arrangements or that their parents and teachers, just because they are parents and teachers, know better. As Habermas would rightly put it, the challenge to existing legitimacy claims put forward by young adults cannot be evaded by a mere invocation of established and unquestionable structures of authority. Rather young people must find the models of fallible yet faithful adults whose identity is realized only in and through roles, so that they may begin to see roles not as external encumbrances but as the very forms though which one becomes an authentic and responsible adult.

What all this suggests is that the hard-won autonomy of the young adult needs to be supplemented by the conscious choice of roles, the conscious acceptance of the degree to which we are always "implicated" with other people. A friend of mine recently overheard an argument between a middle-class mother and her four-year-old child that was taking place in a quintessentially Habermasian language, arguments flying thick and fast between them and voices rising, until the mother finally said, "Because I'm the mother and you're the child, that's why!" Under some circumstances such a response could be an attempt to crush the independence of the child or to refuse the legitimacy of the child's questions altogether. In this case, however, it seemed as though the mother was finally accepting the fact that she was the mother, and that her responsibilities were different from those of the child, something it was probably valuable for the child to learn as well. Thus as we come to accept the fact that we are fathers and mothers, teachers and priests, we more fully understand the virtues that go with those roles, virtues of responsibility, care, and wisdom, which do not subvert but enrich the virtue of autonomy.

When we take these reflections back to the question of the meaning of the church in an individualistic culture, we can well ask when we teach the words of the creed and the catechism, what do they mean? In a society where group boundaries are weak, where families are often incoherent, where individuals do not feel innerly connected to their roles, and where the language of feelings and reasons is much more pervasive than the language of symbol and meaning, then it is hard for people to understand the very idea of the church. I would agree with Stanley Hauerwas that without a strong sense of what it is to be the church it is very hard for people to understand faith, the liturgy, and, ultimately, what we are called on to be and to do as disciples of the crucified Christ.

Without a sense of what might almost be called the physicality of the church, the church as the Body of Christ, people have a very privatized idea of religion, disembodied, psychological, and finally consumerist. The looseness they feel toward their family, their occupation, and their friends is extended to the church. Individual psychological reward becomes the measure, leading to an incredibly distorted notion of discipleship: Take up your cross and follow me — it'll make you feel good.

The most fundamental practice that tells us who we are as Christians is worship. The very concreteness of the sacramental tradition is difficult for free-floating middle-class Americans to understand. If I do not understand who I am as a parent or a child, a teacher or a student, how can I understand that this bread and this wine is the actual body and blood of Christ and that by participating in the Eucharist I become immediately and physically one with the body of Christ?

What I am trying to say is that we cannot just declare ourselves to be resident aliens. We need to engage in an immanent critique of a culture that is incapable of offering even its own professed goods of authenticity and autonomy. We need to show that in every significant area of our lives a more adult understanding of what is required of us is the only basis for the individual meaning that this culture has staked its life on.

Finally, let me say that I cannot accept the third position's claim that we should live in one and only one narrative community. I accept its emphasis on the church as the narrative community that should have priority in our lives and of the very difficult process of reeducation that would make us understand that. But I think we are all also members of a variety of other narrative communities — the Enlightenment community; national, ethnic, and racial communities; political and familial communities — that have a justified claim on us, even though we need to hold them up to the light of criticism coming from our experience as members of the body of Christ. Such a constant critical movement between our religious community and all our other communities is how I would phrase the role of the church in civil society and thus its ability to participate in public life.

Life itself is teaching us, I think, the inner vacuity of an individualistic culture. But we also need the intellectual resources to offer viable alternatives. So let me conclude with a plea for the centrality of theological education. We do not need more alienated, more "academic," theologians. But we are desperately in need of genuinely engaged organic theologians who understand and can speak to the needs of the church and the culture. Such theologians can help us see that we can draw on all three of the answers to the question of the meaning of the church in an individualistic culture in order that a more vital and authentic church can help our culture move from adolescent self-preoccupation to adult responsibility.

Notes

1. This discussion of Habermas's view of religion is based on volume II of *The Theory of Communicative Action* (Boston: Beacon Press, 1987; first German edition, 1981), especially ch. 5, sec. 3, "The Rational Structure of the Linguistification of the

Sacred," pp. 77-111. In his concluding chapter to *Habermas, Modernity, and Public Theology* (New York: Crossroad, 1992), "Transcendence from Within, Transcendence in this World," pp. 226-250, he modifies these views to some extent, recognizing the practical contribution of some Christians and some theologians to the public struggle for social justice. But with respect to the place of religion in modern culture he leaves us with only this rather agnostic statement: "As long as religious language bears with itself inspiring, indeed, unrelinquishable semantic contents which elude (for the moment?) the expressive power of a philosophical language and still await translation into a discourse that gives reasons for its position, philosophy, even its postmetaphysical form, will neither be able to replace nor to repress religion" (p. 237).

2. The importance of the transition symbolized (but certainly not caused) by the Treaty of Westphalia was pointed out to me in an as yet unpublished paper by Brian Hehir in 1992.

3. See, for example, *The Theory of Communicative Action*, vol. II, p. 137, but also elsewhere when he discusses tradition. Unfortunately, tradition is not an entry in the index.

4. Most extensively in Charles Taylor, *Sources of the Self* (Cambridge: Harvard University Press, 1989), but in a somewhat more accessible form in *The Ethics of Authenticity* (Cambridge: Harvard University Press, 1992).

5. See Albert Borgmann, *Technology and the Character of Contemporary Life* (Chicago: University of Chicago Press, 1984).

6. George A. Lindbeck, *The Nature of Doctrine: Religion and Theology in a Postliberal Age* (Philadelphia: Westminster Press, 1984).

7. Stanley Hauerwas and William H. Willimon, *Resident Aliens: Life in the Christian Colony* (Nashville: Abingdon Press, 1989); Stanley Hauerwas, *After Christendom? How the Church Is To Behave if Freedom, Justice and a Christian Nation Are Bad Ideas* (Nashville: Abingdon Press, 1991).

8. John Milbank, *Theology and Social Theory: Beyond Secular Reason* (Oxford: Basil Blackwell, 1990).

9. Harold Bloom, *The American Religion: The Emergence of the Post-Christian Nation* (New York: Simon and Schuster, 1992).

TO WHOM AND HOW ARE WE SPEAKING?

Rodney L. Petersen

In her introductory remarks to the above-titled section, Elizabeth C. Nordbeck, Dean of the Faculty and Vice-President for Academic Affairs at Andover Newton Theological School, reflected upon perceptions of religion, theology, and social science. Such remarks served to draw out issues pertaining to the constituency of theological studies. Acknowledging the differences among these disciplines, clarity about what theology has to contribute to a civil society in distinction from religion and social science is a theme running through the following papers. We might ask what a particular theology has to contribute to a common public life? What is religion in itself in contrast to the ways by which religious language can mask social deprivation or acculturation? We might wonder whether all religion is to be subjected to theological evaluation? Michel Foucault refers to such questioning as "the politics of truth."[1] These questions ask us to be clear about who we are, what it is we wish to communicate, and to whom we are speaking.

Who are we who seek to administer theological education? Who is qualified to teach about religion, which is, by definition, an all-encompassing dimension of life? Who can teach theology? The sixteenth-century theologian John Calvin wrote that we cannot know God apart from a knowledge of ourselves and, on the contrary, we cannot know ourselves apart from God.[2] When we consider the discipline of social science the matter becomes more complex. For now we not only talk about religion and theology, but also about the human community. The way in which

Rodney L. Petersen is Executive Director of the Boston Theological Institute.

these concepts interrelate is as controverted as the sociologies of Auguste Comte, Emile Durkheim, and Max Weber are different. Religion, traditionally integrationist in reach, is restricted in the minds of many to a private sphere in this country not only for constitutional reasons but also through philosophical dispute. Yet many ask if religion has, in fact, been thus restrained or if we are not now worshipping a host of other non-traditional gods in society.[3]

The question of who teaches in our schools is politically important. It always has been. Different constituencies are interested in this question since the future shape of the church is, in part, determined by its leadership. Following the structure of Bellah's remarks we can highlight the following positions. Some in the schools do not see God's activity as taking place primarily in the church. Following models of universalism, they understand God to be active in the world without special regard to either Israel or the church. Others see the life of the individual as fraught with spiritual significance and grounded in the mystery of free will: one may choose to live selfishly or in recognition of others. The struggle of the church in the world mirrors this conflict in the individual and resonates with covenantal, prophetic, or apocalyptic overtones. Still others reject modernity. They find the role of the Christian to be that of "resident alien" in a society characterized by deep spiritual conflict. The church is the primary place of God's activity in the world. It is the community of the elect and the unfailing focus of salvation. Each of these three positions reflects ways in which communities of faith find their place in the world. They are continuous with past models of the church and civil society.[4]

Numerous studies have been done over the past several years on who is attending our seminaries, schools of theology, university divinity schools, and departments of religion today. One study, compiled by James M. Shopshire for the Association of Theological Schools, indicates record growth rates into the 1980s, a surge in second-career students, a doubling of the percentage of women, and significant increases in the variety of racial-ethnic groups.[5] Traditionally places of preparation for the ordained ministry in the churches, many seminarians today include those who are on personal journeys of faith or paths of intellectual discovery after having become awakened to issues pertaining to meaning in life. Groups formerly excluded from seminary training are now being encouraged to attend. This variety of interests makes theological schools often difficult places in which to work for faculty, staff, and students alike.[6] In addition to aspects of a traditional curriculum, schools must adjust their course offerings to meet the demands of churches, the expectations of the university, and the needs of a varying constituency.[7]

The question of who attends theological school is not limited to those sitting as students in the classroom. It includes congregations in churches and meeting houses. This picture is equally complex and changing. One study with respect to Boston indicates an approximate 30 percent decline in mainline church attendance whereas over the same period of time more than two hundred new churches were founded in the city.[8] Teachers in seminaries, perhaps more so than their colleagues in departments of theology or religion, often serve as priests or ministers in local churches as well. Additionally, the audience for theological education includes society at large. Insofar as the people of this land have attended to the prophetic ministry of the churches, "the world," to paraphrase John Wesley's phrase, "has been its parish." To the extent that Christian values prevail in society, Christ can be said to be its sovereign in a variety of typological ways.[9]

Whether as priest, prophet, or sovereign, the mandate given the Christian community in its call as *ecclesia* is not only to love, or listen to, one's neighbor, but also to love God. Loving God means listening to God.[10] To whom are religious educators listening? The form in which this question is answered may take on different aspects reflecting understandings of the nature of God, revelation of Christ, and activity of the Spirit. The three models of theological educators developed in relation to Bellah's conception of the way in which churches are seen in our culture might provide a place to begin. Issues of revelation, tradition, different conceptual models of reason, and philosophies of suspicion all call for new degrees of mature attentiveness. The models of transcendence and immanence with which theological educators have lived since the nineteenth century have intersected in increasingly complex ways as reflected in these issues.[11]

Three specific audiences are addressed in these papers. Each is symbolic of greater diversities. As we listen to each, we might ask whether Bellah's "second language," that embedded in the traditions of republican virtue and biblical insight, is helpful.[12] Or what new language might be needed to address the spiritual needs of a civil society?

Ethicist Max Stackhouse's paper, "Social Theory and Christian Public Morality for the Common Life," offers a nuanced understanding of individualism in the context of contemporary global society. He begins by noting Bellah's opposition to liberal individualism, questioning whether or not individualism is as rampant in our society as is sometimes thought. Stackhouse goes on to illustrate how Bellah's sociology draws from deeper wellsprings than those often evident in what Stackhouse refers to as the contemporary and somewhat undernourished "rights" debates. It reaches back to forms of association, "estates," "orders," or "sectors" of society out of conceptions of Roman *jus gentium*, or *societas naturalis*, with their further philosophical and biblical shaping. These subsystems of society, family, church, etc., like the state, have a natural right to exist. They ought not be swallowed up by the state. They have a "metaphysical-moral reality that transcends their relative autonomy." The health of such institutions, or sectors of society, provides the social safety net required for social stability and cohesion.

Stackhouse's understanding of such institutional plurality, and by inference Bellah's, is not rooted in "racial, class or power analysis" but in "value, meaning and moral ecology as found in fragmentary fashion in three places: first, in the residual consciousness of people who do not always know from whence such things come; second, in the basic, necessary, unavoidable institutions of life that make pluralistic society sustainable; and third, in the symbolism of religion." Ethnicity, economic stratification, and oppressive patterns of gender dominance are framed, Stackhouse argues, by the larger questions of the fragmentation and chaos we face and for which we need an integrated vision. It is the function of religion to provide this vision.[13]

Bellah's answer to this social fragmentation is his "second language." What is not clear, Stackhouse writes, is how this normative and universal picture relates to sociology. We do not have a pattern for the good society that we can discern or to which we can conform. Religion, often interpreted together with sociology, forms one of two pillars for social ethics. However, ethics requires that second pillar, the normative vision provided by a theology, to clarify what is the just, the true, and the holy. The importance of this bipartite foundation for ethics is seen in the moral infrastructures and the macrostructures through which we live. An example of the former is the family. Social ethics calls us to reflect on how we love and how we institutionalize that love. Stackhouse's call is as timely as the moral cynicism that prevails and undermines civil viability. At the global level macrostructures also require this bipartite foundation for intercontextual definitions. Religion may hold a society together but, to paraphrase Stackhouse, in an emerging global social order that is not rooted in the memory of common experience, more is required. Ethics requires theology.[14]

Stackhouse's plea for theology comes out of the inner crises sociology as a discipline is facing in the new global order. In past periods of social transition, "theology, not religion; ethics, not cultural traditions; and new forms of civilizational theory, not national analysis alone," Stackhouse writes, represented the level of abstraction that was required. Theology played its role in shaping the principles that were to guide the encounter and clash of nations. In the face of recurring problems in places like the Balkans, Rwanda, and our cities we face a mounting cynicism that erodes the moral infrastructures and macrostructures which make a humane life impossible apart from a viable theology.[15]

In response to Stackhouse's paper, Preston Williams of Harvard Divinity School noted four concerns. First, the Christian citizen bears a responsibility to help change society. Second, agreeing with Stackhouse that normative standards are important for change, Williams pressed the different question of how we define the norms of a good society. Third, while norms may be muted today, some standards are present. They include, for example, "trust" and "participation." Both are existing norms. They shape and propel Bellah's vision. Still, for Williams, both Bellah's and Stackhouse's conceptions of the problems confronting churches are too much of the "old." Although both place issues of liberation in a larger philosophical framework, they themselves fail to be strong advocates for persons who have been marginalized in Christian social policy. Williams's point is well taken, but it remains to be seen how it is shaped by the issues of value and meaning in addition to the justified claims of racial, class, or other forms of power analysis.[16]

Sociologist Lawrence Mamiya's paper takes up the concerns raised by Williams with reference to Stackhouse and Bellah. In "Christianity and Civil Society: Challenges from a Black Church Perspective," Mamiya remarks on the specific nature of the Afro-American culture and the experience of black Christianity in the United States.[17] Mamiya presents three challenges that the Afro-American community puts before the Christian movement generally. They may also be said to be challenges offered by other marginalized groups as well. He notes that blacks have felt their Chistianity to be more "Christian" than a white or Caucasian Christianity perceived as racist in its theology and practice. If present trajectories continue, the church of the twenty-first century will be characterized by more diverse and less European- or Anglo-appearing congregations. Clearly there is room for further constructive theological work on Mamiya's first point. Furthermore, the black church sees itself as a model for a holistic ministry. The church has played a vital role in all segments of the black community, something once characteristic of earlier white American congregations. However, whether the black church is marginalized by the black community in the future or serves as a model for the reinvigoration of all congregational life in the United States is an open question. Mamiya writes of the pivotal role black churches have had in pushing issues of multiculturalism, a revisionist history, and social change in American society. This third point is well made, but as American society wrestles with issues of moral and theological integration, it will be important to watch how theorists in the black community position themselves in relation to other liberation movements and questions of moral and epistemic integra-

tion. Again, Bellah's "second language" or Stackhouse's concern for integration becomes paramount as issues of personal resentment are weighed
against those of meaning and value in civil society.[18]

Mamiya continues by raising three challenges posed by the general
Christian movement in America to the black or Afro-American church.
First, despite only modest gains made by blacks in American economic
life, the black church is not alleviated of responsibility to the poor. Too
often one sees the tendency of moving up the economic ladder and away
from a concern for the economic plight of the Afro-American community.
This point is socially significant in that part of the challenge of the urban
poor today is the diminishing influence that the black church has with
urban black youth. How issues of social resentment and communal values
are affected by this will be a new factor in American religious history,
particularly if black youths gravitate to religions outside the bounds of
Christian expression.[19] Second, black churches are confronted by the challenge of gender as much as white or other multiracial churches today. This
issue is doubly significant because of the number of black women in the
churches and in theological education. The black church typically has not
been receptive to the leadership of women except in the more spirit-ori-
ented and Pentecostal churches. Finally, although black congregations
have been active in their communities, there is not always a very adept
understanding about the nature of public policy. Accordingly, Mamiya
writes, there is a need in our schools for an emphasis upon learning about
how public policy works. Such will permit us to target better specific
issues for public policy from an ethical perspective.

By way of response, ethicist John H. Cartwright of Boston University
School of Theology noted that one of the challenges faced by the urban
poor is, first, that of the susceptibility of the urban community to the
problems associated with the prison system in the United States. Apart
from the larger discussion of who gets incarcerated in American society,
there is the human toll and the greater need for Christian presence through
an enhanced prison ministry. The United States leads the world in the
incarceration of black men and increasing numbers of women, not to
mention white and other ethnic groups. More needs to be done to develop
an effective program for prison ministry in theological education today.
Additionally, there is a need for more informed patterns of activity between all churches and those in our urban contexts. More knowledge is
needed of organizational systems, changing urban demographics, ways to
cooperate with other civic community services. How values help shape
communities and mobilize congregations for neighborhood renewal are
important concerns here. Finally, we must ask what is the theological
significance of a black church? While its work has been important in the

African-American community, Cartwright goes on to ask whether its very existence is something of an indictment of the larger Christian church? What does it mean to have a separate racial church in our society? In various ways both Williams and Cartwright remind us of the need to find tangible ways to live in light of the Matthean injunction (25:35-36), integrating such into the larger framework of Christian meaning.[20]

After reflecting on contemporary politics in America, historian Richard Lovelace's paper, "The Bible in Public Discourse," takes us into some specific ways in which society, religion, and theology play themselves out in public life. Lovelace begins by noting that we are not a society "gripped by religious decay, indifference, and relativism." Indices of both a secular and religious orientation indicate otherwise.[21] Agreeing with Bellah's description of ours as a post-Westphalian society, Lovelace goes on to contend that America is not a post-Christian society in any sense that reverses Alexis de Tocqueville's analysis. We may be divided as a people, but with the amount of "God-talk" in our culture we are still religiously alive. This life is part of the contemporary "culture war" and sees religious alliances, heretofore unthinkable, being established on the right and left. An example of such is the growing relationship between Evangelicals and Roman Catholics. Additionally, many Evangelicals who look for historical anchorage are becoming Orthodox today rather than joining other Protestant churches.[22] Areas of life once seen as unitive of American culture from local schools to the television and film industry are becoming "ideological targets" by secular humanists, the religious right, or other groups seeking to promote their perception of legitimate social values. Lovelace counsels new areas of unitive activity in ways that are socially and politically involved.[23]

In her response, ethicist Lisa Cahill of Boston College posed a number of questions. For example, "God-talk" may be alive and thriving, but is this real religion or religion to gain a constituency? In calling for more Bible in public discourse, as Lovelace does, how, in fact, she asks are we using biblical language? Are biblical images being used with cynicism by some? How does one determine religious authenticity? What is the proper role for religion? Can we move from communities of faith to a common ethical ground in civil society? Such questions grow out of her own work on the nature of Christian discipleship in relation to sexuality and social conflict.[24] The concerns she raises recall some of the important distinctions in terminology raised by Stackhouse as we seek to find a place for theology in public discourse.

In summary, these questions and the audiences to which they pertain are a unitive thread running through the issues, "To Whom and How Are We Speaking?" What is the nature of theology? Whose theology is it?

Who is the presumed constituency for theological education and prophetic criticism? Stackhouse raises up these questions in light of the moral infrastructure and the macrostructures through which we live our lives. Mamiya draws us to the specificities of ministry in American society, and thereby to the question that is raised of the nature of this civil order. Lovelace reminds us of the ways in which religion uses — and is used by — politics in the United States. These issues speak to the larger moral vision required in America today. Cornel West has called for its recovery through a "politics of conversion." This is not empty patter about transcendence but the vision that alone makes possible authenticity and a sustaining moral commitment.[25] It is a moral vision grounded in conversion to the transcendent but committed to a life in community. It permits the kind of attentiveness to God and neighbor that promotes democratic consciousness. This consciousness is not an end in itself. However, it allows for the calculus of a "principled pluralism," the formula required by a theological education committed to the public arena.

Notes

1. Michel Foucault, *Politics, Philosophy, Culture*, tr. by Alan Sheridan, et al. (New York: Routledge, 1988). Another method for such evaluation is explored by Mortimer J. Adler, *Six Great Ideas: Truth, Goodness, Beauty: Ideas We Judge By, Liberty, Equality, Justice: Ideas We Act On* (New York: Macmillan, 1981); and other books as a part of the Paideia Group. Beginning with the German philosopher Ludwig Feuerbach, a line of social critics that includes Friedrich Nietzsche, Karl Marx, and Sigmund Freud has questioned whether theology contributes any form of knowledge or clear methodological understanding. Adler offers a different point of departure.

2. John Calvin, *Institutes of the Christian Religion*, ed. and transl. by Battles and McNeil (Philadelphia: Westminster Press, 1962), vol. I.1.i.

3. This point raises the debate over secularization, any theory of which must deal adequately with a definition of religion, a point argued by Peter E. Glasner, *The Sociology of Secularization: A Critique of a Concept* (Boston: Routledge & Kegan Paul, 1977) and Richard K. Fenn, *Toward a Theory of Secularization* (Storrs, CT: The Society for the Scientific Study of Religion, 1978); see Jacques Ellul, *The New Demons*, tr. C. Edward Hopkins (New York: Seabury Press, 1975). Ellul writes as a sociologist and theologian, finding new forms of reification in society. This book has stimulated many further studies.

4. Different definitions of the church in relation to the topical motif of *koinonia* are discussed by Lesslie Newbigin, *The Household of God: Lectures on the Nature of the Church* (New York: Friendship Press, 1954), pp. 32-110; or more recently, A. T. and R. P. C. Hanson, *The Identity of the Church: A Guide to Recognizing the Contemporary Church* (London: SCM Press, 1987). Preparations for and discussions following the Fifth World Conference on Faith and Order, 3-14 August 1993, brought the

issue of ecclesiology into prominence. See S. Mark Heim, "Ecumenical Pilgrims: Taking Stock in Santiago," *The Christian Century* (3 November 1993): 1086-1092.

5. James M. Shopshire, "New Faces in Theological Education," *The Christian Century* (6-13 February 1991): 140-142. See also Melinda R. Heppe, "Finding Out Who Seminarians Really Are," *In Trust* (Autumn 1992): 3-4. This study was administered by the Educational Testing Service under a grant from the Lilly Endowment's Quality of Ministerial Candidates Program. See also Eugene F. Hemrick and Dean R. Hoge, *Seminarians in Theology: A National Profile* (United States Catholic Conference, Inc., 1986) and Ellis Larsen and James Shopshire, "A Profile of Contemporary Seminarians," *Theological Education*, vol. XXIV (Spring 1988).

6. Paul Wilkes questions the spiritual and educational health of today's seminarians in "The Hands that Would Shape Our Souls," *The Atlantic Monthly* (December 1990): 59-88; see Mary Harris and Clinton Stockwell's reply in *The Christian Century* (6-13 February 1991): 133, 136.

7. In this regard it would be useful to survey ways in which courses of instruction have changed over the past quarter century.

8. Douglas Hall and Rudy Mitchell, *Christianity in Boston* (Boston: Emmanuel Gospel Center, 1993). Issues of changing demographics and other factors need to be drawn into this analysis. Such figures reflect not only changes in urban ethnicity but also conflict in the churches themselves, often in line with changes in American religion that began in the interwar years. See Martin E. Marty, *Modern American Religion*, vol. II: *The Noise of Conflict, 1919-1941* (Chicago: University of Chicago Press, 1990); reviewed by Mark A. Noll, "The Public Church in the Years of Conflict," *The Christian Century* (15-22 May 1991): 552-559.

9. A classic expression of ways by which the churches interact with culture remains that by H. Richard Niebuhr, *Christ and Culture* (New York: Harper's, 1951); see also Pablo Richard, *Death of Christendoms, Birth of the Church* (Maryknoll: Orbis, 1987).

10. Edward Farley writes of the term "theology" that it implies listening to words about God, *Theologia: The Fragmentation and Unity of Theological Education* (Philadelphia: Fortress Press, 1983), pp. 29-48. Examples of such listening include Thomas Merton, *The Seven Story Mountain* (New York: Harcourt Brace Jovanovich, 1948), *The Way of the Pilgrim*, trans. R. M. French (New York: Seabury Press, 1965), and Joyce Huggett, *Listening to God* (London: Hodder and Stoughton, 1986).

11. Arthur Cushman McGiffert, *Protestant Thought before Kant* (New York: C. Scribner's, 1911); and see for the nineteenth century George Rupp, *Culture-Protestantism: German Liberal Theology at the Turn of the Twentieth Century* (Missoula, Mont.: Scholars Press, 1977).

12. To properly understand the term "republican" see Eugenio Garin, *Italian Humanism: Philosophy and Civic Life in the Renaissance* (New York: Harper and Row, 1965); Hans Baron, *The Crisis of the Italian Renaissance: Civic Humanism and Republican Liberty in an Age of Classicism and Tyranny* (Princeton: Princeton University Press, 1966); and J. G. A. Pocock, *The Machiavellian Moment: Florentine Political Thought and the Atlantic Republican Tradition* (Princeton: Princeton University Press, 1975). For ways in which this republican tradition could come together with biblical insight, see Charles S. McCoy and J. Wayne Baker, *Fountainhead of Federalism: Heinrich Bullinger and the Covenantal Tradition* (Louisville: W/JKP, 1991).

13. Stackhouse's own work has illustrated the ways in which competing religious

perspectives in the world advance or hinder human rights. In his work *Creeds, Society, and Human Rights: A Study in Three Cultures* (Grand Rapids: Eerdmans, 1984), he argues that the public theology developed by "Free-Church Protestantism" offers the intellectual and social resources to make human rights a reality. See also his *Public Theology and Political Economy* (Grand Rapids: Eerdmans, 1987).

14. James M. Gustafson's work reminds us that in the midst of our attempt to find a coherent theology, God will be God; see his *Ethics from a Theocentric Perspective*, vol. I, *Theology and Ethics*; vol. II, *Ethics and Theology* (Chicago: University of Chicago, 1981, 1984).

15. Such theology will need to be spelled out in relation to at least three critical issues facing the churches: first, environmental degradation, or cosmology in relation to questions of nature and grace. One might begin here with Paul Kennedy, *Preparing for the Twenty-first Century* (New York: Random House, 1993); see also Max Oelschlaeger, *Caring for Creation: An Ecumenical Approach to the Environmental Crisis* (New Haven: Yale University Press, 1994). A second issue concerns ecclesial identity and mission, or the place of the church in history. For background one might turn to Samuel Huntington, "The Clash of Civilizations?" *Foreign Affairs* (Summer 1993); and see Dana L. Robert, "From Missions to Mission to Beyond Missions: The Historiography of American Protestant Foreign Missions since World War II," *International Bulletin of Missionary Research*, vol. 18, no. 4 (October 1994): 146-162. Third, issues of advanced medical technology raise the question about the meaning of personhood. For here and elsewhere, see Alvin Toffler, *The Third Wave* (London: William Collins, 1980) and John Naisbitt and Patricia Aburdene, *Megatrends 2000* (London: Sidgwick and Jackson, 1990); see also Hans Küng, *Freud and the Problem of God* (New Haven: Yale University Press, 1990).

16. Preston N. Williams, "Contextualizing the Faith: The African-American Tradition and Martin Luther King, Jr.," in *One Faith, Many Cultures*, Ruy O. Costa, ed. (Maryknoll: Orbis/BTI, 1988), pp. 129-135.

17. C. Eric Lincoln and Lawrence H. Mamiya, *The Black Church in the African-American Experience* (Durham: Duke University Press, 1990).

18. The controversy surrounding such national figures as Minister Louis Farrakhan of the Nation of Islam and the Rev. Benjamin Chavis, former NAACP president, may be seen in this light. See James H. Cone, *Martin & Malcolm & America: A Dream or a Nightmare* (Maryknoll: Orbis, 1991); and cp. Charles J. Sykes, *A Nation of Victims: The Decay of the American Character* (New York: St. Martin's, 1992).

19. James H. Cone, *Martin & Malcolm & America: A Dream or a Nightmare* (Maryknoll: Orbis, 1991).

20. See John H. Cartwright, *An Affirmative Exposition of American Civil Religion* (Evanston, IL: Bureau of Social and Religious Research, Garrett-Evangelical Seminary, 1976). In this regard see Max L. Stackhouse, *Ethics and the Urban Ethos: An Essay in Social Theory and Theological Reconstruction* (Boston: Beacon Press, 1972). Stackhouse seeks to lay bare the ethos, ethics, and related beliefs implicit in urban life.

21. See the published studies by the Gallup Organization, Inc. and the Princeton Religion Research Center (53 Bank St., Princeton, NJ 08540). Further examples include Timothy Jones, "Great Awakenings: Americans are becoming fascinated with prayer and spirituality; Is it time to rejoice?" *Christianity Today* (8 November 1993): 22-25; and Richard N. Ostling, "The Church Search," *Time Magazine* (5 April 1993): 44-51; O. Gruenwald et al., eds., *Religious Resurgence in the Modern World: Social,*

Economic and Political Implications (Santa Monica: Institute for Interdisciplinary Research, 1994).

22. For example, see the work of the son of the American Evangelical apologist and founder of L'Abri, Francis Schaeffer, Frank Schaeffer, *Dancing Alone* (Brookline: Holy Cross Orthodox Press, 1994).

23. Lovelace's search for meaningful Christian renewal in society is explicit in his *Dynamics of Spiritual Life: An Evangelical Theology of Renewal* (Downers Grove, IL: Inter Varsity Press, 1979) and in his interest in the colonial American theologian, Cotton Mather. See his study, *The American Pietism of Cotton Mather: Origins of American Evangelicalism* (Grand Rapids: Christian University Press, 1979).

24. For example, see Lisa Sowle Cahill, *Love Your Enemies: Discipleship, Pacifism, and Just War Theory* (Minneapolis: Fortress Press, 1994).

25. Cornel West, *Prophetic Fragments: Illuminations of the Crisis in American Religion and Culture* (Grand Rapids: Eerdmans, 1988).

2

Social Theory and Christian Public Morality for the Common Life

Max L. Stackhouse

It is a personal pleasure to be able to pick up the dangling threads of an older conversation with Professor Bellah, who as a former teacher has shaped my own work and to whom I am indebted; and to meet again with Professor Mamiya, whose work, like mine, was given impetus by the civil rights movement. But it is also appropriate in a broader sense that this theological consortium join in conversation with sociologists on this anniversary, especially sociologists whose work has focused on the moral fabric of the common life and the historic role of religion in shaping that fabric. The recognition of the inevitable and indispensably intimate connection between religion and the social fabric has been a legacy both of the great post-Marxist sociological thinkers from Weber and Durkheim and Parsons to the present, and of the major ecumenically open theologians from the Protestant Social Gospel through Neo-Orthodoxy, Christian Realism, the Catholic Social encyclicals and Vatican II to the Liberationist, Evangelical, and Pentecostal movements shaping the global church today. In many ways, the preoccupying concerns of modern theology have been sociological. Recognizing that feudalism, patriarchy, serfdom, and slavery are failed patterns and that life will henceforth involve constant change and pluralism, what forms of sociality — of polity and authority,

Max L. Stackhouse is Stephen Colwell Professor of Christian Ethics at Princeton Theological Seminary; he was formerly Herbert Gezork Professor of Christian Social Ethics and Stewardship Studies, Andover Newton Theological School.

of human relations and association, of economic production and distribution, cultural solidarity and opposition — are appropriate to or fundamentally against the way God wants humanity to live under contemporary conditions?

Indeed, the BTI itself was born from the joined passions of ecumenicity and social witness. A quarter of a century ago, the ecclesiastical desire to affirm a common faith and the ethical desire to overcome false social discriminations and to establish an integrated society brought theology and sociology into new conjunctions that we now celebrate and hope to extend. Priests and nuns marched with Protestant theologians and Sunday-school teachers, arm in arm with preachers and deaconesses from store-front churches as a new generation of Christian activists tried to call the nation to live up to the promises of human rights for all that its forebears had anticipated, but not actualized.

The remarkable generation which founded our BTI wanted to transform the moral ecology of church and society. They sought also to lower the walls of suspicion between communions that had been in conflict since (at least) the continental wars of religion, and they wanted to renew the capacity of theology to address the architecture of the common life, even though many believed that if religion entered public life it threatened both peace and reason. However, the twentieth century has turned this fear on its head. The neopaganism of fascism, with the science of the Enlightenment as its tool, and the rationalist secularism of communism, with a humanist theory of meaning at its heart, have engendered more perilous threats to civilization and the human spirit than Christianity ever did. Indeed, after the collapse of national socialism the quest for renewal emerged in Orthodox, Protestant, and Catholic circles around the world, just as it is now emerging as Evangelical, Pentecostal, and Fundamentalist forms.

A quarter of a century ago, that spirit appeared in the United States not only in a new demand for obedience to a higher moral law, such as Martin Luther King, Jr. articulated in his "Letter from a Birmingham Jail," and in a vision of a reconciled future such as he painted in his address "I Have a Dream." Similar motifs reemerged internationally from long trajectories of Christian developments that had been submerged by ethnic nationalism and class warfare to reappear in those worldly replications of canonicity and conciliarity, the Declaration of Human Rights and the formation of the United Nations. For many, such developments renewed the confidence that theologically-grounded first principles, effectively linked to embodied social theory, could mitigate historic evil, strengthen constitutional democracy, more nearly approximate justice, create mutuality in the midst of contention, bring reconciliation in the face of enmity, and constrain the wanton use of force when coercive authority was necessary to preserve civility.

Such ideas had been severely tested by steel, blood, and ideology in this short and hostile century, as already hinted. Whether in the name of the sovereignty of national will rooted in an assertion of ethnic identity and cultural particularity that would reclaim the grandeur of a noble past, or in the name of the "workers of the world" who would be purified of their illusions by their suffering and thus be liberated to bring the future to its fulfillment by overthrowing every domination, modern worldly messianic movements, one based on race and the other on class, both dedicated to power, rekindled passions that lay beneath the veneer of a supposedly "Christian" and "rational" modernity.

These have not been the only ills of our century, of course. New harvesters of death have joined the ancient horsemen of destruction. As far as we can now see into the future, all succeeding generations will face the possibility of nuclear threat, ecological ruin, and immune deficiency syndromes. And the limitation of these perils will require levels of technical prudence, political cooperation, and transcultural moral wisdom that are rare in human history. Nevertheless, the rise and fall of national socialism and now also of proletarian socialism in the twentieth century have unleashed demons not yet exorcised from our world. The assumptions on which they developed pathological programs still generate the categories by which many — perhaps especially in social scientific and ecumenical Christian circles — understand life.

And yet, now that they have collapsed, we experience not a euphoria of triumph but a profound anxiousness, for we struggle with the doubts these movements have induced. Is it possibly that the central claims about theology and ethics that attracted hundreds of intellectuals and theologians to them, and that stand at the depths of these crude ideologies, are in some measure true? Are theology and ethics basically to be understood as projected rationalizations of our ethnicity, manifestations of our national identity, our social location, our psychosexual dispositions, or our group interests? Are we to understand theology and ethics as the superstructural reflections of what is ultimately more real — the material and social constellations of substructure? The problem is this: we know that these horrendous movements have revealed what is in fact the case in some measure. These are the great insights that not only allowed this dying century to unmask the pretentious use of religious symbols to legitimate violence, domination, and exploitation, and the inflated use of particularist claims to simulate universal principles, even while they fed the forces of destruction and deconstruction that define our century. And now that we are on the far side of those movements socially and politically, we ask whether we are, or can be, on the far side of such assumptions intellectually and emotionally.

It is in this context that we renew the conversation between theology and sociology. It is a wonderful opportunity. Robert Bellah, the traditions of social thought from which he draws, and the colleagues with whom he works, always have a deeper agenda in mind than the ideologies of the moment. He has constantly sought the deeper foundations of the common life and he has seen both religion and morality as critical in this sociological quest. What remains a question, at least to me, is whether he has seen the importance of the distinctions between religion and theology, between morality and ethics. That is, how are we to understand the relationship between the descriptive and the prescriptive, the interpretive and the normative? This, of course, is a large question and we cannot raise all its aspects here; but it may be useful to identify two motifs of his thought that bear on this question — one I think is very important but may be overstated by him, and one I believe to be profound and enduring but rather understated.

Bellah shares one characteristic with many radical protests against modern society: he opposes liberal individualism, particularly as it appears in market economies, although he wants the kind of society that supports and defends persons. It is, I agree, surely the case that egoism and selfishness are alive and well in this culture, and are nurtured by parts of it. However, individualism has many faces and not all of them are evil. In his paper for this celebration, he seems to acknowledge that some aspects for the dignity of the person are among the great achievements of modernity. And it is surely the case that modernity is, in these respects, an improvement on societies in which the individual is swallowed up in the heteronomous herds of ethnic, class, or gender stereotypes and predetermined roles.

To be sure, a substantial academic debate has been raging for some time between the "liberals" and the "communitarians," with whom Bellah is most frequently identified. Liberals, as the term is often understood, stress the factual and the moral priority of the free individual over the community's authority. The promise of the future is the liberation of the human personality from the domination of heteronomous imposition, and the lever of liberation is the sovereignty of the rational capacities of the individual mind. The chief threat to freedom, thus, is residual or resurgent irrationality — religious belief, political lust for power, or economic greed. In contrast, the communitarian doubts the power of rationality when it is separated from a base in community loyalty and practice. Freedom as the liberal appeals to it is viewed as an escape from the embedded character of historical responsibility and a fraudulent warrant for licentiousness. The chief threat, in this view, is anomie, rootlessness, and egoism.

We could debate these alternative views with a number of vocabularies. Recently, the eminent scholar of jurisprudence Harold J. Berman showed the relative inadequacy of both the liberal views as presented by Harvard philosopher John Rawls, and the communitarian ones as defined by his colleague Michael Sandmel, for actually guiding the kinds of decisions jurists must make.[1] On grounds of social theory, Mark S. Chadis of Vassar recently published an analysis of Durkheim in relation to certain elements of Rousseau that indicates how both contain individualist and communitarian elements.[2] Drawing more on Germanic traditions, Seyla Benhabib of the New School recently published a defense of a "chastised liberalism" in the tradition of Jürgen Habermas, one able to "take seriously the claims of community, gender, and postmodernism" and nevertheless hold to a post-Enlightenment defense of rational universalism beyond the critique of Alisdair MacIntyre.[3] And, in an analysis of these issues from the standpoint of the philosophy of religious ethics, the superb work of Franklin Gamwell identifies the necessary complementarity of personal integrity and community relationship.[4]

On the basis of such arguments, it is not altogether clear that individualism and its origins are quite as Bellah identifies them. For one thing, the treatment of Locke as the father of all that is evil about modern individualism is such that (as Yogi Berra said of a deceased friend) if he were alive today he would turn over in his grave. With Archbishop Laud on one side and Hobbes on the other, Locke's arguments not only defended the independence of conscience from government manipulation and the right of associations in the face of a sovereign will, but he sought to place coercive power under a moral law, to which he believed every soul had access, to constrain the arbitrary individual will of those who thought they could and should control community power. That is why Puritans such as Jonathan Edwards could draw on him for religious renewal, and Jefferson to form a new kind of constitutional government. In other words, a strong case can be made that Lockean influences were supportive of much that Bellah surely wants to defend. Insofar as liberalism, Christianity, and civic virtue in the form of submission to constitutional law continue to guide (admittedly with tensions) large segments of our common life, we are less removed from that history than he suggests. However, to pursue this argument would take us into historical debates that are not the main focus today.

The wider question is whether, in fact, individualism is so overwhelmingly rampant in all areas of life and theory as Bellah maintains. It is surely so that this generation is, in large measure, anti-institutional — suspicious of church, state, school, marriage, and manners — and that we have just passed through the "me" generation that bought, sold, and dismantled corporations for personal gain. But this may not be due to some influence of Lockean individualism so much as it is due to the incapacity of post-World War II institutions, especially in the suburbs, to socialize and acculturate those whom we call the baby-boomers. This generation may not understand what it takes to establish and sustain a civilization in which humans can flourish with some grace. To be sure, some contemporary theorists of capitalism claim that the individual calculus of cost and benefit is the sufficient logic for understanding all of social reality,[5] but it is more likely that Colin Campbell's study of the relationship between romanticism and consumerism is closer to the mark.[6] He argues that we ought to make a distinction between the productive side of modern economic systems, where disciplined "this-worldly asceticism" and modes of corporate cooperation clearly obtain, and the consumption side, which is less due to the evils of a free market than it is to the relative triumph of a series of cultural influences mediated to the economy by romantic philosophers, poets, and religious leaders and widely established in the modern university as well as in advertising.

Certainly, if we examine the structures of our own lives, there is much evidence that we continue to be relational creatures, enmeshed in networks of interdependency and obligation about which we constantly have to clarify the relation between individual inclinations, responsiveness to family and friends, professional accountability, and general societal duties. The middle classes find their egocentric willfulness constrained by interpersonal, communal, and social networks of obligation and constraint even if some evidence suggests that the super-rich do not have to pay attention to others and the homeless represent a population of disconnected people. The problem may be less that we have a nation of alienated, lonely, isolated, and calculating individuals than that we continue to be in the midst of a major transformation in which communitarian interactions are now modulated and supplemented, not entirely displaced, by complex societal forms of human interdependence.

Of course, it is also true that a number of ideological postures seem to want to portray modernity lopsidedly in the other direction. Many neoconservatives seem preoccupied with an overbearing "*polis* envy," and no few sectarian fideists want to return to enclaves of pious togetherness distinct and separate from the evils of "culture." Thus they too condemn individualism at every juncture. But what appears to be at stake in Bellah's condemnation is neither of these. It is a residual antipathy to modern economic institutions that he and his colleagues read in terms, first, of Karl Polanyi's theory of the corrosive effects of capitalism, which he holds "set off destructive forces which by the middle of the twentieth century had come close to destroying civilization,"[7] but finally in terms of

R. H. Tawney's Fabian-socialist account of the rise and character of modern industry.[8] In the turn to Polanyi and to Tawney, Bellah and his colleagues not only reject the postsocialist tradition of Weber and Parsons, which had informed earlier work, they adopt what could become an antitechnological, antimodernizing ethic of relinquishment, simplicity, and spirituality that avoids engagement with materiality and stands in opposition to the demands of a complex, global society. It is yet to be seen whether these theorists have recognized the fuller implications of the failures of socialism around the world for our understanding of the relationship between morality and the new demands of the economic order.[9]

In any case, the assessment of individualism and the relationship between the person and society remains a decisive question. From the standpoint of Christian ethics, the critique of individualism always has to be guarded by protections for the integrity of the individual conscience, the significance of the moral agency of selves, the inviolability of human persons, which no community, collectivity, or government can compromise with impunity. The human soul finally stands before God and knows itself to be a gift of grace intended to be discipled in an obedience that aids the neighbor and glorifies its source, and thus not to be seen either as a "freedom that finds its fulfillment in independence" nor one that finds its freedom "in active engagement with the society *that creates us.*"[10] Increasingly it appears that even the recovering socialists who still dominate large segments of academia acknowledge that key aspects of individualism must be preserved, insofar as it prompts associations in which people have a measure of participatory choice about how they are to be identified, what discipline they are to accept, which duties they assume, and how they worship. It appears to me that Bellah remains ambiguous on this issue and thus is limited in the normative guidance he can give, although obviously he intends a rather creative mixture of "liberal" and "communitarian" elements in his understanding of the human self.

It would be interesting, in this connection, to see him take up key questions that have plagued religious debates over the centuries. It is not clear, for example, whether he believes in the reality of a "soul" or an "*imago dei.*" Is there something real and inviolable at the deepest levels of the self, something prior to our social relationships that, while it may evoke a profound desire for and need for responsible relationships, does allow us to challenge every definition of the common good that is not rooted in God's law and purpose? There are several relevant ways of posing this question. For example, we might ask whether this way of understanding the human self tells us anything about how humans ought to be related to one another sexually, since issues of homosexuality are among the most heated debates in the churches and in the society today.

Does Bellah (and his colleagues) believe that there is a right and good — and thus a wrong and evil — way to love, and if so what might it be? At another level, one might ask him about the nature and character of conversion, for conversion from one religion to another involves the acknowledgment of a proper individual transcendence over the social, cultural institutions in which one finds oneself — the relative abstraction of the self, as "soul," from institutional and historical tradition, and the formation on the far side of the transition of new patterns of relationship and sociality. In other words, I think it is possible that Bellah and his colleagues may have overstated, in several ways, the problem of individualism. At the least, its assumptions and implications need further clarity.

However, I think that the second and less obvious set of contributions that Bellah has made is more important. Sociology in the tradition from which he draws is rooted in deeper historical, philosophical, and theological veins than those which echo the left critiques of individualism or the right critiques of individualism. Anticipations of the deeper motifs appear in the Roman notions of *jus gentium* and *societas naturalis*, ideas understood by parts of the pre-Reformation church to be an aspect of natural law and often identified with the "estates." Here the view is that key social institutions such as family or school or hospital must be allowed to exist with the support of and without undue interference by political authority, for each has a sacred quality that ought not be violated. Birth and death, science and learning, sickness and health are matters every society must face and to which, inevitably, religious meanings are attached. All people are duty bound to honor, pay attention to, and preserve the institutions and the people in the critical roles who wrestle with these questions. Much of the post-Reformation church regarded these institutional "orders," what we today call "sectors" of society or "departments of life," which could be best understood in terms of "mandates of creation" or "spheres of providential care."[11] Such terms pointed to key institutions in civilization as channels of God's grace. When Bellah and his colleagues introduce their most recent book arguing that "We Live through Institutions," and then focus in a sequence of chapters on the analysis of morality, market and work, law and politics, education and the church, we know that we are in a world of "sectoral analysis," even if the terms of this analysis and their roots are not made fully explicit. It is likely that they represent the rediscovery by the modern social sciences of what theologians have argued for, in other terms, for centuries.

The ancient theories of society that are at stake here presume that souls and civilizations are morally and spiritually shaped by many subsystems of society — subsystems that become more explicit and differentiated in historical development. Each sector of life — family, politics, medicine, law, education, economy — has a distinct integrity, one that is related to the ethos of civilization as a whole. In the course of several centuries, as Bellah knows well and has taught many of us, different ones of these institutions have come to prominence. But the ancient Christian sources saw them as distinct areas prior to their modern emergence. In modernity, to be sure, these and other areas have developed an increasingly independent self-consciousness, their own discipline in the university, their own professional cadre of experts, and their own claims to an autonomy both from religion and from other sciences. But this differentiation did not take place in other cultures in the same ways where religious influence was different, and in all of life these areas are actually interdependent.

Ultimately, they are rooted in a metaphysical-moral reality that transcends their relative autonomy. Thus sociology done in a manner that is sensitive to these matters, as is Bellah's, assumes the task of interpreting how these multiple systems interact to shape the moral fabric of selves and of society as a whole, and of inquiring as to what it takes morally and spiritually to make things work. This is a theory of a pluralistic civility, a "federated" society of associations held together in covenant by common beliefs and moral commitments. If either the integrity of the various parts, or their relative interdependence or their transcendental-ethical rootage is lost, things fall apart and people suffer. Sociology in the tradition Bellah represents thus appears to bear within it an implicit, complex set of assumptions about the foundations of common life. It recovers and recasts a deeper heritage than he and his colleagues document.

I applaud this way of reading the human condition; it makes the contemporary modes of liberation analysis that have come to dominate much of contemporary theology and ethics look thin. This pluralist, institutional way of interpreting the most important features of the common life is not based in racial, class, or power analysis, although it can include and comprehend those ways of interpreting human conflict. Instead, this tradition focuses on value, meaning, and moral ecology as found, often in fragmentary forms, in three places: in the residual consciousness of people who do not always know whence such things come; in the basic, necessary, unavoidable institutions of life that make pluralistic society sustainable; and in the symbolism of religion. These are the loci of analysis in *Habits of the Heart*, for which Bellah and his team are so justly famous, as well as in *The Good Society*. This way of reading the contemporary situation does not presume that the deepest human problem is oppression from which we need liberation. Rather, the deeper problem is fragmentation and chaos, for which we need an integrative commitment, a greater cohesion of organization, a social-ethical fiber, and a coherent vision of the ultimate order and purpose of things that preserves the dignity of all the people

involved. Of course, this does not mean that ethnicity or economic stratification or oppressive patterns of gender domination are not important. It
does mean that they are framed by larger questions that have to do with
the inevitably necessary functions and inescapable structures through
which a common life in civilization must be ordered. Such a theory is of
enormous importance for both personal life in complex civilization and
for the global society into which we are plunging today.

However, all this poses several problems for us in the BTI. While it
takes *religion* seriously, it is not clear what role *theology* is to play in the
society it helped form, in the social theory that it helped generate, or in the
social context this sociological child now interprets. For ourselves, we
need to ask whether Christian theology knows anything indispensable to
these institutions, or about the foundations on which a viable complex
society and all its various sectors must rest. Does theology have anything
distinctive to contribute to the study of contemporary society that is not
better covered by others in the modern university, such as sociology in
this mode? Or is theology the exhausted elder who now sits gently at the
table, sipping its vintage wine while the youthful social sciences and their
middle-aged natural cousins dance with religion?

It is *necessary* to pose this question, lest we confuse sociology, religion, and theology. Sociology and its sister sciences can offer nuanced
interpretations of how human relationships and institutions work, and they
can point to the critical social role of religion in forming and maintaining
the structures of the common life. But it is not clear that it can tell us
whether the religion and the society of which it is the core are fundamentally true and just. The proper sciences for this discernment are theologically rooted, and (if there is anything to them) necessarily transsocietal
and transcultural. It is *possible* to pose this question to the scholarly work
of Bellah and his colleagues for they do not presume, as do a number of
other prominent social theories, that the social sciences can alone explain
the ultimate foundations of sociality. To be sure, there is evidence that
much of what people believe and do is shaped by their psychological
needs, their social location, their political interests, their racial prejudice,
and their cultural reference group. In the last generation, indeed, several
theologians have been preoccupied with just such questions. The tradition
Bellah represents recognizes the influence of upbringing or neurosis, of
social stratification and class consciousness, of legitimation and the political manipulation of religious symbols, and of acculturation and socialization; but it does not presume that this is all that there is to it. This
interpretation recognizes that there is "more" to religion and morality than
that. And this is the question: what more, how much more, what kind of
more, what difference does that more make, and is that more true and just?

At this point, it makes a good bit of difference what the basic definitions are, and it is not clear today whether we have a common definition
of theology. We may well have profound commitments and convictions
among social theorists, but these are not all "theological." We have also
much religion around the world, including powerful and explosive renewal movements of enormous importance, but it is not clear that they are
"theological" either. If theology is to be taken seriously in a pluralistic
world, it must be able to inquire with clarity and confidence into the truth,
justice, and love of God beyond the opinions of specific constituencies
and it must clarify the criteria by which we do so in public discourse. In
many ways, this is what Bellah does; but for religion, not clearly for
theology.

One way to pose the issue I am raising can be put in terms of a key
phrase that Bellah uses: the idea of a "second language." Many will remember that in *Habits of the Heart*, the authors spoke of the first language
Americans use to speak about meaning and morality. It draws, they say,
its vocabulary on the one hand from the psychological, emotive language
of therapy and on the other hand from the managerial, calculative language of utilitarianism. Against this, Bellah and his colleagues pose the
idea of a "second language," one that is constituted by deep traditions of
"republican virtue" and of "biblical insight." In such references, we find
soft echoes of the fact that theology was formed by a long heritage that
wove the reason of the Greco-Roman world together with the revelation of
the Hebraic and Christian scriptures to form a normative if unfinished
understanding of how God wants humanity to live together. That this
second language is becoming dangerously eroded is one of the main lessons of that work; that these foundations are necessary for a viable public
ethic is central to its message.

However, this idea of a second language seems to disappear in *Good
Society* instead of being elaborated in a direct way. References to these
normative motifs are muted. Instead we find an appeal to the traditions of
John Dewey and Walter Lippman — traditions that, while they recognize
that religion continues among the people, and while they speak to public
issues, and while they may have echoes of earlier religious overtones,
have no theological basis for anything really important. To be sure, one
finds in Bellah frequent references to Martin Luther King, Jr., H. Richard
and Reinhold Niebuhr, and John Courtney Murray. These references are
interesting and pertinent, but they have little obvious connection to overt
theological and doctrinal bases. Of course, this is not a book about doctrine; but pressing this issue poses the issue of whether or not that "more"
is necessary so that it must be there, overtly, or whether it is sufficient that
it is present covertly, almost as a matter of optional style and audience.

Insofar as anything normative is there, it is indirect, implied, and veiled, as a reminder of earlier influences, a deep archeological deposit that may bear resources for our identity — not because it is true or just, but because it is part of us.

Perhaps the BTI has been, in principle, on the right track. Perhaps the BTI senses where the deepest and widest public is, and knows that the primary reference for it should be an ecumenically conceived and publicly engaged theology. It is a broader and deeper concept than any particular church or any single society or any sector of society or any social science possesses. Is it not so that wherever it finds a place for orthodox, catholic, evangelical, reformed, and liberal elements, it always reaches beyond itself? Certainly internally, both the *theos* and *logos* of theology drive it toward cosmopolitan perspectives of a normative and universal sort. The only "more" worth worshipping and talking about is, finally, God — who is interested in many things besides our religion, in many peoples besides ourselves, and in many places besides America; and the only theology of enduring interest in our global society seeks the truth, justice, and mercies of God wherever these can be found.

What is not clear is how this normative and universal feature of theology relates today to the kind of sociology that so helpfully exegetes many features of our particular moral ecology and socioreligious heritage. In sociology we find few references to the question of how God wants us to live. Indeed, Bellah wrote: "(T)here is no pattern of a good society that we or anyone else can simply discern and then expect people to conform to. . . . [I]t is central to the notion of a good society that it is an open quest, actively involving all its members." [12] And at the end of the study, he writes: "In the theoretical perspective we have developed, we see our present configuration of institutions not as sociologically 'necessary' but as historically contingent, open to critical reflection and significant reform." [13] And of course the question is whether or not there is a normative vision to which critical reflection has access, and whether there is a normative form by which to measure the relative adequacy of any reforms we make.

Quite practically, we can ask whether it is possible to reform a society and its institutions with such an unguided quest and such disclaimers, and without explicitly normative and universal content. How does the transformation of an ethos take place in social history, especially since the regnant twentieth-century ideologies of change have collapsed? So far as I know, no enduring restructuring of religion or of institutions or of civilizations or of personal character has ever occurred because of the denial of a normative vision or of the capacity of humans to know one. The history of Moses, the prophets, or the early church does not suggest that such change happens. Nor can we find evidence for the reform of the church in any age by inviting all to join a rudderless quest toward an indeterminate goal. The Ecumenical Councils, the Gregorian Reforms, and the Protestant Reformations did not develop from such roots. And in our nation's history, I cannot imagine Jefferson writing: "We hold this hypothesis to be likely, that all persons are equally to participate in an open process." Nor can we imagine Lincoln ending his second inaugural address by saying: "With malice toward none; with charity for all; let us press on to whatever we decide we need to do, since there is no pattern of a good society that we can discern or to which we can expect people to conform."

But there may be such a pattern and the current resurgence of religion, even in its militant forms, may be the quest for it. And here a brief note must be made of the enlarged public to which our public discourse must be directed today. Bellah is well aware of the changes in the role of America in the world, and he directs his considerable wisdom to guiding a prudent national policy toward the well-being of the wider world; but it is not clear yet that he has fully encountered the fact that we face a world of multiple religions and cultural traditions that cannot all be equally valid. At this level, to appeal to the power and significance of our religion in our context simply does not suffice. After all, the distinctive feature of religion is that it claims to have some insight about a real, other world that is manifest in or related to this one. And the distinctive claim of theology is that it can critically assess and evaluate those claims with the recognition that some of them may be valid even if many are false or even evil. If this is not possible, if theology cannot reach cross-culturally, cross-historically, cross-religiously, and finally transcendentally, even religion loses sight of the character and content of its "more," and sinks into the collective consciousness of what is going on in this or that social history, serving only as the totemic flag of all those mundane interests which preoccupy the world without God.

We can put the matter this way: the moral ecologies of human communities have an important if limited viability on their own. All the moral humanists and ethical philosophers in the world already know this, and theological ethics is on weak ground if it fails to take the careful study of this into account in its work. Yet what they do not know is how feeble a moral ecology is. It must be supported and sustained by many institutions, including religious ones, and by committed human attentiveness, as Bellah and his associates say. But ethics needs, finally, not one pillar of support, but two — and the second of these is theology — that kind of theology which clarifies the criteria by which we know what is true and just and holy.

Nowhere does this seem to be more important than in two areas of life that we must face in the future — one in the moral infrastructure of our social lives and the other in the moral macrostructure. One of these areas is the family. Nearly all the major denominations have experienced major and bruising debates about the character of human sexuality and its implications for the family today, and much of this debate has been more sociological than theological. In the coming years this debate will become a political and ideological battleground if all present indicators are valid. It is simply not clear that we in church or society know, today, how we ought to love, and how the normative patterns of love ought to be institutionalized in our moral ecology — in part because our culture, under the influence of the social sciences, has removed this area from theological guidance.

And at a quite different level we face the ongoing processes of globalization — of the economy, of communication, of law, of technology, of politics, and of medicine and education. These bring with them new demands for intercontextual definitions of justice, fresh patterns of cross-cultural cooperation and mutuality, and more universalistic modes of interaction than previous interpretations thought were possible. In several ways, humans are learning to relate to one another in a wide variety of styles, situations, cultures, and locales. And these developments have today brought us to a new, more direct encounter with the great world religions — especially Hinduism, Confucianism, and Islam — which represent the most important, powerful, and profound representations of alternative religious and ethical systems that have ever been able to form enduring civilizations. These are much greater and much more serious challenges to Christianity than fascism or communism precisely because they more nearly approximate the overt, principled universalism present in profound religious consciousness, and they have shown that they can, as has Christianity, form complex civilizations over many centuries. In the face of these, we must articulate the foundations of our confidence in our faith again, refining it where it is faulty, obscure, or incapable of guiding lives and cultures, not because we are Americans with a specific tradition, but because we live in a new global civilization where just these things are under suspicion.

In this context, more than religion is required. Religion may hold a particular society together, but we live in a matrix of particular societies that is being formed and transformed by an emergent global society. This emergent global society is not rooted in common memory or on a common historical experience. Insofar as it is developing as a *novum*, it exists as an artifact based on certain widely-accepted abstract principles that disrupt and detract all who participate in it from the historic traditions that have informed life's meanings. In the face of this, only some religions can support a fascination with and a commitment to such abstractions. Theology, not religion; ethics, not cultural tradition; and new forms of civilizational theory, not national analysis alone represent that abstraction.[14]

In the past, theology played a major role in shaping the principles that were to guide the encounter and clash of societies, although such concerns have not been central to theology for generations. What ought we do when we face the creation of a world society that presents us with a common future without a common past. Religion by itself is insufficient. We face something like the situation of the Christians in the Roman Empire who had to encounter frames of reference that were, by all appearances, more universal than what the biblical message seemed to be — a small group with a large idea making its way by touching the people one by one and encountering by the development of theology the intellectual and moral and social forces of that cosmopolis. They did this not only by reflecting on the faith that was in their cultural heritage, but more by engaging in the task of testing whether the core of that heritage was, at its root, more universal than the best philosophy and broadest social theory and widest empire history had known. Today, given the global role into which the United States has been thrust, we may be forced again to seek what is true and just beyond the ordinary limits of our own religious confession, cultural heritage, social contract, historical experience, and national interest.

The capacity to speak effectively to such issues of the common life surely will require renewal of the ecumenical spirit linked to a renewed engagement with such theorists as Bellah, but it shall also require a broader sense of "public," and therefore a revival of the encounter between sociology and theology at new levels. If this is successful, we in the BTI shall not only learn how to read the moral ecology of our ethos as it is embodied in the multiple institutions and interactions of our emerging complex global civilization, but we shall be better enabled to help persons find their ways in life and to speak discerningly of the laws and purposes of God in the midst of it. May God grant that it be so. Then we can have another celebration — twenty-five years hence.

Notes

1. See his "Toward an Integrative Jurisprudence: Politics, Morality and History," *California Law Review* 76:4 (July 1988): 779-801.

2. "Rousseau and Durkheim: The Relation between the Public and the Private," *Journal of Religious Ethics*, 21:1 (Spring 1993): 1-25. See also his *A Communitarian Defense of Liberalism: Emile Durkheim and Contemporary Social Theory* (Stanford: Stanford University Press, 1992).

3. See her *Situating the Self* (New York: Routledge, 1992).

4. See his *The Divine Good: Modern Moral Theory and the Necessity of God* (San Francisco: Harper San Francisco, 1990).

5. Gary S. Becker has indeed won the most recent Nobel Prize in economics for arguing just this point, and his arguments have been taken as the guide to normative thinking in several areas. See, for example, Judge Richard Posner, *The Economic Analysis of Law*, 3rd ed. (Boston: Little, Brown, 1986) and *Sex and Reason* (Cambridge: Harvard University Press, 1992).

6. See his *The Romantic Ethic and the Spirit of Modern Consumerism* (London: Basil Blackwell, 1987).

7. Robert Bellah, et al., *The Good Society* (New York: Knopf, 1991), 291.

8. Ibid., 292.

9. See my "Brunner's *Christianity and Civilization* Revisited: Its Significance after the Collapse of Socialism," in *Theologie und Ökonomie: Symposium zum 100. Geburtstag von Emil Brunner*, ed. H. Ruh (Zurich: Theologische Verlag, 1992), 163-186.

10. Ibid., 245. Italics added.

11. See my "Religion, Society and the Independent Sector: Key Elements of a General Theory," in *Religion, the Independent Sector and American Culture*, ed. C. Cherry and R. A. Sherrill (Atlanta: Scholars Press, 1992), 11-30. The more elaborated, cross-cultural use of such categories of analysis appears in my *Creeds, Society and Human Rights* (Grand Rapids: Eerdmans, 1986).

12. *The Good Society*, op. cit., p. 8. In the appendix the authors affirm again that they want to draw on "important elements in biblical religion and civic republicanism" which have always moderated individualism, but the grounds beyond their social functionality in a culture already shaped by these influences are not emphasized.

13. Ibid., 292.

14. See especially Rolland Robertson, *Globalization: Social Theory and Global Culture* (London: Sage, 1992) and R. Robertson and W. R. Garrett, *Religion and Global Order* (New York: Paragon House, 1991). Cf. also M. Featherstone, *Global Culture* (London: Sage, 1990), especially Peter Beyer, "Privitization and the Public Influence of Religion in Global Society," 373-396.

3

A Black Church Challenge to
and Perspective on
Christianity and Civil Society

Lawrence H. Mamiya

As-salaam alaikum! Shalom alecheim! Pax Vobiscum! Peace be unto you! Good morning! I want to thank Dr. Rodney Petersen, Executive Director of the BTI, Professor Preston Williams of Harvard Divinity, President David Shannon of Andover Newton, and all of the BTI faculty for the kind invitation to participate in celebrating the twenty-fifth anniversary of the BTI by addressing you this morning on the topic of "Christianity and Civil Society from the Perspective of Black Churches." I also bring greetings from my coauthor and colleague, Professor C. Eric Lincoln. I also want to thank Professor John Cartwright of the School of Theology of Boston University for responding to my paper.[1] It is a rare privilege indeed to take part in a symposium with Professor Robert Bellah whom I have always regarded as one of my mentors and former teacher and certainly one of the most creative minds in the fields of the sociology of religion and the study of American religious life.

"Man makes himself even his own body. The human body a historical variable."[2] The quote is from Norman O. Brown's *Love's Body*, a text that we graduate students at Berkeley were reading in Bellah's seminar when Governor Ronald Reagan ordered the National Guard to drop tear gas from helicopters on the students and to flood the campus with troops

---

Lawrence H. Mamiya is Professor of Religion and African Studies at Vassar College.

during the People's Park demonstrations in 1969. It is good to see Bob again in a somewhat more peaceful setting.

This paper will be divided into two sections. Part I will include several challenges from the perspective of black churches to Christianity and civil society in the United States. There are some important lessons to be learned from the history and sociology of black churches. Part II includes challenges to the black churches, some important factors that African-American Christians and others need to pay attention to in the decade of the 1990s.

Part I: Challenges from Black Churches to Christianity and Civil Society

As a result of the national study of black churches that Eric Lincoln and I completed, *The Black Church in the African American Experience*, I was given the task of reflecting upon the theme of this conference from the perspective of black churches, both historically and currently.[3] Obviously, from the point of view of enslaved Africans, the major terms of the theme of this conference, "Christianity and Civil Society," were already rendered problematic. From the beginnings of the North Atlantic slave trade in 1506, Christianity provided the major legitimation for slavery, both as a means to convert "pagan" Africans to Christian salvation and to provide economic wealth for the royalty and venture capitalists of slave-trading countries. For example, in the Latin American, Caribbean, and North American colonies claimed by Catholic countries, Catholic priests met the slave ships and administered the rite of baptism into the Christian faith to the startled and puzzled Africans who walked off the gangplanks in chains. Protestants, on the other hand, were much more ambivalent regarding the religious status of the African slaves, who were not officially baptized until the colonies of Virginia and Maryland led the way in 1667 with legal statutes that declared baptism into the Christian faith would not lead to the freedom of the slaves. Slavery was deemed to be "durante vita," a status and condition for all of life, passed on from generation to generation.[4] It was not until 1701 when the Society for the Propagation of the Gospel of the Anglican Church applied for permission from plantation owners to spread the gospel among Indians and African slaves that the real efforts of missionary work among the Africans began. The Anglican missionaries succeeded in convincing the slave owners that Christian slaves would make docile and obedient laborers. The Apostle Paul's injunctions in Romans to the good master and good slave were often quoted. This effort at Christian evangelism would culminate in the massive revivals of the First (1790s) and Second (1830s) Awakenings when the major-

ity of the slaves were converted, largely by Baptist and Methodist evangelists and circuit riders. For the first one hundred years, Africans survived with the traditional African or Islamic practices they brought with
them. But the system of plantation slavery, which stripped slaves of their
language and customs, eventually led to the demise of traditional religions, whose remnants were later incorporated into the African American
practice of Christianity.[5]

Although Africans fought in the American Revolutionary War, they did
not share in the original definition of "citizen" written into the documents
of the American Constitution and the Declaration of Independence. While
all women and Native Americans were excluded, Africans were considered subhuman property or three-fifths of the political worth of a white
European male. The Constitution was only the first of many attempts to
deny the benefits and rights of citizenship to African Americans in American society, no matter how many times they had fought for and died to
secure those rights. While Africans themselves had practiced their own
forms of slavery in their own lands, they did not match the brutality and
destructiveness of the system of chattel slavery that developed in the
United States. It is estimated that for every slave who survived in the
plantation system, at least five others died; the toll of millions is of holo-
caust proportions.[6] According to Raboteau and Wills, from the seventeenth to the mid-nineteenth centuries, more Africans were crossing the
Atlantic Ocean than Europeans.[7] Although there is much debate and great
uncertainty about the numbers of Africans taken as slaves during the
North Atlantic slave trade, the best estimates run into the millions. This
presence of a greater African consciousness in the Americas will require a
rewriting of history to account for their presence.

The African slaves turned the religion they had adopted into a weapon for
their own survival and liberation. African American Christianity was not
merely Christianity with a black patina; it was suffused with the traditions,
values, and practices of African American culture. Although their beliefs
and doctrines were the same as white Christians, the worship practices, the
call-and-response preaching style, and even the songs and music of African
American Christians began to differ.[8] In fact, the black churches were the
first major institutional products of a developing African American culture,
which was made up of elements from African and Euro-American cultures
blended in a unique way. Since the process of cultural development is too
complex to detail in a short paper, let us assume that such a process took
place from the seventeenth to the twentieth centuries as other scholars have
documented, given the rigid racial segregation that was imposed upon African Americans in the North as well as in the South.[9] Before the Constitution
of the United States was written, from 1750 to the 1780s, the "Invisible

Institution" of slave religion, often practiced clandestinely by slaves in the brush arbors, bayous, and backwoods of plantations, became the visible independent black churches. The Bluestone Church on the Byrd plantation in Virginia, Silver Bluff in South Carolina, Springfield in Augusta and First African in Savannah, Georgia were founded by African American Baptists, while Bethel-Baltimore, Mother Bethel in Philadelphia, and Mother Zion in New York City were among the earliest churches established by African Methodists. Spurred by the onset of abolitionist activity in the early nineteenth century, these churches also organized themselves into the first independent black church denominations, with the African Methodist Episcopal Church (1816) and the African Methodist Episcopal Zion Church (1821) as the first national black organizations. The formation of these independent churches took place because African American Christians were often treated as second-class members within white churches, forced to sit in the upstairs balconies, which were called "nigger heavens" in the South, or outside by the windows. Black clergy were often treated contemptuously by their white counterparts and they had to sleep in church pews and bring their own food when the denomination held a conference that lasted for several days. Restaurants, lodging houses, and the homes of white members were barred to them.[10] But above all, African American clergy and church members desired the independence to make their own decisions and plans. Thus black churches became the most independent institutional sector in black communities, a situation that still prevails at the present time.

Next to the black family and extended kinship network, black churches became the earliest and the central social institution within black communities. Much of black history can be viewed through the lens of this institutional sector, because black clergy and their congregations have been involved in all of the crisis points that have affected African Americans. The first challenge from black churches to American society concerns their strong anti-racial discrimination stance. From their origins to the present, there has been a uncompromising challenge to the deeply embedded racism of the larger society. Black church members have often asserted that their clergy should be "race men and women," speaking up publicly at the occurrence of racial incidents. On this score, many black Christians have often felt that their form and practice of Christianity has been more authentic, more humane, and more accepting of racial differences. White Christians can attend any black church and they will be warmly welcomed, but the same cannot be said about the acceptance of African Americans in some white congregations, even to this day. While overt forms of racial discrimination such as lynchings, beatings, and attacks will still be of some concern, the major challenge for black churches and all Americans will focus on the covert, subtle types of racism institutionalized in the forms of admissions and employment policies, budget decisions, membership in private country clubs and corporate boards, etc. The struggles of the Civil Rights movement have been carried from the political arena of voting rights and the desegregation of public accommodations to the economic sphere. Twenty-five years after the Civil Rights movement, there is very little evidence that those with power and wealth are willing to share it. Even with Bill Clinton's victory, much of the evidence still points in the opposite direction.

A second challenge concerns the holistic type of ministry that black churches have been involved in throughout their history. As we have argued in our book, black churches have been involved in all of the life spheres of the black community. Beginning with a strong grounding in spiritual matters, the ministry of black churches has also encompassed involvement in economics, politics, education, physical and mental health, music and other artistic endeavors, recreation, and leadership training. As Lincoln has eloquently written:

> The black pilgrimage in America was made less onerous because of their religion. Their religion was the organizing principle around which their life was structured. Their church was their school, their forum, their political arena, their social club, their art gallery, their conservatory of music. It was lyceum and gymnasium as well as sanctum sanctorum. Their religion was the peculiar sustaining force that gave them the strength to endure when endurance gave no promise, and the courage to be creative in the face of their own dehumanization.[11]

Since the Rev. Jesse Jackson's two presidential races in 1984 and 1988 have been highlighted by the media, the political role of black churches has become more widely known. Black churches have been acknowledged as a training ground for leadership skills that can apply to the political realm as well as the religious. They have also been quite successful in mobilizing resources, funds, and voters in political and Civil Rights campaigns.[12] But very few people know about the role of black churches in the economic sphere. While churches and synagogues among other ethnic groups have played a role in economics, largely on the basis of the economic ethic and values they preached, black churches went further — they were also involved in creating and establishing economic institutions. From 1888 until the Great Depression, black churches along with the fraternal orders and mutual aid societies provided the leadership and the capital base to establish more than fifty black-owned banks and several black life insurance companies. When whites started discriminating against black people by not

providing bank loans for mortgages or small businesses, or by their unwill-
ingness to sell life insurance to African Americans, the black clergy and
their congregations moved in to fill the void. While much of the economic
activity by churches ended with the Depression because their focus shifted
to an emerging Civil Rights movement after World War II, there has been a
resurgence in economic development activity over the past twenty years.
Under the leadership of the Rev. Leon Sullivan one of the largest job
training programs, the Occupational Industrialization Centers (OIC), was
created. Black clergy were intimately involved in the leadership of the OIC
programs, which attempted to instill moral values and black pride besides
teaching job skills. Through a link with the federal government more than
700,000 persons received job training before OIC funding was cut by the
Reagan administration. Sullivan also mobilized four hundred black
churches in the Philadelphia area to provide the capital to build the first and
largest black-owned shopping mall in Progress Plaza. Black churches have
also been among the leading builders of housing for senior citizens, the
poor, and moderate-income persons. These examples are only the tip of the
iceberg of economic involvement by black churches. Yet, they also under-
score the notion of a holistic ministry because economic empowerment in
black communities has emerged as the most pressing issue in the decade of
the 1990s.

   In an analysis of the economic, political, and cultural roles of black
churches, it is important to stress their dualistic and dialectical functions
of "accommodation and resistance" in regard to the larger civil society. As
Manning Marable pointed out, the crucial axis of black history consisted
of two decisive political options, that of "resistance versus accommodation." [13] Every black person and every black institution has participated in
making compromises between these two polarities. The pole of accommodation means to be influenced by the larger society and to take part in
aspects of it, however marginal that participation may be. In their accommodative role, black churches have been one of the major cultural brokers
of the norms, values, and expectations of white society. Black churches
are viewed as "mediating institutions." [14] For example, after the Civil War,
the church was the main mediating and socializing vehicle for millions of
former slaves, teaching them economic rationality, urging them to save
money and get an education, helping them to keep their families together,
and providing the spiritual and political leadership for early black communities. Sometimes accommodation also meant that black preachers were
manipulated and used by whites. But the pole of resistance also meant that
it was possible to resist the accommodative forces and pressures of the
American mainstream. Resistance meant affirming one's own cultural
heritage, in this case an African American or black heritage. As one of the

few black-controlled, black-owned, and independent institutions, black churches have played a major role in resistance. Politically, resistance has included both self-determination and self-affirmation. Since the Civil Rights movement and the attempts to desegregate American society, the accommodative pressures on black people and black institutions have grown considerably. One of the major roles of black churches in the future will be as historic reservoirs of black culture and as examples of resistance and independence.

The third challenge from the perspective of black churches to American Christianity and civil society concerns their pivotal role in introducing and pushing for multiculturalism at all levels of society. Diversity has always been present from the beginnings of American society, with Native Americans and African Americans among Euro-Americans, but that diversity has never been recognized or institutionalized until recently. It took the Civil Rights and the Black Consciousness movements of the 1960s to provide the leverage and the opening wedge toward an expanded notion of democracy for all groups and peoples that had been excluded, neglected, disenfranchised, and disempowered by mainstream American culture. So women, Hispanics, Jews, Native Americans, Asians, gays and lesbians, senior citizens, and even the disabled joined African Americans in pushing for an expansion of democracy. Multiculturalism also led to revisionist history and Black Theology as intellectual perspectives. Revisionist history meant that African Americans were not only the objects of history but also the subjects, the makers and creators of their own history, which had been suppressed by the old way of doing mainstream American history. In the same manner, the Black Theology movement announced that the theological reflections of black people, even illiterate slave preachers, were just as important as sources for theological reflection as the writings of Karl Barth, Paul Tillich, and Reinhold Niebuhr. And yes, diverse figures like Dr. Martin Luther King, Jr., Minister Malcolm X, and writer Zora Neale Hurston could also be added to the list. Furthermore, Black Theology also emphasized the need to take seriously the particularities of a person's social context and not jump to an easy reconciling universalism, or "cheap grace" as Bonhoeffer would call it. Until the realities of the pain of racial, class, and gender oppression are seriously dealt with and overcome, authentic reconciliation is not possible.

Multiculturalism also assumes a bicultural model of socialization as opposed to the monocultural or "melting pot" view. Biculturalism means that a person is socialized by the mainstream American culture via educational institutions, the media, language (American English), and the majority population. But it also means that a person is also socialized at the same time via black religious and educational institutions (i.e., the historic black colleges or classes in African American history), the black family, black newspapers, music, food, clothing, hair styles, and the community. A dual process of socialization is going on. This bicultural model also is a critique of monocultural views of American culture such as the one expressed by Bellah et al. in *Habits of the Heart*, where the authors assert that individualistic values of mainstream middle-class white culture affect all parts of the society.[15] While that is true to some degree, the analysis cannot end there. Mainstream middle-class white culture is also affected by other cultures in the society, particularly black culture. The clearest examples of this reverse influence are found in music and dancing. Much of what is called American music has been derived from black culture — the various versions of rock and roll, pop, jazz, blues, soul, rap, and hip-hop. Even the style of dancing of most white middle-class teenagers is a free-form style that was once called "dirty dancing" in the 1950s because it embodied the sensuous movements, rhythm, and free-form style that came from black culture. In the arena of religion, the spirituals and gospel music influenced white congregations. Elvis Presley made Thomas Doresey's "Precious Lord, Take My Hand" famous. It is also curious to see the mega-church congregations of white evangelicals immersed in modern gospel music, adjusted to their tastes, of course. The same could be said of the worship styles of Pentecostals. Pentecostalism has been the fastest growing area of religion in the United States and in African, Asian, and Latin American countries. Few people are aware that modern Pentecostalism has black roots, stemming from the Azusa Street revival in Los Angeles in 1906, led by a charismatic black preacher named William Seymour. Running day and night for three years, Azusa Street was one of the longest-lasting revivals in American history, influencing the founders of the Assemblies of God and many visiting international leaders. Even Bishop C. H. Mason, founder of the Church of God in Christ, was so affected by the event that he led his predominantly black members from the Holiness movement into Pentecostalism. The enthusiastic forms of worship and music, hand-clapping, shouting, and falling out, which had characterized early African American Christianity influenced the whole Pentecostal movement. With the broad media attention given to black preachers such as Dr. Martin Luther King, Jr., Minister Malcolm X, and Rev. Jesse Jackson, the black preaching and oratorical style has also influenced the mainstream. These are just some examples of the more complex and dynamic interactions that occur between mainstream and African American forms of Christianity.

For African Americans the individualism of American society tends to be counterbalanced by the communalism of African American culture. While freedom for white Americans has meant a freedom to do your own thing, to pursue individual interests, freedom for African Americans has had a greater communal emphasis — for an oppressed people, no one is free until all are free. The nature of racism in American society has been to treat African Americans (or any other minority) as representatives of a race or ethnic group, and seldom as individuals. "They all look alike" or "You are one of them" are common stereotypes. The communalism of black culture is also bolstered by the bonds of racial solidarity in the face of racial oppression. Thus, kinship terms from the network of the black extended family are also applied — "brother," "sister," "aunt," "uncle," etc. — even to those who may not be blood relatives. Black religious groups have represented the institutional symbols of community. Ordinary time and space are suspended in sacred worship and for a brief instance of eternity, they come together as a holy family. Black churches have also used kinship terminology within their hierarchy, designating a "Mother of the church," usually an older, well-respected woman who often wields countervailing power to that of the pastor.

Bellah's Analysis and Black Churches

In response to Professor Robert Bellah's paper and presentation at Marsh Chapel, there are two major points from the perspective of black churches. First, Bellah used the phrase "resident aliens," borrowed from Hauerwas and Willimons, to describe the position of Christians in a post-modern, secular world. In many ways the phrase "resident aliens" is more aptly applied to the situation of many African Americans to describe their existence in American society — that even after several centuries of living, working, and even dying for this country in all of its wars, they are still treated as aliens, as those who don't quite belong. How else do we explain the fact that twenty-five years after the Civil Rights movement, American society is more deeply segregated in terms of religion, residence, and education than ever before? As Cornel West eloquently argued, "race matters" and the whole society bears the moral responsibility for its failure to confront seriously the racism that is deeply embedded in its institutions and value systems, thereby threatening the future of American democracy itself.[16] While Bellah's paper is more interested in delineating the theoretical background and a three-part typology of the relationship between Christianity, individualism, and civil society, he should also be gently reminded of his concerns in an earlier work, *The Broken Covenant*, which pointed out the contradictions between the ideals of American democracy and the brutal exploitation and mistreatment of Native Americans and Africans.[17]

Second, the majority of black churches would generally fit type two of

Bellah's schema, where through an immanent critique, they attempt to "rescue the valid moral insights of our individualistic culture while helping it move beyond itself through a deeper apprehension of the meaning of the church." As we have pointed out in our earlier analysis, black churches have played a continuing dialectical and dualistic role in black culture. In their role as cultural brokers, especially after the Civil War, they transmitted the individualistic values of the Protestant ethic to the newly freed slaves, exhorting them to get an education, save their money, work hard, and live the straight and narrow life. "The Lord helps those who help themselves." But black churches have also been the carriers and preservers of the communal nature of African American culture, realizing that the fates and lives of all black people were bound up together. Above all, black churches — clergy and laity alike — have played prophetic roles in constantly criticizing and attacking the racism and the narrow definitions of American democracy found in the larger society. Moreover, the seven major historical black church denominations have not suffered the severe decline in membership (from one-third to one-half) that some mainline Protestant denominations, such as the United Presbyterians, Episcopalians, and Disciples of Christ, have experienced over the past two decades.[18]

In concluding Part I, the three challenges to mainstream Christianity and civil society from the history and sociology of black churches include: the anti-racism stance of black churches, which has been proclaimed by all of the major historic black denominations; their holistic ministry, which stresses becoming involved in all of the spheres of life, especially the political and economic arenas, which have an enormous impact upon the lives of African Americans; finally, the multicultural challenge to all Americans to expand the horizons of democracy. All of these challenges and others could not be carried out without the strong anchor that African American Christians had in a biblical God whose presence was manifested in Jesus of Nazareth. Their spiritual strength has provided the foundations for one of the most remarkable institutions ever developed on the American continent. As part of the "immanent critique" involved in Bellah's second model, we now turn to some challenges facing the black churches and all other churches during the decade of the 1990s.

Part II: Challenges to Black Churches (and Others) during the Decade of the 1990s

Someone once said that if you have ever served an inner-city church you will quickly learn that everything is in crisis — family life, housing, welfare, health care, schools, drugs, violence, gangs, food, water, air, streets. Out of the numerous challenges and problems facing black churches, it seems presumptuous to choose only three. However, I have chosen the following three challenges because they relate to the future of black churches in the 1990s and the twenty-first century, and they are relevant to the type of training and theological education for ministry that future students at the Boston Theological Institute will be receiving. The three challenges are: ministry to the urban poor; the gender issue in the ministry of black churches; and the need for public policy analysis in the education of all clergy.

A. Ministry to the Urban Poor

In the last chapter of our book, Lincoln and I pointed to the problems posed to black churches and the national black community of a growing class split among African Americans — the danger of developing two Black Americas or two nations within a nation. At the present time, demographic data points to the fact that two-thirds of African Americans are within the middle-income category, a "coping" black middle class and a "fragile" black working class. The final third is composed of a "crisis" sector of the black poor, or what some social scientists have called a permanent "underclass," representing several generations of poverty. In the largest recent study of the urban poor, *The Truly Disadvantaged*, William Julius Wilson has asserted that poor blacks are more socially isolated than they have ever been before.[19] The institutional network of traditional black communities, of churches, schools, small businesses, social and recreational centers is rapidly disappearing as the more upwardly mobile African Americans have moved out of the ghetto. For example, 48 percent of the residents of central Atlanta have moved to the suburbs or surrounding counties. Only the very poor are left behind. This social isolation of the poor has meant that the traditional models of working adults no longer exist for poor black children to emulate. Instead, they see the ravages of poverty, scores of unemployed black men and teenagers hanging out on street corners, women selling their bodies, people of all ages puffing on crack pipes waiting for that blissful transcendence which will allow escape for some moments.

For black churches, the situation is critical. Most of the church members of the historic black denominations are in the middle-income category, although each church will have some poor members. But the fact is that the rates for the unchurched are highest among poor urban black males and a growing number of females as well. For the first time in black history we are seeing the development of unchurched generations of young people who have no knowledge of nor respect for black church traditions or clergy. In the decade of the 1990s this sector of the crisis poor among African Americans will produce more than 60 percent of all black children. The future of black churches and the future of American society in this decade and the next century hangs in the balance with regard to the treatment of the urban poor.

In another paper given at the Urban Ministry Conference at the Yale Divinity School, I indicated some concrete steps that black churches and clergy and all others could take in their ministry to the urban poor.[20] I will briefly summarize these steps here:

1. All churches can send missionaries to bring the Christian gospel to the poor who live in public housing projects and rundown tenements. They can begin with "apartment" churches or "house" churches, "where two or three are gathered in my name." Studies have shown that religion is a good means of introducing "order and discipline" into the lives of poor people who live in the midst of chaotic conditions. A study by Richard Freeman, a black economist at Harvard, has shown the high correlation that exists between church attendance and their chances of getting out of the ghetto among black teenage urban males.[21] Why? Church attendance requires a rational calculated use of time and disciplined behavior. Religion can introduce an ethic of upward mobility into people's lives, as Max Weber and others have argued. Furthermore, poor young people can meet role models of working adults at these churches. The New Testament command to preach the gospel is the first step in organizing the poor.

2. The methods, techniques, and strategies of community organizing need to be taught to all urban clergy. Although community organizing was a rage in the 1960s, the problem is that not enough of it has gone on, especially in poverty areas. Community organizing is a tool to empower the poor, to use the collective power of organized poor people against the collective structures and bureaucracies that serve to keep them down. Furthermore, community organizing does not produce dependency or paternalism since the task of the organizer is to train leaders among the poor. Poor people are stirred from their fatalistic attitudes to take actions that can alter their conditions. A disorganized poor community remains poor; an organized one at least has a fighting chance. One recent example of a successful community organizing project is the Nehemiah Houses, more than two hundred low- to moderate-income houses sponsored by the coalition of the East Brooklyn Churches which is headed by a black clergyman, the Rev. Johnny Youngblood. Community organizing is a tough and difficult task and it can be dangerous at times because the organizer is often targeted as an "outside agitator"; but the cross of the poor in American society remains, who will pick it up and carry it?

3. Ministry in prisons has become a pressing need in black urban com-

munities. The United States leads the world in incarcerating its citizens and close to half of these prisoners are black. One out of every four black men is in a prison, jail, or holding pen at any time of the year and it is estimated that one out of two black males will experience some form of incarceration during his lifetime. While far fewer women are in prison, the imprisonment rate of black women has increased 150 percent and half of all women prisoners are black. The poorest of the poor are in prison and less than half of the inmates receive any outside visitors. It is estimated that more than 90 percent of all black churches have no form of prison ministry. All urban churches can pool their resources and adopt a nearby prison or jail and begin a regular program of visitation, especially by the laity. A cycle of one visit a month or every six weeks can be worked out cooperatively so that each week is covered. Once a visitation program has begun, other alternatives can also be added to the program such as working with the families of inmates, providing employment counseling and help with housing, discussion and support groups for former inmates, drug and alcohol therapy, etc. Again, the New Testament imperative is there: "I was in prison and you did not visit me. . . . If you have not done it to the least of these, my brethren, you have not done it unto me."

4. The final step for urban ministry in black churches is the most critical of all. There is a pressing need to bolster the self-identity and self-esteem of all young black children, regardless of class. Recent studies of the Doll Choice Tests, pioneered by Drs. Kenneth and Mamie Clark, have indicated a reversion to the scores of the pre-Civil Rights era when as many as 67 percent of all black children misidentified themselves and chose the white doll when they were asked "to choose the doll that looks like you." [22] Even more devastating were the results of the open-ended interviews when both black and white children tended to describe the black doll as "dirty" and "bad." The widespread lack of self-identity and self-esteem among black children in modern American society strikes at the core of the doctrine of personhood that African-American Christians have long endorsed. Amidst the most trying circumstances during slavery, black churches have affirmed the idea that each person is a child of God, a human being. Yet fulfilling the basic commands of Christianity "to love God and your neighbor as yourself" becomes very difficult when one cannot affirm and accept oneself.

Black churches can begin to work on this issue by pooling their resources and by developing after-school classes or Saturday classes on black heritage and culture and provide other tutorial help. Five to ten churches in one urban area can support one school. Churches cannot wait for public schools to develop a truly multicultural curriculum — they need to lead the way. Project Spirit is a more elaborate program and it is sponsored by the Congress of National Black Churches and funded by the Carnegie and Lilly foundations. Project Spirit holds daily black history and culture classes and tutorial sessions in selected churches in six cities. It also works with the parents to become better advocates for their children in the school system, and it teaches black clergy counseling techniques in dealing with the problems of teenage sexuality and drug use. Since Project Spirit is still in the experimental stage, black churches can begin with less elaborate programs and use their tradition of self-help. The lack of identity and of self-esteem among black children not only reflects the racism of the larger society, but it is also a dimension of the spiritual problems within black communities that all Christians need to come to grips with.

B. The Gender Issue within Black Churches

In chapter 10 of our book, "The Pulpit and the Pew: The Black Church and Women," we explored the gender issue more fully, and some insights bear repeating. Black congregations have an inordinately large number of women members, anywhere from 70 to 90 percent female depending on the congregation, and yet there remains a largely male leadership. The explanation for this phenomenon is tied to two issues: first, the historical background of slavery, which deprived black men of all of the normal routes of leadership and power, except through the ministry in black churches; second, the extremely high rates of unemployment among black males, which may reach as high as 50 percent, if those who have dropped out of the labor market and become discouraged are counted. High unemployment leads to decreased participation in mainstream institutions. Except for fraternal orders and college fraternities, all of the major black organizations like the NAACP and Urban League, as well as the churches, suffer from a dearth of black male membership. However, black churches are also faced with a major problem of what to do with all of the black women who have begun to attend seminaries and divinity schools in increasingly large numbers — their presence has increased 676 percent, more than double the 300 percent increase among white women.

The results of our study have shown strong feelings of hostility toward black women as preachers and pastors, particularly among Baptist and Pentecostal male clergy. In reaction to the difficulties of being ordained and accepted by some of the historic black denominations, black women have shown a trend of switching to predominantly white denominations for their ordination and ministry. However, as Delores Carpenter's study has shown, the switch to white denominations has not been entirely satisfactory since a number of black women clergy have encountered incidents of racism within white churches and some feel uncomfortable being treated as the token black person by their denominational leaders.[23] Most of the women expressed a deep desire to serve the black community via ministry in black churches. For women in the Methodist denominations, while acceptance has been very good, they have expressed the frustration of lacking mobility in their appointments, which have tended to be largely lateral moves. Men are still appointed to the large urban Methodist churches, which are pathways to the bishopric.

A major problem confronting black churches is the fact that a growing pool of black women clergy will continue to push the boundaries and strictures placed on them; they will not be denied. In the past, black church denominations were the result of the racism expressed by white Christians and churches. The future may likely see new schisms and new denominations created as a result of the gender issue that is brewing in black churches. We now turn to the final challenge for black and all clergy and their congregations in their need for training in public policy analysis.

C. The Challenge of Public Policy Analysis for All Clergy and Churches

Since the second half of the anniversary theme of this BTI conference involves "Theological Education and Public Life," let me conclude this presentation with a proposal that covers both elements and recommends adding training in public policy analysis to the theological curriculum of the schools of the BTI. I will be reiterating comments that I made recently at Yale because the need for change is great and the proposal needs to be disseminated.[24]

The Deputy Mayor of New York City and one of the most astute political minds in the country, Bill Lynch, who is African American, once said in a conversation that black churches and clergy were good at mobilizing people in crisis situations, i.e. getting people out on the streets for a protest, but that they were ineffective in suggesting any public policy options for city officials to act on. Lynch felt that the clergy and churches did not know much about the public policy process and did not contribute much in that arena. In terms of the daily operations of city, state, and federal governments and their relationships to minority communities, it is public policy that reigns.

In terms of ministering to the needs of urban populations, all churches need to support "enlightened public policies" that would lead to the empowerment of their people and communities. However, this capacity has not been institutionalized in any of the major denominations, black or white. Furthermore and even more serious is the fact that black and white clergy do not receive any training in public policy analysis in their theological education, even at the best seminaries. Thus, the clergy and their congregations remain ignorant of the public policy arena. I know of this situation since I speak from the personal experience of my own theological education. Even at the Union Theological Seminary, the home of Reinhold Niebuhr who encouraged Christians to become involved in the political sphere and to use the "tainted tools" of politics, there were no courses on public policy analysis (even to the present day). I was one of the fortunate few to receive any training in this area while at Union, but it happened by default. Three Union students were chosen to participate in Columbia University's International Fellows Program, sponsored by the School of International Affairs. We were given a high-powered, intense year of training in international relations with an emphasis on policy analysis. It was a well-funded and well-connected program; we had a closed-door session with Secretary of State Dean Rusk on his administration's Vietnam policies and a meeting at the Pentagon with some admirals and generals on their strategies for prosecuting the Vietnam war. These meetings forced all of us to bring our best ethical reflections and critiques to the policies and policy-makers of our country.

The payoff of the sociological dimension is found in the arena of public policy. Sociologists are not merely interested in the collection of data and statistics. They are ultimately interested in the questions: What are the public policy implications of the data? What does this study tell us about our options in the future? What concrete plans and strategies can be devised to improve this situation? If they are really involved in ministry, i.e. serving and caring for people, then all urban clergy should be concerned about the same questions regarding the public good. Because it is public policy that will determine the distribution of a city's budget and resources, policy will affect who gets jobs and who doesn't, whose garbage is picked up, etc. All of the things that concern human well-being on a daily basis are affected by public policy. So when Deputy Mayor Bill Lynch of New York City says that the black clergy and indeed almost all clergy are not involved in the public policy process and do not contribute anything in that arena, it is a major indictment both of theological education and of training for urban ministry. This lack of knowledge and involvement means that the urban clergy and their congregations are merely "reacting" to the policy initiatives put forth by others. They are not "proactive," proposing policy options that would lead to the empowerment of their people or bring healing to bruised and broken lives. It is time to move beyond the rhetoric of the pulpit to concrete action and solutions; it is time to move beyond the crisis mentality that predominates in urban ministry. But let me also warn that public policy is not the utopia of urban ministry

— all utopias are beyond history. It will involve the nitty-gritty of hard negotiations and hard thinking, of pushing and pressuring, all of the dynamics of the political sphere.

Conclusion

Part I of this paper presented three challenges to Christianity and civil society from the perspective of black churches. The first challenge concerned the historic anti-racism stance of all black churches as part of their constant critique of white Christianity and American society. The second challenge involved the holistic ministry of black churches, to minister to the needs and cares of black people in all of the spheres of life, including politics and economics. Black churches did not withdraw from these more public spheres of life nor did they acquiesce to the split between public and private that some white churches upheld. White churches could afford to withdraw into a privatized sphere because other white institutions dominated the politics and economics of their society. Black people only had their churches, but the model of a holistic ministry that derives from the example of black churches is a profound one that needs to be studied and replicated in a complex technological society. The ministry remains one of the few areas for generalists in a society that calls for increasing specialization. The third challenge is reflected in the push for multiculturalism in American society as one of the main results of the Civil Rights and Black Consciousness movements. While diversity has always been present in this society, it has only been recently that it has been recognized and embraced as a principle for education and as a public good. Black churches have also been among the main vehicles for socialization among black people, accommodating some major values and resisting others by emphasizing the preservation of black history and culture. A bicultural model of socialization is proposed as the most adequate way of minority groups and hyphenated Americans where a person is socialized by mainstream American society, but at the same time is also socialized into ethnic culture and heritage. This bicultural model is important in understanding how minority groups both assimilate and critique the central value system of American individualism, a problem that Professor Bellah addressed in his main essay. Part I concluded with some reflections on Bellah's typology in relation to black churches.

Part II elaborated on three major challenges facing black churches and all other churches in the future. These challenges include ministry to the urban poor, the gender issue of ordaining and accepting black women as preachers and pastors, and the need for involvement in the public policy process.

Let me point out that this last decade of the twentieth century is a crucial turning point for the black church. There is a struggle going on now for the souls and allegiance of poor black men and women and youth. The Muslims have been far more active in the prisons and in the streets than the black churches have ever been. If the black church should ask itself why it needs to be reconnected with the hard-core urban black poor, the answer is as simple as it is obvious: one-third of the black population will be responsible for about 60 percent of all black children growing up in the decade of the 1990s. The future of the black church in the twenty-first century will depend as much on how it responds to the poor in its midst as to the externals of racism, the abstractions of ecumenism, or the competitive threat of a resurgent Islam. Past tradition has cast the black church as the proverbial "rock in a weary land" — the first and the last sure refuge of those who call it home, and all those who live in the shadow of its promise.

Notes

1. The remarks of my respondent, Professor John Cartwright of the School of Theology of Boston University, basically agreed with the thrust of this paper. He expanded on the need to develop the relationship of seminary education to the urban scene and to hone the relevant skills of urban clergy so that they can develop active churches. He stressed the theological significance of the black church and its presence as an indictment of Christianity, which I pointed to in my historical overview.

2. Norman O. Brown, *Love's Body* (New York: Random House, Vintage Books, 1968), 127.

3. C. Eric Lincoln and Lawrence H. Mamiya, *The Black Church in the African American Experience* (Durham: Duke University Press, 1990).

4. Albert Raboteau, *Slave Religion: The Invisible Institution in the Antebellum South* (New York: Oxford Press, 1978).

5. There is a scholarly debate here regarding the degree of African cultural survivals both in the African American family and religion. E. Franklin Frazier has asserted that during slavery all African practices and customs were stripped away and lost. Melville Herskovits has argued for African survivals in a developing African American culture. See Raboteau, *Slave Religion*, for the best resolution of this debate.

6. Although there is much debate and great uncertainty about the numbers of Africans taken as slaves during the North Atlantic slave trade, the best estimates run into the millions. See Walter Rodney's *How Europe Underdeveloped Africa* (London: Bogle-L'Ouverture, 1972) for the chart on Basil Davidson's estimates.

7. Albert Raboteau and David Wills, editors of an African American Documentary Religious History project, reported on some of their findings at a session of the African American Religious History section of the American Academy of Religion in New Orleans, November 1990. Publication of the first volume is expected in 1993.

8. For an elaboration of these differences, see chapter 1 of Lincoln and Mamiya, *The Black Church in the African American Experience*.

9. For an anthropological description of cultural development among black families, see Herbert Gutman, *The Black Family in Slavery and Freedom, 1750-1925* (New York: Pantheon, 1976). Also see Lawrence Levine, *Black Culture and Black Consciousness* (New York: Oxford, 1978). For a description of the social construction of the black sacred cosmos from the sociological perspective of Peter Berger and Thomas Luckmann, see chapter 1 of Lincoln and Mamiya, *The Black Church in the African American Experience*. Also see Mechal Sobel, *Trabelin' On: The Slave Journey to an Afro-Baptist Faith* (Westport, CT: Greenwood, 1979).

10. See David Swift, *Black Prophets of Justice: Activist Clergy before the Civil War* (Baton Rouge: Louisiana State University, 1989). Swift describes the treatment of black Presbyterian clergy.

11. C. Eric Lincoln in the foreword to Gayraud Wilmore's *Black Religion and Black Radicalism*, 2nd ed. (Maryknoll: Orbis, 1983).

12. For a broad summary of the political role of black churches, see chapter 8 of Lincoln and Mamiya. Also see Aldon Morris's analysis of the mobilizing background provided by the churches during the Civil Rights movement. Aldon Morris, *The Origins of the Civil Rights Movement: Black Communities Organizing for Change* (New York: Free Press, 1984).

13. Manning Marable, *How Capitalism Underdeveloped Black America* (Boston: South End Press, 1983).

14. For a sociological elaboration of the idea of "mediating structures" in society, see Peter L. Berger and John Richard Neuhaus, *To Empower People: The Role of Mediating Structures in Public Policy* (Washington, DC: American Enterprise Institute for Public Policy Research, 1977).

15. Robert N. Bellah, Richard Madsen, William M. Sullivan, Ann Swindler, and Steven M. Tipton, *Habits of the Heart* (Berkeley: University of California Press, 1985).

16. Cornel West, *Race Matters* (Boston: Beacon Press, 1993).

17. Robert N. Bellah, *The Broken Covenant* (New York: Seabury Press, 1975).

18. The estimates of decline in membership among white mainstream churches were derived from the research group on Congregational Studies, sponsored by the Lilly Endowment. Also see Wade Clark Roof and William McKinney, *American Mainline Religion: Its Changing Shape and Future* (New Brunswick: Rutgers University Press, 1987).

19. William Julius Wilson, *The Truly Disadvantaged* (Chicago: University of Chicago Press, 1988).

20. Lawrence H. Mamiya, "The Sociological Dimension: Reading the Signs," unpublished paper given at the Urban Ministry Conference at Yale Divinity School, 29 November 1992.

21. Richard B. Freeman and Harry J. Holzer, eds., *The Black Youth Employment Crisis* (Chicago: University of Chicago Press, 1986), and Freeman and David A. Wise, eds., *The Youth Labor Market Problem: Its Nature, Causes, and Consequences* (Chicago: University of Chicago Press, 1982).

22. For a summary of the recent Doll Choice Tests, see "In My Mother's House: The Black Church and Young People," chap. 11 in Lincoln and Mamiya, *The Black Church in the African American Experience*.

23. See "The Pulpit and the Pew," chap. 10 in Lincoln and Mamiya. Also see Delores Carpenter's "The Effects of Sect-Typeness upon the Professionalization of

Black Female Masters of Divinity Graduates, 1972-1984" Ph.D. diss., Department of Sociology, Rutgers University, 1986.

24. These comments were first made at the Urban Ministry Conference held at the Yale Divinity School, 29 November 1992.

4

The Bible in Public Discourse

Richard Lovelace

When I was asked to produce this essay last spring, I thought that the subject called for a biblical studies specialist, not a historian of church renewal. But perhaps what the conference really wanted was a theological voice from a self-consciously "angelical" seminary, reflecting this movement's distinctive concerns, and also its failures, in making biblical faith impact society.

What was energizing my mind last spring was the growing role of Christianity in the 1992 presidential campaign. So I agreed to write a case study on the use of scripture and religious discourse in the campaign, ending with some conclusions about projecting strong biblical convictions into the public arena.

Religion entered the campaign early from a familiar direction. In January, George Bush spoke to the annual meeting of the National Religious Broadcasters, thanking Evangelicals "for helping America, as Christ ordained, to be a light unto the world," and explaining the need to improve the balance of trade by citing scripture: "The Bible reminds us, by thy works shall ye know them."

Muslims and Jews reacted nervously. But now it appeared that the Religious Right was disenchanted with Bush. One broadcaster commented, "He's a typical political. He's talking to us, so he's talking our language." Richard Cizik of the National Association of Evangelicals observed that conservatives feel they are in "the back of the bus with the Bush administration and are likely to stay there," and warned that they

Richard Lovelace is Professor of Church History at Gordon-Conwell Theological Seminary.

may "decide to vote their pocketbooks," since Bush apparently cannot or will not deliver on social issues like abortion.[1]

In March, Bob Dugan, the NAE's Washington liaison, said that the Evangelicals want Bush to speak out against homosexual rights, radical feminism, and federal funding of the arts — all elements in what Dugan called a "culture war." Bush had been told what he should stand for if he wants Evangelical support, but Dugan felt that this community now gave him no higher grade than a C.[2]

At the NAE Convention in March, Bush reiterated his support of "traditional values," including religious liberty, educational choice, voluntary school prayer, antipornography efforts, profamily legislation, and opposition to racism. But in April, *Christianity Today* complained that the Bush administration had met with the Gay and Lesbian Task Force, had not supported its own proposals for educational choice and private schools, and had coddled the NEA until Pat Buchanan had put on the pressure.[3]

H. Ross Perot's entry into the presidential race did not inject any additional religious element in the campaign, although Perot is an active member of the Evangelical Highland Park Presbyterian Church in Dallas, the planet Jupiter of Presbyterian congregations. In June, James Wall complained that both politicians and reporters were steering clear of biblical and theological roots and anchoring the discourse in moralistic phrases like "family values." "To fill the vacuum left by the departure of religion from our public realm, with its diminution of spiritual goals, ideals and priorities, we have adopted a language that is ethically neutral." [4] But the rest of the campaign calls in question Wall's assumption that we are in a secular society in which religion has been drained from public discourse.

Christianity Today, like most conservative Republicans, seemed to prefer Dan Quayle to George Bush. In June, the magazine interviewed Quayle, a member of the Evangelical Fourth Presbyterian Church in Washington. Quayle showed that he is immersed in Washington's evangelical life and handles the language of personal salvation easily, though he did not refer to scripture.[5]

By September, *CT* evidently felt it had to give the Democrats equal time, and it interviewed Al Gore. Gore's political approach claimed to be theologically grounded:

The foundation of all of my work on the environment is my faith in Jesus Christ and my conviction that the purpose of life is indeed as I learned in Baptist Sunday School so many years ago: To glorify God. Heaping contempt upon God's creation is inconsistent with the duty to live one's life in a way that glorifies God. Destroying that

which God has pronounced pleasing and good is an act with implications for one's attitude toward the Creator.

This at least sounds like piety, not the usual political moralism. Gore
goes on to expound familiar scripture with a new twist:

> In three of the four Gospels we see the parable of the unfaithful
> servant, where the master leaves on a journey and tells his servant to
> care for the house. The master says, "If, while I'm gone, vandals
> come and ransack this house or thieves come and steal my belong-
> ings, it will not be a sufficient excuse if you tell me you were
> asleep." There are many ways of sleeping. Christ speaks of those
> who have eyes but do not see and ears but do not hear. And he
> commands us, in this context, to watch. . . . If we are witness to the
> destruction of the earth's ecological integrity, it will not be a suffi-
> cient excuse for us to say we were asleep. . . .
> Yet our God is a God of miracles. . . . And I am one who believes
> that the Spirit is moving very strongly in this post-cold-war world,
> with the Berlin Wall torn down and the statues of Lenin shattered by
> free men and women.[6]

Gore puts a spin on the gospel passage, extracting it from its eschato-
logical context and focusing on the need to stay awake — not just to be
ready for the *parousia*, but also to be good stewards in the period "between the times."

In July, however, *Christianity Today* had projected Bush the winner,
due to a new post-Falwell grassroots activism, a kind of stealth Moral
Majority, composed of groups like Pat Robertson's Christian Coalition,
Concerned Women for America, Focus on the Family, and Citizens for
Excellence in Education. At this point 60 percent of both Evangelicals and
mainline Protestants were logging in for Bush, along with more than half
of Roman Catholics.[7]

The political conventions, however, may have changed all that. Neither
of them proved James Wall wrong. The Democrats gave a platform to
Jesse Jackson and Mario Cuomo, but their usual ethical passion was
muted. The extreme platform position on abortion and the profusion of
radical groups alienated many Catholics, Evangelicals, and perhaps also
some mainline Protestants.

But the Republican convention was equally problematic: a polar extreme in the platform position on abortion, a blatant display of homopho-
bia, virulent antifeminism concentrated on an attractive and capable

working mother. In a column called "Merchants of Hate," Anthony Lewis commented:

> I remember Joe McCarthy. I have been going to national political conventions since his day, and I do not recall one as mean in spirit as this one. God was much spoken of. But He was a God without compassion, a God of intolerance. . . . Barry Goldwater is a moderate compared to those in charge now.

As the *Chicago Tribune* put it, perhaps "the GOP needs a Kremlin to bash." [8]

Voters may have been put off by the undercurrent of rage and violence in all of this. Pat Buchanan characterized the two parties as diametrical opponents in a religiously-based "cultural war." Pat Robertson commented that Europeans had "gotten rid" of their liberals, and that perhaps we should do the same.

The Democratic and Republican campaigns emerging from both conventions were exercises in convergence on the center after experiments testing extremes. The convergence included an important religious dimension, most visible in the Clinton campaign.

Clinton's motto for his proposed administration, "The New Covenant," had caused problems. Even Martin Nolan of the *Globe* found it "theologically questionable." My wife responded to it with the same disquiet she has when she thinks about the natural foods store in Ipswich that calls itself Bread of Life.

But what is going on here? Are religious concepts being secularized? Or are politicians simply trying to raise their sails in a rising wind of popular Christianity? Perhaps both are happening. And there is some promise in the fact that the Democrats have worked their way up from "The New Deal," an image out of a poker game; through "The New Frontier" and "The Great Society," images out of history and sociology; into the covenant image, which is rooted in the Bible but also in our Puritan heritage.

Immediately after the convention Clinton interacted with religious voters on the Vision Interfaith Satellite network, fielding questions from Temple Israel in Boston, black Methodists in Los Angeles, Presbyterians in West Virginia, and Roman Catholics in Texas. "This is a historic first that two days after the nomination a candidate approaches the religious community," said the president of Temple Israel. [9]

Clinton returned from his bus campaigns in September to focus on the Catholic constituency. At Notre Dame University Clinton used scripture to argue that it is not inconsistent to combine pluralism and diversity with adherence to a core of biblical values centered in community:

> Everything in the Old Testament concerns not isolated individuals, but a people, a community. . . . In the Christian tradition, that emphasis on community continues, since the Acts, the Gospels, and the Epistles all come from early Christian communities, and recount to us their problems, their failures, their strengths, but, above all, their unity. Echoing down the ages is the simple but powerful truth that no grace of God was ever given me for me alone. To the terrible question of Cain — am I my brother's keeper? — the only possible answer for us is God's thunderous yes.
>
> Our individual rights flow from our essential dignity as a creation of God. But each of us reaches our fullness as a human being by being of service to our fellow men and women.
>
> All of us must respect the reflection of God's image in every man and woman. And so we must value their freedom, not just their political freedom, but their freedom of conscience — in matters of philosophy and family and faith.

In contrast to this call for unity without uniformity, Clinton condemned "voices of intolerance" that:

> proclaim some families are not real families, some Americans are not "real Americans," and what this country needs is a "religious war." America does not need a religious war. America needs a reaffirmation of the values that, for most of us, are rooted in our religious faith.[10]

This may be serious theological reflection of the sort that Jim Wall was calling for. In a later interview with Catholic News Service, Clinton claimed some indebtedness to his Jesuit schooling:

> The Catholic influence on me . . . [was] manifested in two ways. First of all, a real sense that we are morally obligated to try to live out our religious convictions in the world, that our obligation to social mission is connected to religious life. . . . That I got out of my Catholic training more than from the Baptist Church, which is much more rooted in the notion that salvation is a matter of personal relationship between an individual and God. . . . And the other thing I got . . . is real respect for the obligation to develop one's mind, that religious convictions involve more than emotions . . . that if you

have a mind you have an obligation to develop it, to learn to think and to know things and then to act on those things more powerfully because you know more and because you can think better. That's something the Jesuits did for me as much as anything else. . . . I love the Jesuits. You know, one of my good friends to this day is a Jesuit priest.

With or without his speech writer, Clinton functions well theologically, although we may have traded a president who cannot speak English for one who cannot stop speaking it. Clinton does not just dredge up scripture texts to misapply in speeches. Asked if he had any favorite scripture passages, Clinton replied, "A lot of them. Galatians 6:9. 'Let us not grow weary while doing good for in due season we shall reap, but do not lose heart.' It's a wonderful scripture." And a text exactly suited for the stress he was enduring at the moment — if Democratic campaigning is considered "doing good." [11]

Fr. Andrew Greely commented that both parties were courting Catholic voters, but with unequal success. "The Catholic vote continues to be Democratic whether the Democratic leadership wants it or not. . . . But the Democrats will never win another presidential election unless they recognize how important that Catholic vote is." Greely said Catholics would vote without much attention to official church direction. "The national media each year at election time become worried about Catholics voting the way their church tells them to vote on the abortion issue. In fact . . . they don't vote on that issue and never have . . . Catholic church leaders generally could not deliver a pack of hungry vampires to a blood bank." [12]

The Evangelical right became increasingly harsh against Clinton as the campaign wore on. Pat Robertson's Christian Coalition distributed thousands of tracts comparing the three candidates on the issues, presenting Bush as the only safe choice. (In a 1991 book on *The New World Order*, Robertson warned that Bush had become an unwitting tool of the Illuminati, a conspiracy of Satanists, Masons, secular humanists, and occultists; but presumably Clinton and Gore were even worse.) [13]

Late in the campaign, Randall Terry of Operation Rescue distributed a flier to pastors calling on them to urge their congregations to vote against Clinton. After proving that Clinton's positions contradicted a long string of scriptures, Terry concluded:

Clinton has a veneer of Christianity — but on close inspection one sees it is the height of hypocrisy. For example, in his acceptance speech, he flagrantly twisted scripture. Even more frightening, Clinton spoke of his "new covenant": a humanistic pact that has nothing to do with biblical Christianity. What would his sacraments be? The body and blood of dismembered babies? . . . Do we really want to compound our economic problems by putting a neo-pagan at the head of our government?

This portrait of Clinton as warlock was followed by comments from endorsers, including Catholic clergy who suggested that excommunication was appropriate for those voting Democratic.[14]

People the American Way and other watchdogs on the left were outraged. But what is most interesting is that the tract was "leaked" to Churchnews International by InterVarsity Fellowship, a neo-Evangelical ministry. Someone ought to poll the Evangelical community to determine what percentage was turned off by the religious component of the Republican campaign, and how many of these ended up voting for Clinton in reaction to their own right wing.

After the Republican convention, a study done at the University of Akron predicted that Bush would win the election based on religious factors, gaining 68 percent of the Evangelical voting block (23.3 percent of the general voting population); 64 percent of the mainline Protestant vote (21 percent of the population); 56 percent of the Roman Catholic vote (23.5 percent of the population); 23 percent of the Jewish vote; and 53 percent of those not closely identified with organized religion (15.5 percent of the population).[15]

By 14 October, however, a Vision International Satellite Network poll was projecting a win for Clinton. Of those polled, 74 percent indicated that economics weighed more than religion in voting, although 69 percent said they could not vote for an atheist; 12 percent could not vote for Clinton because of his position on abortion, but 17 percent could not vote for Bush for the same reason! Strikingly, while 36 percent of black and white biblical conservatives now favored Bush, 37 percent favored Clinton. And while white Evangelicals still favored Bush 41 to 31 percent, persons attending church five or more times in September favored Clinton 64 to 34 percent. Apparently strongly committed Christians had come to favor Clinton by two to one.[16]

According to Ed McAteer, a conservative leader, voters were not ignoring religious issues to vote their pocketbooks. Religion continues to be a major factor because "there are 100 million people who are religious people in this country, and that's a big market. Both candidates are making a play for that market."[17]

A post-election network poll showed an atypical distribution of votes. Among white Evangelicals, Bush won by 61 percent (down from 81 percent in 1988), with Clinton at 23 percent and Perot at 15 percent. Among mainline Protestants, who usually vote 60 to 70 percent Republican, Bush and Clinton tied with 38 percent, and Perot scored 24 percent. Roman Catholics gave Clinton 44 percent, with Bush at 36 percent and Perot at 20 percent. Catholics had favored Bush over Dukakis by a margin of 5 percent in 1988.[18] This was the fifth presidential election in which Catholics picked the winner — and we only have data for five elections.[19]

What does all this say about the ultimate audience to whom we are speaking? It is certainly not an America gripped by religious decay, indifference, and relativism. It is indeed a post-Westphalian society, as Dr. Bellah says, but it is not a post-Christian society in any sense that reverses de Tocqueville. Any political landscape with this much God-talk going on may be divided, but it is religiously alive.

In fact, I would suggest that we are in the midst of a bull market in religion. The exploding New Age movement shows that Theodore Roszak was right: 1960s religiosity was just the entering wedge of a cultural shift away from technological secularism and toward sources of spiritual meaning.[20] And when the game is religion, Christians may hold trumps. I am willing to bet that in the last fifteen years, more books on Christian spirituality have appeared than were published in the rest of the twentieth century.

Religious bull markets, however, are often divisive and disorderly. The literal religious wars after the Reformation shocked Europe into pluralism and secularism. Now, at least in America, we have progressed to the point where we have symbolic wars — culture wars. We need to ask whether the results of this are likely to be favorable or unfavorable to the Christian cause.

The Religious Right, as everyone is commenting, is not going to fade out this time like the Moral Majority. Instead, it is in an ideal situation to raise money and expand, because militant Evangelicals always prosper when there are monsters to be slain.[21] (Mainline renewal groups, for instance, are like white corpuscles; they positively multiply in the presence of germs. An American Baptist renewal group went out of business because things improved too much; now there are problems again, and a new one has appeared.)

The escalating arms race among religious factions is disquieting. Pat Robertson and People the American Way are using *each other* in their promotional literature to provoke contributions. The harder either side is attacked, the more money rolls in.[22]

The noise of this combat may be an alarm clock for the Clinton team, which until now has paid minimal attention to the religious voting base. But if we can gain their attention, this administration may be able to hear at least some of our concerns. Clinton and Gore have demonstrated some spiritual sensitivity which does not appear to be mere civil religion. George Stephanopoulos, Clinton's former press secretary, is the son and grandson of Orthodox priests; he says he learned his social concern from his parents' involvement in the National Council of Churches.[23]

We have elected two Southern Baptists to our highest office — Jimmy Carter squared — and one of them has been trained by Jesuits. There are worse things than a White House open to moderate Southern Baptists and liberal Catholics. It is true that both men are on the losing side of the inerrancy war in the Southern Baptist Convention, but they are on the same side as, say, Bill Moyers and (quietly) Billy Graham — who believes in biblical inerrancy but does not like to see this theological instrument used to bludgeon other Christians.

Some years ago at Southwestern Seminary I was told that Bill Moyers talks for an hour every other week with one of his old seminary professors. I would like to be that professor now; Gordon-Conwell could really get an oar into public policy.

But since I am not Bill Moyers's mentor, how can I speak into the current religious turmoil? Certainly by helping shape a seminary that will project biblical truth in the midst of imbalance and confusion. I want to say just a little about this from a confessional standpoint, as part of an Evangelical faculty, realizing that other institutions travel other roads.

Neo-Evangelicalism is a reform movement that has tried to recover the theological balance of Evangelical Protestantism before it disintegrated into Fundamentalism. That balance included various elements: biblically reformed theology; Christian humanism integrating theology with culture; a call for spiritual awakening in the church; evangelism and social reform as inseparable forms of holistic mission; and Christian unity as an instrument both of mission and spiritual nurture.

The New Evangelicalism has imperfectly recovered these elements. It has made progress in confronting modernity, in theology and cultural integration, though at times it falls into a rationalistic head-trip, or simply photocopies Protestant scholastics. Its parachurch groups do effective evangelism, but Edwards's and Wesley's stress on spiritual renewal is mostly visible among Pentecostals and Charismatics. Social reform is given lip service as part of the mix, but is practically ignored by most neo-Evangelicals. As for Christian unity, birds of exactly the same feather may flock together, but anything beyond this may imperil your funding base.

My calling at Gordon-Conwell Seminary has been to encourage students to recover all the elements of Classical Evangelicalism. I take particular care to stress ecumenism and social reforming Church History Surveys, and I teach courses on Edwards, Pietism, and Catholic Spirituality to reinforce these concerns with a call for spiritual awakening. Although I do not teach exegesis, it is my hope that students will start hearing the Bible speak to them about some of the missing or weaker elements in the current Evangelical mix.

I respect and appreciate my seminary's approach to scripture. Our biblical scholars are trying to continue a task that the great neo-orthodox theologians, for all their brilliance and their vital engagement with modern culture, were unable to tackle: sifting the huge deposit of critical speculation about scripture, from Reimarus to Bultmann, sorting out what is helpful, but discarding whatever impedes our hearing of the whole counsel of God and subtracts from the deposit of faith.

Theologians at Gordon-Conwell are sometimes captivated by the problems and formulations of Reformed scholasticism, but their real effort is to reestablish a thorough grounding in the Reformers' own faith, and to use this faith not only to refute modern heresies but to engage contemporary culture in dialogue. All in all, the seminary does seek to embody Barth's alternation between the Bible and the daily newspaper. Sometimes it may be yesterday's newspaper, but it is never yesterday's Bible.

Mainline Presbyterians sometimes attend Gordon-Conwell because they think they can get better instruction in Calvinism there than in the Presbyterian schools. And I am not prepared to say that they are wrong: for much of Evangelicalism is simply Old School Presbyterianism extracted from its ecclesiastical base.

How do Gordon-Conwell faculty and students feel about the new political administration? Most probably voted for Bush or Perot, because they come from a subculture that has been Republican since D. L. Moody shifted the funding base of Evangelicalism from progressive layman to conservative business leaders.

How do they feel about the Religious Right? Almost all endorse its agenda, though many are uneasy with tactics or particular spokespersons.

And this reflects neo-Evangelicalism as a whole. *Christianity Today* and the National Association of Evangelicals are main instruments of the New Evangelicalism, but their social policy is identified with that of the Religious Right. An on-target cartoon depicted the leader at an NAE convention declaring that the movement is free from party affiliation. As he is followed on the podium by Charles Colson and Ronald Reagan, his nose grows longer and longer until it becomes an elephant's trunk.

Liberal critics dismiss the Religious Right as an obnoxious form of moralism with bad manners. It is, however, trying to do something that was a standard feature of the nineteenth-century Evangelical awakenings.

C. C. Cole, in *The Social Ideas of the Northern Evangelists*, notes that the Second Evangelical Awakening began with a widespread movement of personal evangelism, which then provided the popular base for five further waves of development: a wave of home and foreign missions; a wave of edifying literature to nourish converts; a wave of new educational institutions to train them; a wave of moral reform to make the culture ethically livable; and a wave of social reform to satisfy God's justice and avert his judgment.[24]

Note that moral reform was an integral part of this pattern. William Wilberforce wrote in his diary in 1787, "God Almighty has set before me two great objects, the suppression of the slave trade and the reformation of manners."[25] The efforts of John Newton and the Clapham Sect to evangelize England, to clean it up morally and to liberate the Empire's slaves, to abolish wage slavery and other social ills — all these were integrally connected and motivated by a biblical theology of liberation, which included moral reform as a form of release from institutional sin.

The Religious Right has read about the Second Awakening.[26] This is one of the reasons Falwell and the rest have abandoned the politically passive stance of Fundamentalism and opted for activism. But they have reproduced the nineteenth-century concerns with great imbalance. They have specialized in moral reform, the reformation of manners, except for their interest in a single justice issue — the rights of the unborn. They have avoided other social issues, partly because they perceive them as the province of their politically correct enemies, the liberal Democrats. This has left us with a very unhealthy political schizophrenia, in which Republicans specialize in morality and Democrats promote justice.

Even so, conservative Protestants have transcended their sectarian past to join forces with many Roman Catholics on the abortion issue, on aid to private religious schools, on homosexual rights, and on a variety of moral issues.

I am increasingly convinced that Pat Buchanan was right when he said that America is engaged in a religious and moral cultural war — although this is a classic instance of the right message and the wrong messenger. A recent book by Evangelical sociologist James Davison Hunter, *Cultural Wars*, spells this out. Hunter notes that the original *Kulturkampf* resulted from Bismarck's effort to force cultural conformity on a territory with a mixture of Catholics and Protestants. He suggests that post-Westphalian secularism is making the same mistake within a fundamentally religious America.[27]

But there are ironic differences. Now the resistance movement is led by a coalition of conservative Catholics and Protestants, by those who were formerly enemies. But this is a *very* broad coalition; there are also conservative Jews, like Michael Medved, whose *Hollywood versus America* is so sympathetic to the Christian right that it includes a rigorous critique of the Christology in *The Last Temptation of Christ*.[28]

The ideological targets of the conservative resistance are secular humanism and the New Age Movement, two opponents who are themselves in unstable opposition. The resistance has identified two instruments through which these forces impose their values on the more conservative religious society: the film and television media, and the public schools. Boston University professor William Kilpatrick's *Why Johnny Can't Tell Right from Wrong* is a good statement of the case against the school system, which began as a disguised conduit for Protestant values, but ultimately became an indoctrinating agent for humanist relativism.[29]

Up against this onslaught of cultural pollution, *all* Evangelical Protestants — not just Fundamentalists and Pentecostals — feel imperiled, especially as they seek to raise their families. Like Dr. Bellah, many are tempted by the Anabaptist cultural solution; they may even envy the Amish! There is no doubt that they regard themselves as Resident Aliens. The only question is whether they will continue to reside on earth, or move their families to some kind of metaphorical Space Station.

But it is increasingly evident that they are not going to emulate past models of Fundamental withdrawal. They may shore up their bunker walls, but leaders like Pat Robertson are going to move out in political mission, working and praying to change institutions that are deforming their culture. And when the chips are down, almost all Evangelicals are going to fall in behind Robertson's leadership — not because they feel his agenda is perfect, but because they agree with it as far as it goes.

Part of my task as an Evangelical seminary teacher is to try to enlarge and rebalance this agenda, to alert my students and other Evangelicals to what is missing in our moralistic version of the Second Awakening reforms. I must also try to convince mainline Protestants, who carry a full program for justice, that moral reform is a legitimate concern and in fact a crying need.

Ruth Graham has said that if God does not judge America, he will have to apologize to Sodom and Gomorrah. Here is the authentic voice of nineteenth-century reform — the sense that God holds nations accountable for moral decay and social injustice. Our common goal as Christian educators may well be to get our students, and their future congregations, to sense the current distance between God's holiness and the unholiness in American society, and to try to change things to lessen that distance.

That means that the left and right wings of American Christianity must close ranks, so far as that is possible. At the moment we are engaged in isometric exercises — the left adopts some cause that the right considers an abomination, or vice versa, and the two hands strain against one another fruitlessly.

Perhaps the next few years will lead beyond this impasse. Catholic and

Evangelical voters may have lost confidence in some causes at the top of the Religious Right's agenda. A national consensus seems to be emerging that abortion ought to be permitted, but only under conditions discouraging its use as substitute contraception. (This is probably where Clinton and Gore stand, although the administration's support of the Right to Life Bill is a contradictory sign.) Christians may have concluded that with safe chemical abortifacients available, this is no longer a winnable war — or that if it can be won, the cure will be worse than the disease, as in the Prohibition era.

Regarding homosexual rights, the second most sensitive issue for the Religious Right — eventually it is going to sink in that one class of sinners should not be singled out for special judgment. "The love that dare not speak its name" has become the love that cannot shut up about itself — partly because, in a homophobic society, its job is at risk. We have got to take away that risk, but demand courtesy and discretion in return. Flaunting one's sexuality, whether straight or gay, should continue to put one at risk. Does this mean "back in the closet"? No, just back in the bedroom with the door closed, which should be the single standard for all sexual orientations. "Don't Ask, Don't Tell" could turn out to be the standard not only for the Army, but also for society at large.

If we can get our attention off these two issues, we can focus on more dangerous hazards, such as the global AIDS pandemic, rooted increasingly in heterosexual transmission. Tipper Gore's "cultural environmentalism," trying to clean up song lyrics, is a gesture in the right direction. Nineteenth-century Evangelicals would respond by mounting a sexual counterrevolution based in renovated educational systems. Tax assistance for Christian schools is not the half of it; younger Gordon-Conwell faculty are home-schooling their children to guarantee their moral formation in today's polluted culture. Perhaps we should just bite the bullet, pay the tab for public schools, but invest in alternative systems that can reshape public education by competitive pressure — the voucher system without the vouchers.

Catholics and Protestants might well cooperate on this. Evangelical historian Timothy Smith has remarked that while the Catholics and Protestants were fighting each other at the turn of the last century, the humanists took over the educational system. It is time to reverse that move, which created the greatest secularizing force in history.

Handling the global environmental crisis is certainly on a par in importance with the antislavery campaigns of the last century. It will take great skill to persuade all parties that this issue can be solved without stifling the economy either in the developed or the developing countries. But if Gore feels the spiritual wind that leveled the Berlin wall is now blowing in this direction, his administration may develop that skill.

Without that wind, our usual mode of muddling through world problems may be terminally inept — and we have not even mentioned the reconstruction of post-communist Asia and Europe. The great evangelist Charles Finney, who led the charge against slavery in this country, used to worry that reform would outrun the revival. It did, and the result was the Civil War.

What we are involved in now may not yet be a revival, although it is certainly a numerical multiplication of different kinds of committed Christians. Perhaps the most salient effort seminary educators can make is to call on our communities to pray for a transcendent spiritual energy that will harmonize our clashing efforts and give us a visible unity in mission. John 17:21 assures us that when the world sees that unity, the result will not just be changes in public policy, but evangelization.

Does it make any sense for lowly seminary professors to grapple with problems on this scale? Perhaps not. However, the chairman of the Gordon-Conwell Trustees is not Bill Moyers, but another Southern Baptist, Billy Graham. After all the flirtations with Nixon, Ford, Reagan, and Bush, now may finally be the moment when Graham can be useful in the White House, and not merely used.

That, at least, will be our prayer, because the new administration needs exposure from the religious center. If it fails to seek this exposure, if it continues to make "politically correct" moves that are eccentric to the popular moral consensus, it is in for increasingly traumatic encounters with the Religious Right.

Notes

1. "Where is the Religious Right?" *Christian Century* (26 February 1992), 216.

2. "Evangelical Politics," *Christian Century* (11 March 1992), 270-71.

3. "Evangelicals Offer Uneasy Support to Bush," *Christianity Today* (6 April 1992), 84-85.

4. James M. Wall, "Blending Commitment and Politics," *Christian Century* (17-24 June 1992), 603.

5. Dan Quayle, "Where Dan Quayle Stands," interview by Charles Colson, *Christianity Today* (22 June 1992), 28-31.

6. Al Gore, "Preserving God's 'Very Good' Earth," interview by David Neff, *Christianity Today* (14 September 1992), 26-28.

7. Kim Lawson, "The New Face(s) of the Religious Right," *Christianity Today* (20 July 1992), 42-45.

8. *Chicago Tribune* (21 August 1992), p. 25.

9. *The Boston Globe* (20 July 1992), p. 9.

10. U.S. NEWSWIRE [GT 42] via NewsNet (14 September 1992).

11. CATHOLIC NEWS SERVICE [CN01] via NewsNet (26 October 1992).

12. Ibid. (1 September 1992).

13. Religious News Service DAILY NEWS REPORTS [SS07] via NewsNet (20 August 1992): RNS16996.

14. CHURCHNEWS INTERNATIONAL [SS05] via NewsNet, 21 October 1992.

15. Religious News Service DAILY NEWS REPORTS [SS07] via NewsNet (31 August 1992): RSN>17055.

16. Ibid. (14 October 1992): RNS>17310.

17. Ibid. (23 October 1992): RNS>17372.

18. Ibid. (6 November 1992): RNS>17446.

19. Ibid. (19 October 1992): RNS>17339.

20. Theodore Roszak, *The Making of a Counter Culture* (Garden City: Doubleday, 1969); *Where the Wasteland Ends* (Garden City: Doubleday, 1972).

21. Religious News Service DAILY NEWS REPORTS [SS07] via NewsNet, 4 November 1992: RNS>17293.

22. Ibid. (12 October 1992): RNS>17293.

23. CHURCHNEWS INTERNATIONAL [SS05] via NewsNet, 18 November 1992.

24. C. C. Cole, *The Social Ideas of the Northern Evangelicals, 1826-1860* (New York: Columbia University Press, 1954), 102.

25. E. M. Howse, *Saints in Public* (London: Allen, 1953), 32.

26. See, for example, Jerry Falwell, *The Fundamentalist Phenomenon*, eds. Edward Hindson and Ed Dobson (Garden City: Doubleday, 1981).

27. James Davison Hunter, *Culture Wars: The Struggle to Define America* (New York: Basic Books, 1991).

28. Michael Medved, *Hollywood versus America: Popular Culture and the War against Traditional Values* (New York: HarperCollins, 1992).

29. William Kilpatrick, *Why Johnny Can't Tell Right from Wrong: Overcoming Moral Illiteracy* (New York: Simon & Schuster, 1992).

WHAT AND HOW
ARE WE LEARNING?

Rodney L. Petersen

In her introductory remarks, Clarissa Atkinson, Associate Dean for Academic Affairs at Harvard Divinity School, reflected upon the question of "What and How Are We Learning." Initially it might be said that the "what" concerns speech about God, *theos logos*. The "we" is just as clear on the surface of things but complex if we begin to probe more deeply. It is we who teach. Teachers impact their students in a variety of ways. Thus the biblical injunction follows that not many should presume to be teachers (James 3:1). Teachers can contribute to constructive or dysfunctional church leaders. The key to effectiveness in the seminary remains character and spiritual integrity as much as the ability to pass on useful and insightful knowledge. It is well recognized today that the profession of theological educators stands as much in need of a code of ethics as do all other professions.[1]

Christian theological education began with the first disciples of Christ. However, it was the Cappadocians from Asia Minor who in the fourth century first set the more extensive pattern for relating classical learning with the Christian tradition.[2] A certain normative form was given to theological education for the West through the reflections of Augustine of Hippo and the vast learning of the ascetic Jerome. In his book *On Christian Doctrine,* Augustine outlines a vision for understanding God and Christian faith. After a charge that we learn to listen to one another since each can bear the inspiration of the Spirit, Augustine presents what has come to be called the fourfold model of theological education as centered around theology, history, biblical interpretation, and rhetoric or the practical disciplines.[3] Following Greek and medieval philosophical tendencies, the language of theology tended toward analogical expression. By way of inference and similarity one might come to know something of the nature of God whose essence was beyond comprehension. This God had chosen to reveal himself through his works, or energies (e.g., Exod. 3:14). This precluded a univocal, or direct, knowledge of God, as Aquinas argued, but so also such knowledge as there was was not subject to doubt.[4]

Controversy would continue in the developing schools of the West, particularly in the twelfth and thirteenth centuries, over whether the philosophical assumptions of Augustine, Thomas Aquinas, or Averroës (Ibn Rushd) were to underlay theological understanding. The first appeared to lay primacy of understanding upon the mystical presence of God, the latter upon the potentiality of matter apart from God. Based upon Aristotelian precedent, Aquinas defended their philosophical co-mingling.[5] Such controversy would continue well into the period of Protestant and Catholic reform when new epistemological and ecclesial controversies gave form to theological education. This curriculum, shaped by religious polemic and then reordered in the West through the influence of pietism and deism among Protestants, and with the appearance of new orders and oratories among Roman Catholics, would continue as such into the nineteenth century when the effects of rationalism and romanticism provided new grids through which theology was to be understood and taught.[6]

The fourfold theological curriculum, inherited from Augustine, has undergone continual transpositions into our own day in relation to different social and epistemic constructions of reality. Each of these shifts in forms of expression has nuanced theological understanding differently so that conceptions of Christology, trinity, anthropology, history, grace and salvation, sanctification, ecclesiology, and eschatology have been raised into prominence differently. Presently we stand in the middle of another paradigm shift in theological understanding. Issues of cosmology, mission and ecclesial identity, and theological anthropology are among the most pressing to be addressed theologically. The "what we are learning" today incorporates not only the foundational curriculum inherited through the fourfold model of instruction, but also such substantive issues as are basic to modernity's definition of knowledge and understanding. In the contemporary climate of cultural conflict and confusion such background as this can prepare one to lead a congregation as it seeks to live out Christ's mission in civil society.[7] As such, the theological community has much to learn from the natural scientific and philosophical disciplines about the place of faith and personal commitment in relation to Christian theology and understanding.[8]

Theology incorporates not only a claim to knowledge, but also to behavior. The bifurcation in theological discipline that has been followed in the past, that of scholastic theology and moral theology, is a separation in pedagogy but not in life. It issues from the Sinai prescription and Jesus' injunction to love God and neighbor (Matt. 22:34-40). Issues of formation come to the fore not only in terms of the mind of the theologian, but also of the heart. Love of God and love of neighbor require that we not only live intelligently but also compassionately. On the verge of the twenty-first century this twofold nature of theological education asks us to look at the place of the church in civil society in relation to these two distinct but related roles. Who our neighbor is, is not unrelated to the philosophical forms through which we understand individuality and community.[9]

Indeed, the very question of what a person is has come to the fore in a way hitherto unseen since the theological controversies of the third and fourth centuries formulated our received ideas about the nature of person-hood.[10] This debate was set in a classical framework that understood the highest of interpersonal relations to have been defined by what came to be called the cardinal virtues or strengths. In the instruction of the Roman rhetor Cicero to his son Marcus, Cicero argued that the really difficult knowledge to impart to another is not so much how to do as how to be. The four virtues of prudence (or wisdom), temperance, fortitude (or courage), and justice constitute the "strengths" that separate us, at least by degree, from the rest of sensate life.[11] Christians, conscious of their inheritance in Christ, would add to these cardinal strengths the theological virtues of faith, hope, and love as articulated by Paul in his first letter to the church at Corinth (I Cor. 13:13).

In surveying three modes of moral inquiry and evaluation today, the encyclopedia, genealogical, and traditional, Alasdair MacIntyre offers a modern restatement of the traditional Thomist position, as described above, in relation to a metaphysics of morality.[12] Although challenged by Cornel West to be more realistic in his assessment of human proclivities, to be more processive in his view of life and history, and inclusive in moral outlook, MacIntyre's project is given some consideration in contemporary society.[13] Both Catholic MacIntyre and Protestant West require us to ask about what kind of persons we are trying to form through theological education. The failure of the ideologies fo change in the twentieth century has deepened this traditional Orthodox concern in the lands of traditional Orthodoxy and its diaspora.[14] Is there an image to which we should become conformed? Scripture counsels our having been made in the image of God by intent (Gen. 1:27), but requiring the grace of God through Christ for its realization (Col. 3:1-11). This grace, or virtue, needed for the completion of our identity raises the debate of who we are by nature, nurture, or might be by grace.

By the late Middle Ages Aristotle's understanding of virtue, as seen in the instruction of Cicero to his son Marcus, had so conditioned Western

Christian conceptions of sanctification as preceding salvation that it appeared to Martin Luther that the basic fiduciary element of faith in
Christ's work yielding our justification for salvation had been lost. Based
upon the teachings of Aquinas, theories of habitual grace, that conveyed
through the sacraments, and actual grace, whether condign (debtor's) or
congruous, had come to replace a more diffuse understanding of the reception of grace implicit in Augustinian mysticism. Protestantism, often
riding the crest of philosophical nominalism, argued that all virtue is
empty and useless unless the heart is rightly trusting in Christ. Only then,
as formed by the gospel (in Lutheranism) or as shaped by the law of
Christ (the *Lex Christi* among the Reformed), could one be said to bear
that rightousness which yields salvation. Different communities of Christian expression rallied around this debate over nature and grace. New
churches appeared with different postures of support or hostility to civil
society as shaped by varying social conditions.[15]

The two talks that were given at the BTI symposium, together with
their respondents, were intended to address the issues of scholastic and
moral theology as sketched in the foregoing discussion. David Hollenbach, S.J., begins his paper, "The Foundation of Theological Knowledge,"
by reflecting on the spirit of anti-foundationalism and contemporary dilemmas in theological epistemology. By this Hollenbach means reflection
upon whether philosophy can give us a clear understanding of the basis
for faith. We live in a world that has not only given us individuality, but
also a Kantian grid for epistemology that in our postmodern period is
undergoing revisionist challenges.[16] Questions are being raised about the
assumptions for verifiability and for standards of judgment. Each of these
questions takes us back to medieval debate over Augustine, Aquinas, and
Averroës or forward into issues of historical methodology and explanation.[17]

Hollenbach raises up two perspectives on this dilemma in understanding. The first is that of Karl Barth with his stress upon the autonomy
of theology and its demand that we be faithful as people or in the context
of the church to the covenant. The second is that of "Post-Liberalism"
with its stress upon the application of the Christian story as cultural critique to the ways by which we lead our lives. These positions are sketched
out in the persons of, first, George Lindbeck for whom it might be said the
text absorbs the world. God, as understood in scripture, sets the terms for
theological discussion. The narrative theologian tries to recover the proper
form of the story's language and perception for Christian understanding.
The problem with this assumed autonomy of theology, according to
Hollenbach, lies in translating Christian understanding into meaningful
categories for contemporary culture.

The second person Hollenbach cites is Ronald F. Thiemann. It might be said the problem left off with in Lindbeck is one with which Thiemann begins, i.e., the problem of translation. In Thiemann's opinion there is no common normative language or experiential paradigm out of which to translate Christian meaning. Thiemann raises a concern for maintaining the oneness of truth. It is important that theology remain in dialogue with other academic disciplines for the university and seminary to speak meaningfully to each other. This is of pointed concern if we are to construct a public theology or common civic language of normative values. Christian faith for Thiemann has public import, and as such he stands against the sectarian tendencies of narrative theology. In light of these commitments, in Thiemann's opinion the nature of theology today is of necessity *ad hoc* or fragmentary. The Bible and its story somehow absorb the world, but our understanding of this is limited and partial.[18]

Hollenbach offers several points for our consideration as it grows out of the above discussion. First, he is concerned about the way in which we think or talk about the truths of faith. The problem with the narrativist approach, he argues, is demonstrated in terms of Christian apology, or evangelism. From the narrativist perspective the only way to demonstrate the truth of one's understanding of scripture is to socialize another into one's own community. Through entering into the group's language and life sense can be made of it for the one now, formerly, outside of it. However, according to Hollenbach, this method can take on the character of indoctrination or promote cultural passivity in the outsider. Roman Catholics have struggled with such a narrative theology since Vatican II with its deepened emphasis upon Christian thought and life under scripture. A similar struggle has occurred for Protestants dissatisfied with the dichotomies of fundamentalism and liberalism and needing a fresh way to recast neo-orthodoxy. In Hollenbach's perspective the narrativist approach never adequately affirms the truth of Christianity. Accordingly, religious faith is not simply learned, but discovered. Coming to believe is more active than learning a language. It requires a mutually critical interaction for which neo-Barthian categories are inadequate. Some form of foundationalism or philosophical demonstration of Christian truth is implicitly mandated.

In the end, Hollenbach contends that a purely narrativist approach to truth is not possible. The likelihood of isolating the full meaning of the biblical story is questionable. Biblical texts have polyvalent meanings that are sometimes in conflict with each other. Drawing upon his work as an ethicist, Hollenbach argues that this can be seen in the conflict over advocating Christian nonviolence in contrast with the theological defense of just wars. It can be seen, he believes, in controversy over whether proper biblical counsel calls for the subordination of women or clearly mandates

forthright declarations of gender equality. In light of such apparent antino-
mies in understanding, the task of theology will never be finished.[19]

In his response to Hollenbach's paper, Ronald F. Thiemann, Dean of
the Harvard Divinity School, laid out three considerations. He began by
focusing his criticism on Lindbeck's position, favoring the "thick description" of culture as described by Clifford Geertz or Emmanuel Le Roy
Ladurie, requiring theology to attend to the particularities of religious life
and practice. Such attention is the first step in the making of normative
proposals. Yet the question emerges, he asked, from where do we draw
the critical principles by which to evaluate different cultures? Here narrative theology as represented by the work of Lindbeck and others is inadequate. Thiemann's intention is to make propositions about Christian belief
and practice descriptive, evaluative, and of a reforming nature. He agrees
with Lindbeck in not drawing upon the idea of language games as in
Ludwig Wittgenstein.[20]

In light of this Lindbeck moves toward the idea of an autonomous
theology, but one need not follow him there. In Thiemann's opinion, theology as an autonomous discipline that absorbs the world is a theology that
cannot be adopted since theological thinking is never a unidirectional activity. However, if we deny the aspirations of a foundational theology, Thiemann argues that this does not mean that a sectarian approach is all that is
open to us. Lacking confidence in the neo-liberal approach, Thiemann
recognizes the dilemma that is now reached of how to bring together real
diversity and one truth. On this point the neo-liberalism of David Tracy is
not seen to be helpful according to Thiemann.[21] Founded upon the idea of a
mutually critical correlation grounded in a religious essence that is in each
of us (assuming a *homo religiosis*), the effort has been made since the
Enlightenment to try to identify a core religious nature and then to evaluate
it. However, according to Thiemann, this position merely sees diversity as
an epiphenomenon and never quite takes diversity seriously. Insofar as
Hollenbach's position is open-ended and invitational, Thiemann argues,
there lies the possibility for conversation and collaboration about the goals
that we share in common. This becomes a basis for public theology.

The remarks by Hollenbach and Thiemann raise the issue of the unity
of truth and whether education for the ministry can be founded upon a
restricted or privileged domain of understanding. The implications for
ethical norms in civic life are considerable. Both argue against the separation of theology from the rest of academic discourse for the sake of theology, and by implication the university.[22] A line of Christian theology that
extends back to the early Christian theologian, Justin Martyr (c.100-
c.165), would agree. In Justin's writings the Stoic idea of the *logos* was
personified in Jesus Christ. As such, it became the symbolic, but also real,

source for and final embodiment of truth. This conception was central to the Christian medieval university.[23] Some sense of the recovery of this idea can be seen in the study made by Gabriel Fackre of contemporary efforts in theological instruction.[24] The discipline of Christian theology must first remember what it is and what it is about before there can be legitimate innovation to meet the needs of our day.[25] In fact, without this retrieval it can be argued that the university loses a sense of its own coherence apart from a generalized moral purpose to serve humanity, a concept that may be difficult at times to define.[26] Beyond a recovery of itself for the sake of the church and university, for theology to be fully engaged with the problems of modernity, this recovery or retrieval must deal with the intricacies of a comparative philosophy of religion.[27] Theology cannot become fully public theology apart from this engagement. Both the infrastructures and the macrostructures through which we live, as identified by Stackhouse, mandate this discussion in the context of a principled pluralism.

The search for an engaged theology in Hollenbach and Thiemann meets its formative counterpart in contemporary emphases upon "formation for ministry," the title of the talk and article by Brian O. McDermott, Academic Dean of the Weston Jesuit School of Theology. He cites four areas for consideration in thoughts about living responsibly before God. First, a goal of theological education is to enable us to pay attention to the things that really matter in life. Such attention calls for understanding in relation to the challenges of contemporary society. We are called to be, in McDermott's words, "Reflective Practitioners," not simply theological technicians. This calls, second, for a special kind of formation as persons, those who know the word and seek to be doers of it as well. Third, such formation has as an end the fostering of the ability to make responsible choices. A practical spirituality is needed today, one that is grounded in prayer and seeks God in all things. This requires the integration of knowledge and person, always the intent of the wedding of scholastic and moral theology. In this way discernment is fostered toward recognizing what God desires for our world. This discernment cannot simply be individualistic, it calls for discernment in community. Finally, the end of this preparation for ministry is the enablement we receive and courage we are given to live out the choices we make before God. This will enable us to bridge the world of theological education and public life. It will foster a spirituality capable of being lived in the public arena. People yearn for wisdom in their personal lives and to do right service commensurate with the good. For reasons such as these it is vital that theological schools find their place in the context of other professional schools. It is here that formation for ministry must begin in our world as presently organized.[28]

In his response, ethicist Stanley Harakas, of Holy Cross Greek Ortho-dox School of Theology, drew out four threads from McDermott's com-ments. First, there is an enabling function that is central to theological education. Such education is not simply toward the end of providing facts, but is to enable others to function to their fullest capacity. In saying this Harakas is underscoring a point from an Orthodox perspective that has become central to theological education in the last half of the twentieth century, that theological education is "to motivate, equip, and enable the people of God to develop their gifts and give their lives in meaningful service." [29] The way in which this purpose has been put is something of a *novum* for seminaries and other schools offering religious education that has developed since the middle of the twentieth century.[30] Second, reflec-tive practitioners are to be characterized both by a developed intellect and developed skills to do that which the church is called to do. Third, theo-logical education must nurture a "call." The form of theological education must never become a substitute for the claims of the call to ministry by God.[31] Finally, there is an adaptive task. We are to prepare and form people who can bring forth the commitment to creative engagement with a changing society, but a commitment also tied to a fidelity to the gospel, i.e., to the reigning reality of God.[32]

It must be added that this last emphasis upon formation promotes ideas of individuality, about which this volume has been so concerned, but it is always individuality in context and for something. The context is the church, itself contextualized in its settings in the world.[33] The beginning is with our call to worship the one God of all contexts (Ps. 24). The end is formation by the Spirit through the redemptive economy opened up by Christ enabling us to be that which we were intended to be from the start, men and women made in the image and likeness of God.[34] Keeping the idea of the *imago dei* in mind, the Orthodox community has much to contribute to theological discussion with respect to the nature of the per-son whether seen at the beginning of life, subject to the vicissitudes and violence that are so much a part of our world, or the medical complexities surrounding the end of life as we know it.[35]

Notes

1. James P. Wind, Russell Burck, Paul F. Camenisch, and Dennis P. McCann, eds., *Clergy Ethics in a Changing Society: Mapping the Terrain*. A publication of The Park Ridge Center for the Study of Health, Faith, and Ethics (Louisville: W/JKP, 1991). The Association of Theological Field Education, Catholic Association for Field Education, and the Evangelical Association of Theological Field Educators have encouraged their members for the past several years to deal pointedly with issues of professional ethics in

the ministry. For perspective on ethics in the professions generally, see W. Gellermann, M. S. Frankel, and R. Ladenson, *Values and Ethics in Organization and Human Systems Development: Responding to Dilemmas in Professional Life* (San Francisco: Jossey-Bass, 1990).

2. For example, see on Macrina, Gregory of Nazianzus, Gregory of Nyssa, and Basil of Caesarea in Jaroslav Pelikan, *Christianity and Classical Culture: The Metamorphosis of Natural Theology in the Christian Encounter with Hellenism* (New Haven: Yale University Press, 1993), pp. 58-59, 175-176.

3. Augustine, *On Christine Doctrine*, transl. by D. W. Robertson, Jr. (Indianapolis: Bobbs-Merrill, 1983). These are books I-IV. Ways in which this has been shaped differently can be seen in Patrick Henry, ed., *Schools of Thought in the Christian Tradition* (Philadelphia: Fortress Press, 1984).

4. Thomas Aquinas, *Summa Theologica* (Question 13). Aquinas cites Exodus 3:13-14.

5. Harry Austryn Wolfson, *The Philosophy of the Church Fathers* (Cambridge: Harvard University Press, 1970).

6. Edward Farley, *Theologia*, pp. 29-48, 49ff.; and cp. Glenn T. Miller, "Professionals and Pedagogues: A Survey of Theological Education," in David Lotz, ed., *Altered Landscapes: Christianity in America, 1935-1985* (Grand Rapids: Eerdmans, 1989), pp. 189-208.

7. Lesslie Newbigin sketches ways in which this may be done in *Foolishness to the Greeks: The Gospel and Western Culture* (Geneva: WCC, 1986). See the agenda for theological education in Petersen, "Local Ecumenism and the Neo-Patristic Synthesis of Father Georges Florovsky," in *On Theology and the Ecumenical Movement: Essays in Honor of Georges Florovsky*, George Papademetriou, ed. (Brookline: Holy Cross Press, 1995).

8. Michael Polanyi, *Personal Knowledge: Towards a Post-Critical Philosophy* (New York: Harper & Row, 1964); Thomas Kuhn, *The Structure of Scientific Revolutions* (Chicago: University of Chicago Press, 1973); and Wolfhart Pannenberg, *Toward a Theology of Nature: Essays on Science and Faith* (Louisville: W/JKP, 1993).

9. In terms of discussion in the schools, one might begin with Alasdair MacIntyre, *Whose Justice? Which Rationality?* (Notre Dame: University of Notre Dame Press, 1988); idem, *Three Rival Versions of Moral Enquiry: Encyclopaedia, Genealogy, and Tradition* (Notre Dame: University of Notre Dame Press, 1990). The discussion draws upon theories of virtue and ethics from each of the periods of intellectual history and is nuanced by different tonalities of Christian perception. One might begin with Stanley Hauerwas, *Character and the Christian Life: A Study in Theological Ethics* (San Antonio: Trinity University Press, 1975); with respect to moral spheres of responsibility in the contemporary world, see Peter A. French, *The Spectrum of Responsibility* (New York: St. Martin's Press, 1991).

10. Different aspects in theological instruction may be seen in the following: Preston N. Williams, ed., *Symposium on the Identity and Dignity of Man* (Cambridge, MA: Schenkman, 1973); Lisa Sowle Cahill and Thomas A. Shannon, *Religion and Artificial Reproduction: An Inquiry into the Vatican "Instruction on Respect for Human Life in its Origin and on the Dignity of Human Reproduction"* (New York: Crossroad, 1988). Debate over the issue of gender continues; see the work of John Boswell, and most recently *Same-Sex Unions in Pre-Modern Europe* (New York: Villard, 1994), but note the review by Brent D. Shaw, "A Groom of One's Own?" in

The New Republic (18 and 25 July 1994): 33-41, in which Boswell's work is scored as tendentious and misleading. Jean Zizioulas, *Being as Communion: Studies in Person-hood and the Church* (Crestwood, NY: St. Vladimir's Seminary Press, 1985).

11. Cicero, *De Officiis*, transl. by Walter Miller (Cambridge: Harvard University Press, 1975), I.i-v. See William J. Prior, *Virtue and Knowledge: An Introduction to Ancient Greek Ethics* (New York: Routledge, 1991).

12. Alasdair MacIntyre, *Three Rival Versions of Moral Enquiry: Encyclopaedia, Genealogy, and Tradition* (Notre Dame: University of Notre Dame Press, 1990); see also his *After Virtue* (Notre Dame: University of Notre Dame Press, 1981).

13. Cornel West, "Alasdair MacIntyre, Liberalism, and Socialism: A Christian Perspective," in Bruce Grelle and David A. Krueger, eds., *Christianity and Capitalism: Perspectives on Religion, Liberalism, and the Economy* (Chicago: Center for the Scientific Study of Religion, 1985).

14. Anthony Ugolnik, "Living on the Borders: Eastern Orthodoxy and World Disorder," in *First Things* (June/July 1993): 15-23.

15. For a discussion of grace, justification, sanctification, and salvation in the late Middle Ages, see Heiko Oberman, *The Harvest of Medieval Theology: Gabriel Biel and Late Medieval Nominalism* (Grand Rapids: Eerdmans, 1967). See George H. Williams, *The Radical Reformation*, third revised edition (Kirksville, MO: Sixteenth Century Essays and Studies, 1992).

16. Hans Frei classifies modern theologians, profoundly shaped by Kant's work, by whether they see Christian theology as primarily an academic discipline or as an internal activity of Christian communities in *Types of Christian Theology*, George Hunsinger and William C. Placher, eds. (New Haven: Yale University Press, 1992), pp. 29-55.

17. Such issues, particularly as they touch upon the adequacy of narrative for historical explanation, are raised by Christopher Lloyd, *The Structures of History* (Oxford: Blackwell, 1993).

18. Ronald F. Thiemann, *Revelation and Theology: The Gospel as Narrated Promise* (Notre Dame: University of Notre Dame Press, 1985). The significance of this theology for public life is written about in *Constructing a Public Theology: The Church in a Pluralistic Culture* (Louisville: W/JKP, 1991), pp. 133-139.

19. See David Hollenbach and R. Bruce Douglass, eds., *Catholicism and Liberalism: Contributions to American Public Philosophy* (New York: Cambridge University Press, 1994).

20. A helpful introduction to the importance of philosophical description to theology is given by Anthony C. Thiselton, *The Two Horizons: New Testament Hermeneutics and Philosophical Description* (Grand Rapids: Eerdmans, 1980), pp. 3-23; on Wittgenstein, pp. 357-385.

21. See in David Tracy, *The Anagogical Imagination: Christian Theology and the Culture of Pluralism* (New York, 1981); cf. Richard Lints, "The Postpositivist Choice: Tracy or Lindbeck?" *Journal of the American Academy of Religion*, vol. LXI, no. 4 (Autumn 1993): 655-677.

22. Ronald F. Thiemann, "Toward a Critical Theological Education," *Harvard Theological Review*, vol. 80, no. 1 (1987): 1-13; and "The Future of an Illusion: An Inquiry into the Contrast between Theological and Religious Studies," *Theological Education*, vol. XXVI, no. 2 (Spring 1990): 66-85. See also his "The Scholarly Vocation: Its Future, Challenges and Threats," *Theological Education*, vol. XXIV, no. 1 (Autumn 1987): 86-101; cp. Marjorie Hewitt Suchocki, "A Learned Ministry?" *Quar-*

terly Review (Summer 1993): 3-17; and Ernest L. Boyer, *Scholarship Reconsidered: Priorities of the Professoriate* (Princeton: Carnegie Foundation, 1990).

23. This would include the early development of American college and university life as well. See George H. Williams, *The Theological Idea of the University* (New York: NCC, 1958); and cf. Marsden, *The Soul of the American University*, pp. 48-67.

24. Gabriel Fackre, "The Surge in Systematics: A Commentary on Current Works," *The Journal of Religion* (1993); and "Reorientation and Retrieval in Systematic Theology," *The Christian Century* (26 June-3 July 1991): 653-656. See the earlier "Analysis of Systematic Theology Courses, B.T.I." by Owen Thomas and Edward Kilmartin. A study under the auspices of the Luce Foundation (June, 1970). See also David Wells, *No Place for Truth: Or Whatever Happened to Evangelical Theology?* (Grand Rapids: Eerdmans, 1993); and Thomas C. Oden, *After Modernity . . . What? Agenda for Theology* (Grand Rapids: Zondervan, 1990); Gabriel Fackre, *Ecumenical Faith in Evangelical Perspective* (Grand Rapids: Eerdmans, 1993).

25. Such appears to be the assumption of many ecclesial renewal groups. See the recent works of such church scholars as, e.g., Elizabeth Achtemeier, Carl Braaten, Gabriel Fackre, Thomas Oden, and David Wells. A similar effort seems evident in the recent work of Robert C. Neville, but in the context of recognizing the larger world of religious symbolism. See his chapter in this volume and *The Truth of Broken Symbols* (forthcoming).

26. The defense of such moral purpose is offered by Jaroslav Pelikan in *The Idea of the University: A Reexamination* (New Haven: Yale University Press, 1991); see the review by George M. Marsden, "Christian Schooling: Beyond the Multiversity," *The Christian Century* (7 October 1992): 873-875. In addition to Marsden's own study, *The Soul of the University* (1994), the significance of Christian theology in the formation of American university development is documented with respect to Harvard University by George H. Williams, *Divinings: Religion at Harvard, 1636-1992: The University in the Context of New England Church History* (Cleveland: Pilgrim Press, 1995 (forthcoming)).

27. Drawing upon Michael Polanyi, Alasdair MacIntyre, and Robert Wuthnow, among others, Lesslie Newbigin argues for this in *The Gospel in a Pluralist Society* (Grand Rapids: Eerdmans, 1989). This discussion can be seen to be framed by the theological arguments of pluralism, inclusivism, and exclusivism in John Hick and Paul F. Knitter, eds., *The Myth of Christian Uniqueness: Toward a Pluralistic Theology of Religions* (Maryknoll: Orbis, 1987), on the one hand, and in Gavin D'Costa, ed., *Christian Uniqueness Reconsidered: The Myth of a Pluralistic Theology of Religions* (Maryknoll: Orbis, 1990).

28. Brian O. McDermott relates such activity to grace in *What Are They Saying about the Grace of Christ?* (New York: Paulist Press, 1984). Katarina Schuth, O.S.F., *Reason for the Hope; The Futures of Roman Catholic Theologates* (Wilmington: Michael Glazier, Inc., 1989), see her chapter on "Formation Programs for Future Ministers," pp. 137-200.

29. Ross Kinsler, *Ministry by the People* (Maryknoll: WCC/Orbis Books, 1983). A variety of perspectives is presented in Samuel Amirtham and Robin Pryor, eds., *Resources for Spiritual Formation in Theological Education* (Geneva: WCC, 1990), a volume based on a consultation sponsored by the Program on Theological Education of the World Council of Churches (1989).

30. Although grounded in Protestant thought pertaining to the priesthood of all

believers, a significant reemphasis upon the importance of empowering the laity was given by the Roman Catholic Yves Congar in his study, *Lay People in the Church: A Study for a Theology of the Laity*, tr. D. Attwater (Westminster, MD: Newman Press, 1957).

31. Alkiviadis Calivas, "Orthodox Theology and Theologians: Reflections on the Nature, Task, and Mission of the Theological Enterprise," *The Greek Orthodox Theological Review*, vol. 37, nos. 3-4 (1992): 293-300.

32. Stanley Samuel Harakas, *Living the Faith: The Praxis of Eastern Orthodox Ethics* (Minneapolis: Light and Life, 1992). This is the second of an envisioned trilogy by Harakas on the "theoria" of Orthodox ethics, the ethic of personal and ecclesial life, and a volume on social ethics.

33. For an Orthodox perspective, see Georges Florovsky, "The Church: Her Nature and Task," in volume I of his *Collected Works, Bible, Church, Tradition: An Eastern Orthodox View* (Belmont: Nordland, 1972), pp. 57-72; and cf. Judo Poerwowidagdo, "Theological Education in 'Glocol' Context," in James Massey, ed., *Contextual Theological Education* (Delhi: SPCK CTE, 1993), pp. 1-14; and The Fund for Theological Education, *Learning in Context* (Bromley, Kent, 1973).

34. Vladimir Lossky, *The Image and Likeness of God* (Crestwood, NY: St. Vladimir's Seminary Press, 1974).

35. Jean Zizioulas, *Being as Communion: Studies in Personhood and the Church* (Crestwood, NY: St. Vladimir's Seminary Press, 1985).

5

The Foundation
of Theological Knowledge

David Hollenbach

The planning committee for this symposium has assigned me the impossible task of saying something coherent about the foundation of theological knowledge in the short space of twenty minutes.[1] Each term in the title of this session is highly problematic in the contemporary intellectual and cultural environment. The anti-foundationalist currents in postmodern discourse challenge the notion that theological knowledge — or any other form of knowing for that matter — has a *foundation* at all. The alienation of large parts of the academy from theistic belief suggests that, whatever knowledge is achievable through academic inquiry, it cannot be *theological* knowledge. And the propensity of the movers and shakers of public debate to use the term "theology" to describe the most speculative aspects of strategic military issues such as nuclear deterrence or of economic debates about supply-side versus guided-investment industrial policies implies that whatever theology is, it is not *knowledge*, but at best conjecture or at worst self-deception.

Since the Enlightenment, theologians have been grappling with such challenges to their effort to give a reasoned account of the Christian faith. Numerous strategies to secure a place for Christian faith in modern culture have been pursued. For example, Schleiermacher's appeal to the inner experience of absolute dependence sought to protect faith against the solvents of modern scientific and historical understanding. Pre-Vatican II

David Hollenbach, S.J., is Margaret O'Brian Flatley Professor of Ethics at Boston College.

Catholicism adopted an aggressively defensive strategy that sought to create an alternative to modernity by constructing a theological/philosophical worldview based on a form of Thomism and a self-contained ecclesial community structured by papal authority. Twentieth-century Protestants like Tillich and Bultmann relied on idealist and existentialist philosophy to find a foothold for faith, while Catholics like Rahner and Lonergan appealed to transcendental analysis to make Christian belief intelligible in light of a philosophical understanding of the human subject. More recently, thinkers like James Gustafson have been seeking to reconstruct classical Christian beliefs in light of scientific work in the areas of astrophysics, sociobiology, and ecology. Feminist and liberation thinkers are engaged in similar efforts at reconstruction — some would say deconstruction — of Christian tradition in light of a praxis that seeks to overturn all forms of oppression and injustice. And, of course, there have been neoconservative responses to these efforts that have recently arisen across denominational lines.

What is one to make of all this? I can hardly attempt to analyze the strengths and weaknesses of all these efforts to give the theological task a coherent basis. I do think there is at least one identifiable characteristic that is shared by all of them, namely, they all attempt to show that Christian faith is understandable and credible within the intellectual and cultural world shaped by modern notions of rationality, history, and science. I propose to explore the topic of the foundation of theological knowledge by first noting that Karl Barth frontally challenged the legitimacy of such a theological procedure. For Barth, Christian faith, if it is authentic, is an obedient response to the gracious Word of God, i.e. to the gracious covenant of reconciliation offered to humanity in Jesus Christ. This covenant cannot be understood or made credible in any other terms than those in which God offers it, i.e. in the words that tell the story of the Word, the story of Jesus Christ.

This Barthian emphasis on theology's autonomy from philosophy, science, and other forms of understanding and imagination present in our culture fell into considerable disfavor in the 1950s and 1960s. But it has been undergoing a notable revival over the past several decades, particularly in the work of narrative theologians such as Hans Frei, George Lindbeck, John Howard Yoder, Stanley Hauerwas, and others. These so-called postliberal thinkers are frequently contrasted with a group of thinkers that includes David Tracy, Langdon Gilkey, Schubert Ogden, and Paul Ricoeur. According to this second school, theology cannot be content with describing the meaning of the Christian faith by presenting an exposition of the story of Israel and of Jesus. It also has the task of mediating the meaning of the Christian story by bringing it into mutually critical correlation with cultural self-understandings. This latter approach is sometimes called neoliberal.

Let me briefly sketch George Lindbeck's version of the postliberal, narrative approach to the theological task. Relying on thinkers such as Ludwig Wittgenstein in philosophy and Clifford Geertz in anthropology, Lindbeck's theory compares religion to a language or cultural system. Like language and culture, a religious tradition provides a framework that shapes the way those who have learned it perceive reality, speak about reality, and order their lives in action.[2] Tradition is formative of and embedded in experience itself. Experience is never "raw" or uninterpreted. The languages and conceptual frameworks as well as the paradigmatic persons and events of a historical tradition are already present, shaping the world of the experiencing subject and thus experience itself.[3]

The cultural-linguistic theory of religion also helps explain how symbolic and conceptual traditions have a powerful influence on the way human beings reason about their lives and their world. The structure of rational argumentation is affected by the historical and cultural traditions available to the reasoner. Any reasoned argument that a particular conviction is true must appeal to other, already existing convictions to justify the argument's conclusion.[4] For example, in our efforts to reason about who God is or about our own humanness, we necessarily rely on languages and conceptual frameworks that we have not invented but learned. Thus theological reasoning is not an exercise of pure logic leading from timeless starting points to timeless conclusions. Theological reasoning is itself historical and tradition-dependent.

Considerations such as these have led Lindbeck to argue that the meaning of a religion and the ethical way of life it proposes is *entirely* contained in the normative texts of the religion. In the cultural-linguistic view, efforts to understand a religion or religious ethic depend on a willingness to be schooled in the tradition of that religion, much as an apprentice is schooled by a master craftsman. Indeed, it is just as impossible to learn the meaning of a religion from some standpoint outside the framework of the religion's normative texts as it is to learn the Chinese language by studying English translations of Chinese literature.[5] This, I take it, is the meaning of the claim that theology is autonomous in relation to the meanings contained in contemporary experiences, philosophies, and sciences. Efforts to translate the biblical narrative into nonbiblical languages are bound to fail to give an adequate account of what Christianity actually is. Such efforts at translation are futile because all meaning is immanent *within* the specific uses of a particular language. Just as the meanings of individual words are dependent on their place within the total system of the language they are part of, so the meanings of particular religious beliefs and ethical norms are a function of their place within a religion as a total way of life. Meaning is "intratextual."

Thus the Christian meaning of "God" is determined by examining how the word operates within the Christian story and how it shapes the world and experience of faithful Christians. The meaning of "God" for Christians is not specified by identifying some object to which this word refers and describing that object in a language other than that which tells the Christian story.

Lindbeck therefore recommends abandoning the attempt to translate scripture into extrascriptural categories in the hope of discovering a common meaning that can bridge the gap between the Christian story and contemporary culture. The proper task for the Christian theologian is to describe reality as it is portrayed within the scriptural framework and to discover the behavioral implications of this description. The task for Christians is to "allow their cultural conditions and highly diverse affections to be molded by the set of Biblical stories that stretches from creation to eschaton and culminates in Jesus' passion and resurrection."[6] Thus Lindbeck ends up endorsing something very much like Luther's *sola Scriptura* principle. The text of the Bible — taken in its entirety — has primacy among the sources of theology and ethics. "Intratextual theology redescribes reality within the scriptural framework rather than translating scripture into extrascriptural categories. It is the text, so to speak, which absorbs the world, rather than the world the text."[7] This leads David Tracy to observe that "Lindbeck's substantive theological position is a methodologically sophisticated version of Barthian confessionalism. The hands may be the hands of Wittgenstein and Geertz but the voice is the voice of Karl Barth."[8]

Lindbeck's cultural-linguistic approach to these questions takes pluralism in deadly earnest. It views pluralism, however, not as a challenge to develop universal perspectives but rather as a call to faithfulness to the particularity of Christian belief. It stresses the distinctive meaning of Christianity as the unsurpassable contribution Christians can make to a divided world. In order to make this contribution to a pluralistic, increasingly secularized society, Christians should band together to form "communal enclaves that socialize their members into highly particular outlooks supportive of concern for others."[9] The attempt to find common ground with non-Christians threatens to weaken the strength of such communities and their power to contribute to the larger, pluralistic society.

Ronald Thiemann shares some of Lindbeck's convictions, as do narrative ethicists John Howard Yoder and Stanley Hauerwas. Thiemann, however, suggests an additional pragmatic reason for opposing efforts to translate or mediate the meaning of Christian faith into categories of contemporary culture. This effort simply will not work, because there is no single cultural experience, language, or notion of rationality into which the Christian story can be translated or to which it can be mediated by theological reflection. In our world, experiences, languages, and understandings of rationality are radically plural. Thus theology must be in some sense Barthian, for there is no coherent culture to which it can relate the Christian story. But Thiemann is a vigorous opponent of those aspects of the narrativism of Lindbeck, Hauerwas, or Yoder that would lead to a sectarian privatization of Christian faith. Thiemann holds strongly that the Christian faith has *public* import.[10] Such an effort to relate the meaning of the Christian story to public life, however, cannot be systematic — it cannot be based on a correlation of the Christian story with a systematic philosophy or a unified cultural vision. The public task of the theologian, therefore, must necessarily be a series of *ad hoc* encounters between a person deeply formed by the Christian story and a variety of partial and fragmentary meanings present in the political, economic, and other dimensions of social existence today. So despite his resistance to sectarianism, it remains true for Thiemann as for Lindbeck that the text of the Bible must absorb the world rather than the world the text of the Bible. It is just that for Thiemann this absorption necessarily occurs in a more piecemeal way than the language of Lindbeck implies.

I am quite sympathetic to the overall agenda of the narrative theologians. One of the most salutary effects of the Second Vatican Council in Catholic circles was its strong insistence that both Christian life and Christian theology stand under the word of God proclaimed in scripture.[11] It is no accident, I think, that the emergence of liberation theology and Catholic participation in efforts at liberating practice in Latin America, as well as the efforts of the United States Catholic bishops to address crucial questions of war and economic injustice, have very explicit connections with the renewal of Bible reading in Christian base communities and of scholarly study of the social and political implications of the biblical proclamation. Nevertheless, I remain unconvinced that it is either desirable or possible that the movement between the meaning of normative biblical texts on the one hand and cultural self-understanding and social praxis on the other be all in one direction.

Such a one-way movement is not desirable because a purely narrativist approach to the theological task, even one that seeks to show the *ad hoc* significance of the Christian story for public life, fails to take the question of the truth of that story seriously enough.[12] Lindbeck, Hauerwas, and some of the other pure narrativists[13] are clearly convinced of the truth of Christianity, and they maintain that this truth will be confirmed in the experience of those who undertake to live by it. But because of his intratextual understanding of the meaning of Christianity, the only avenue that appears to be open in the effort to persuade others of this truth is that of "socializing" them into a Christian linguistic enclave and its corresponding form of life. This comes uncomfortably close to viewing the proclamation of the gospel as a form of indoctrination.

It also rests on a peculiarly passive view of religious understanding and of faith. The process of coming to believe is a more active one than is learning a language. Believing is an act of judgment and commitment. Avery Dulles has written eloquently about the analogy that exists between the genesis of religious faith and the processes of scientific or artistic discovery. Religious faith is not simply learned; it is discovered through active engagement with the most fundamental human and cosmic questions. In Dulles's words:

> The religious quest, like the scientific, begins with passionate questioning. Persons sensitive to the dimension of ultimacy in human experience, unwilling to rest in the merely proximate explanations that might satisfy more superficial minds, persistently ask whether life and the world, in the final analysis, issue into a meaningless void, or whether the proximate meanings disclosed in everyday experience point to an ultimate and abiding significance.[14]

In order to understand a religious text or tradition one must be able to grasp the point of such questions. To believe in Christ one must be grasped by these questions as matters of overriding personal importance and find responses to them in the story of Jesus of Nazareth. The believer cannot discover meaning in Christianity or come to a decision about its truth without actively entering into this quest for ultimate meaning. The process by which Christian identity is formed is not only one of receptivity to the texts that tell the Christian story; it is also one of pursuit of ultimate meaning through questioning, and ultimately decision. Human experience and reason are actively engaged from the start in coming to understand and believe any religion, Christianity included. If this active engagement of the self does not occur, religious belief will not be faith at all but rather a mere piece of cultural baggage. Lindbeck's model of religion is curiously silent about this active process of coming to believe. And Lindbeck's "communal enclaves" will have to have very high walls indeed if they are to survive in our pluralistic culture. The narrative approach to the theological task is quite right in stressing that Christian identity must be shaped by the Biblical story in its fullness. However, in David Tracy's words, "this crucial insight does not mean that we should, in effect, abandon half the dialectic" by maintaining that the meaning and truth of Christianity as a way of life can be apprehended by a process of simple retrieval from scripture and tradition.[15] Tracy insists, rightly I believe, that a judgment that Christianity is true and worthy of belief calls for a "*mutually critical* correlation" between an interpretation of the meaning of the Biblical story on the one hand and the potential believer's already existing self-understanding on the other. The neo-Barthian approach of pure narrativism is inadequate to this task.

Second, I do not think that a one-way movement from biblical story to personal or cultural self-understanding is even possible. The pure narrativist approach appears to presuppose that it is possible to identify a unified block of meaning in the biblical texts, a meaning it calls the "biblical story." I think the matter is considerably more complex than this. The biblical texts have polyvalent meanings that call us to pursue and enact a number of different values that are sometimes in conflict with each other. For example, there has been a sustained argument throughout the history of Christianity about whether the biblical story implies that Christians should be committed to an ethic of non-violence or whether in tragic circumstances Christians might be called to defend their innocent neighbors against injustice by the use of force. Good cases have been and continue to be made on both sides of this argument. I mention it here, not to settle it, but simply to suggest that on this question one cannot simply "apply" or "enact" the biblical story in personal or cultural activity. One must take the risk of interpreting it. And such interpretation means relying on experiences, self-understandings, and concepts of rationality that are inevitably drawn from the culture in which one lives.

It is also the case that the biblical texts are not simply disclosive of God and of a truly human form of life. In these texts we also "confront meanings which distort and conceal rather than disclose."[16] For example, the subordination of women to men that is present in much Christian ethical and theological tradition, including the Bible, has led theologians such as Mary Daly to reject this tradition altogether. Others, such as Rosemary Ruether, Phyllis Trible, and Elisabeth Schüssler Fiorenza have been led into a process of reinterpretation that is based on an acknowledgment of the polyvalent meaning of the tradition. In Ruether's words, "I believe we must recognize two things: (1) Practically all the inherited culture we have received from a male system of tradition has been biased. It tends either to ignore or directly sanction sexism; (2) All significant works of culture have depth and power to the extent that they are doing *something else* besides just sanctioning sexism."[17] This something else, in Ruether's view, is the response that the texts of Biblical faith provide to fear of death, estrangement, and oppression and their power as sources of hope for life, reconciliation, and liberation. In other words, the tradition's ability to provide ultimate meaning and guidance for fitting moral action is at

the root of Christian feminists' desire *both* to retrieve *and* to reconstruct
this tradition. Their goal is to make the central religious and moral meaning of the Christian story fully available to contemporary women — and
to men in their relations with women as well. This task calls not only for
retrieval but also for critical revision.

Contemporary understanding and experience, of course, do not themselves generate Christian faith apart from retrieval of the Christian story
from the Bible and tradition. But shaping one's life by this story depends
on being able to give reasons why this story provides guidance in grappling with life's ultimate questions. The content of this story must be open
to rational assessment (which is different from rationalistic proof). It must
also open up a "seriously imaginable" vision of the right way to live
within the context of the wider culture.[18] This story, of course, can and
does challenge deeply held cultural convictions in significant ways. But if
this challenge is finally perceived as a flat-out contradiction of one's most
fundamental self-understanding and already existing convictions, it cannot
be received as good news. Rather it will be experienced as a form of
violence against the self.[19] Any claim, therefore, that the Christian story
should form experience and guide moral reasoning in a way that leads to
the violation of the equal dignity of women is neither rationally defensible
nor seriously imaginable for many women and men today. This negative
judgment serves as a critical principle for the retrieval of the Christian
story. It will insist on reconstructing those elements of the tradition which
legitimate sexism, precisely in order to retrieve the good news of the God
of Jesus Christ as a word addressed to men and women today. A purely
narrativist understanding of the task of theology, I submit, will find it
impossible to deal with this task of reconstruction.

This means that the task of theology will never be finished so long as
history lasts. The life of a Christian in this world is never closed or finished
but is always moving beyond what it has already become to the reality of
the God whom St. Augustine called both ever old and ever new. Christian
faith is not yet the full vision of God, but it is the firm conviction that in
Jesus Christ we have the guide to and promise of that vision. Christian life
is always life "on the way." Therefore, as Avery Dulles has written,

> The Christian is defined as a person on the way to discovery, on the
> way to a revelation not yet given, or at least not yet given in final
> form. . . . The Christian trusts that, in following the crucified and
> risen Christ, he is on the route to the one disclosure that will fully
> satisfy the yearning of the human spirit. This confidence is sustained
> by a series of lesser disclosures that occur on the way, and are
> tokens or promises of the revelation yet to come.[20]

Since Christian theology is the effort to understand how to live this life-on-the-way, it too must also be always ready to welcome fresh discoveries of God's gifts of freedom and reconciliation. It will be able to recognize them as coming from the hand of the God of Jesus Christ only if it has been schooled in the story of that God. This is the truth in the narrativist approach to theological knowledge. But when it has been so schooled, it will also be ready to recognize in new cultural insights the lesser disclosures that anticipate the final and full gift that God intends to give us — God's own self. The hermeneutical task, in other words, is the intellectual counterpart in Christian theology to the challenge of discipleship in Christian living. It is such discipleship, in both thought and action, that is the ultimate foundation of theological knowledge.

Notes

1. These remarks are an adaptation and refinement of ideas I have previously presented in "Fundamental Theology and the Christian Moral Life," in Leo J. O'Donovan and T. Howard Sanks, eds., *Faithful Witness: Foundations of Theology for Today's Church* (New York: Crossroad, 1989), 167-84.

2. George Lindbeck, *The Nature of Doctrine: Religion and Theology in a Postliberal Age* (Philadelphia: Westminster, 1984), 33.

3. See Francis Schüssler Fiorenza, *Foundational Theology: Jesus and the Church* (New York: Crossroad, 1985), 296.

4. Ibid., 287-88.

5. Lindbeck, *The Nature of Doctrine*, 129.

6. Ibid., 84.

7. Ibid., 118.

8. David Tracy, "Lindbeck's New Program for Theology: A Reflection," *Thomist* 49 (1985): 465.

9. Lindbeck, *The Nature of Doctrine*, 127.

10. Ronald Thiemann, *Constructing a Public Theology: The Church in a Pluralistic Culture* (Louisville: Westminster/John Knox, 1991). See especially the essay "Karl Barth and the Task of Constructing a Public Theology," 75-95.

11. See especially Vatican Council II, *Dogmatic Constitution on Divine Revelation (Dei Verbum)*.

12. See David Tracy, "Lindbeck's New Program for Theology," 461.

13. I use the term "pure narrativist" here, following Gary L. Comstock, to distinguish Lindbeck et al. from Tracy and other theologians who affirm the crucially important role of narrative in theology, even though they do not think theology should be purely narrative discourse. Comstock calls those who follow the lead of Tracy and Ricoeur "impure narrativists." See his "Two Types of Narrative Theology," *Journal of the American Academy of Religion* 55 (1987): 687-717.

14. Avery Dulles, "Revelation and Discovery," in William J. Kelly, ed., *Theology and Discovery: Essays in Honor of Karl Rahner* (Milwaukee: Marquette University

Press, 1980), 10. See also Vatican Council II, *Pastoral Constitution on the Church in the Modern World (Gaudium et Spes)*, nos. 10 and 11; and Tracy, *Plurality and Ambiguity: Hermeneutics, Religion, Hope* (San Francisco: Harper & Row, 1987), 49.

15. Tracy, "Lindbeck's New Program for Theology, " 464.

16. Thomas Ogletree, *Hospitality to the Stranger: Dimensions of Moral Understanding* (Philadelphia: Fortress Press, 1985), 114. The entire chapter in Ogletree's book entitled "The Activity of Interpreting in Moral Judgment" makes a valuable contribution to the matter here treated briefly.

17. Rosemary Radford Ruether, "A Religion for Women: Sources and Strategies," *Christianity and Crisis* (10 December 1979): 309.

18. David H. Kelsey, *The Uses of Scripture in Recent Theology* (Philadelphia: Fortress Press, 1975), 170-75.

19. Margaret A. Farley, "Feminist Consciousness and the Interpretation of Scripture," in Letty M. Russell, ed., *Feminist Interpretation and the Bible* (Philadelphia: Westminster, 1985), 41-51.

20. Dulles, "Revelation and Discovery," 27.

6

Formation for Ministry
in the Nineties

Brian O. McDermott

In these reflections I want to remain faithful to our overarching theme, which bears on society and public life, as well as to my own assigned topic, which concerns formation for ministry. I would like to focus particularly on spiritual formation for ministry in relation to what I perceive to be the heart of theological education as it seeks to provide resources to ministers intent upon serving women and men engaged in the public arena.

I. The Core of Theological Education

I take it that the ultimate goal of theological education is to assist individuals to acquire the resources that will allow them to exercise ministerial leadership in various ways. The fundamental focus of that leadership is helping persons and communities to participate more and more in the divine action in history whose goal is what Jesus called the Reign of God. Among the resources are academic learning, emotional maturity, profound and persistent desiring for the good and holy "more," a capacity for wise decisions and courageous actions, and an explicitly conscious relationship with God in Christ through the Spirit. None of these are "fixed assets" but need themselves to grow continually.

Brian O. McDermott, S.J., is Dean of Academic Affairs at Weston Jesuit School of Theology.

Theological education is the process of paying attention, seeking understanding, assessing the truth of that understanding, becoming responsible by making responsible choices and acting out those choices for the sake of God's reign among us. And that divine action in history claims all of each person: body, psyche, spirit, and the personal, interpersonal, and social-structural dimensions of human life.

Theological education is about intelligence, competence, learning. It is about the critical and creative appropriation of one's tradition as that tradition is drawn into conversation with its surrounding world, as it increases the number of conversation partners and the depth of encounter with them.

Theological education is also about healing of blindness and deafness, the blindness to one's biases and deafness to the call of the "other," whether the other is a student in class who is raising hard issues, or a suburban Christian in Newton who has lost her job, or a newly arrived Cambodian immigrant who is the object of racial attacks in Lowell.

It is also about the growth of that holiness which makes the healing of blindness and deafness worth risking, because I am in love with the One who loves me infinitely, passionately, forever, to the exclusion of no other. The transcendent love that has been poured into my heart by the Holy Spirit can make the stripping away of the false self a work of love, a crucifying work of love, that is mysteriously worthwhile for all the pain. And there will be a correlation between the soundness of my theology and the crucifying of my prejudices and biases in the increase of faith, charity, and hope.

Theological education is about nurturing a call and claim of God on the individual, a call and claim that lands a new student in the divinity school at great cost to self and often with no clear sense of the future of that call and claim. The student is on mission, called, accompanied, and to-be-sent. And that is all about God, the living God, the obscure but compelling call of God.

Theological education in the form of coursework, assignments, examinations, term papers, comprehensives, supervised ministry, can become a huge displacement, or replacement, for the sense of call and claim from God and for the ongoing relationship with God that is needed to keep the call and claim the orienting arrow, the lodestone, the magnet, that it is meant to be during, and after, ministerial studies. Some, right in the halls of divinity school, will counter that religious experience is not to be trusted; human reason in its analytic power must be allowed to stand in final judgment on the words we utter prior to becoming silent before the Holy Mystery of our lives, whom we call God. Critical theology has its place, a most important place in ministerial formation. But if it prevents ongoing relationship with the Mystery of God by virtue of fostering a self-sufficient intellectualism, it has betrayed itself as theology.

The ability to trust one's own experience of God, one's own experience of God's outer word, Jesus Christ, in the openness of God's inner word, the Holy Spirit, is at the center of Christian ministerial identity. Not to speak of God simply "from memory" or simply in quotation marks, however exalted or holy or ancient or contemporary the authority quoted, but to speak of God as present to one and as the One to whom the minister is present: that is required of the minister of the gospel.

The ministry involves Word and Sacrament: prophecy, teaching, and symbol, ritual. The minister stands in a particular tradition of church, has tried to enter into the feel and fiber of that tradition, not as a safe, isolated, place of light and comfort but as the necessary orientation to the ever greater light of God that cannot be encapsulated in any particular tradition. Paradoxically, one cannot relate to our multicredal and multicultural world with success or grace, unless one enters that world by way of a particular history and lens. Ministerial formation involves a narrow door, but still a door. Students are drawn more deeply into a corporate life to which they belonged before beginning their studies, breathe its air, and feel its rhythms, as well as criticize its blind spots and lament its shortcomings. But it is theirs, and they are its, and the argument is first of all "family." This belonging is crucial, and at times it can be cruciform.

II. Theological Education and Adaptive Challenges

Divinity schools face in some respects fundamental issues that are presently being dealt with by other professional schools. The traditional understanding that there is a certain body of knowledge that can be learned and then applied in a rather routine way to a variety of situations has yielded in, for example, medical school to a sense that the student must early on begin to learn in the here and now how to diagnose situations in real life and not wait until the last years of medical school or internship.

Some writers have termed this the education of the "reflective practitioner" who operates in an informed way in the here and now, but who is not simply applying a body of acquired knowledge to new situations in a routine way, no matter how sophisticated.[1]

The explosion of medical knowledge has made it impossible for a physician to rely exclusively on a set of routines, however complex they might be. He or she is confronted not simply with routine or technical work, but with adaptive challenges, which call for unpredictable and unforeseen work in order adequately to respond to the new situations that arise, even in the very framing of the issues to be dealt with.

When a physician gives a patient an injection of antibiotic for an infection, that is routine work. But when a physician challenges a patient who seems on the verge of a heart attack to change his or her lifestyle, such a tactic involves some routine elements but mainly invites the "patient" to adaptive work, which will involve a certain amount of disequilibrium, patience, and responsible life-altering choices on the part of the patient. When the physician is attending a patient who is about to die, the work involved is completely adaptive, it involves new ways of acting that never occurred in the patient's life before, like saying goodby to a spouse, and to parents or children, and to friends. None of this is routine, rather all is adaptive challenge, adaptive work.[2]

In our world of profoundly changing boundaries regarding the most basic issues of life — sexuality, men-women relations, religious identity, family life, learning how collaboration can and must occur between women and men, clergy and lay — again and again the very definition of the problem or issue or set of issues needs to be developed, the framing of the confronting issue needs to be explored. This not-knowing can evoke immense anxiety and disequilibrium, but it must be part of the process.

We would all agree schools of theology are not about the graduating of technicians, but it has been the case that theological education has at times viewed itself as being about the business of "forming" persons who were meant to apply their acquired knowledge to new situations that were in many ways routine. The minister was oriented to the congregation, or to the college or hospital chaplaincy, and the work involved was routine, which is not synonymous with simple or unsophisticated.

Today the churches live in a time of immense adaptive challenges, challenges that cannot be reduced to technical problems or routine solutions, however sophisticated or complex. All manner of hitherto tight boundaries are looser now; the church learns from the world and serves it as well and — in its other graced moments — challenges it and provokes it. The challenge of multiculturalism, of globalization, of gender studies, of religious pluralism, of liberation theology, of feminism, of public and interpersonal and social-structural issues, all these confront the minister to be.

Are we sufficiently about the business of educating students to become "reflective practitioners," or, to use an older vocabulary, "contemplatives in action," who are able to move back and through from the dance floor of engaged action to the balcony of reflective appraisal of the larger dynamics occurring in a situation, and do both in the "here and now," not simply in passing from the workday to the weekend? Do we as faculty live that way ourselves?

III. Spirituality and the Minister in a Time of Adaptive Challenge

While the term "formation" in my title is capable of very broad definition, I would like to focus at this point on the question of spiritual disciplines, or practical spirituality, as an essential dimension of theological education. I realize that by doing so I am moving into an area that will reflect my own background and training. I recognize further that different divinity schools have different histories of involvement with, or distance from, spiritual disciplines, and that the question of integrating spirituality into the total educational climate of divinity school students is very new to some traditions.

But I shall launch ahead, nonetheless! Perhaps there was a reason why a Jesuit working at a school composed of Jesuits and laymen and women was invited to offer this particular essay. The spirituality that traces its origin to Ignatius of Loyola of sixteenth-century Spain is one that in its seminal stage — his composition of the *Spiritual Exercises* — occurred while he was still a layman.[3] Indeed, his spirituality is designed for active people working in the world, not for monks or nuns in cloistered life. And Ignatian spirituality has addressed the longings of not just men and women in active religious orders but laymen and laywomen, married and single, Protestants as well as Catholics.

What I would like to offer at this point are reflections on basic spiritual disciplines that I am convinced need to be ingredient in any integral process of theological education.

The purpose of these disciplines is to dispose an individual to be available to God's gracious action in his or her life. Insofar as they do that disposing of a person, they are already ways in which God is affecting the individual. Times of prayer, processes of "letting go" of enslaving attachments, learning to discern "spirits" and to seek God's will and desire, all these are means meant to help one cooperate with God's action in history — action that bears not only on the authentic prospering of persons but on the genuine flourishing of human-friendly institutions and structures.

Prayerfulness: Finding God in All Things

There is psychological need for us to have a rhythm in our lives, a rhythm of engagement and withdrawal, of "going to the well" and living off what we imbibed at the well. This is a psychological imperative, and we know many ministers of the gospel who, in the name of the god (idol!) of availability try to imitate the real God's infinite availability to the undoing of themselves and those they serve.

It is not the same in the spiritual journey, at least not for someone like Ignatius of Loyola. For him, it is possible to seek and find God right in the midst of action, of busyness, and this is as important — at times more important — than seeking and finding God "on retreat." For Ignatius and the spirituality he represents, the most important thing in life is not profound contemplation, or extraordinary mystical graces, but deeds of service on behalf of the neighbor rooted in, and expressive of, the divinely given virtue of charity or love. All spiritual means are aimed at facilitating, encouraging, sustaining, or expressing those love-rooted deeds. Thus we are finding God when we act on behalf of the neighbor in love, even when we are not explicitly thinking about the divine.

Now there is a way in which a person can grow into an awareness of God "in the corner of the eye." This sensitivity to God's presence and action while we are engaged in activity is a developed sense that comes from three sources: from giving time to God in explicit prayer; by becoming free of disorienting and ensnaring attachments (addictions, we might say these days); and from desiring, and asking for, this gift of sensitivity from God.

Why would one want this awareness of God "in the corner of the eye"? What would be its cash-value, to speak crudely but pragmatically?

One of its principal helps would be that such a coawareness would tend to keep a person connected to purpose when tasks start to pile up and obscure one's vision. Even engaging in ministerial tasks with the question (i.e., the desire to know) "what does what I and we are doing here and now mean to God?" can have a centering effect, even if we do not always receive a felt sense of what the work and struggle mean to God.

Our Godwardness can be fostered. Ultimately, and first of all, God does the fostering. But we are asked to cooperate with God in the fostering. A growing awareness of God in "the corner of your eye" is one form of our experienced Godwardness.

But there are other ways.

A regular habit of quiet presence to God with Jesus in the Spirit is necessary. Now this may seem to contradict my distinction above between psychological need for a rhythm of withdrawal and return and a spiritual capacity to find God even in busyness. Rather, the point is that we need to seek and find God (with Jesus in the Spirit) in times of quiet and times of action, because our concrete humanity takes both forms! If in action we experience God as fashioning us as partners in the divine project in the world, in quiet we can experience God as totally other than the world, as God who is not supreme, or the highest exemplar of Being, or superior to all else, but God who IS, simply.

In quiet we can also experience God as addressing our hearts in our deepest yearnings and fears, as extending hospitality to our sinfulness and negativity, our resistances and attractions. The hospitality (which we don't always extend to these portions of ourselves) is but a first step, of course. Once they are accepted in their humanity God in Christ touches them, transforms them, makes them part of the divine project as it moves into the future.

Discernment: Recognizing God's Desires for Our World

Closely connected to prayerfulness, indeed, impossible without it, is Christian discernment of spirits, and discernment of God's will (what I call God's desire for our world).

In the Old Testament and the New, in the traditions of the early fathers and mothers, in patristic times, in medieval and post-medieval saints and theologians, up until our day there is a tradition of discernment of spirits. This tradition acknowledges that in the individual who is going "from bad to worse" there are different interior movements prevailing than in the person who is basically living as a disciple of Christ, whose life is fundamentally (not totally) rooted in living faith, love, and hope. We come to recognize these various movements, the direction they are leading one toward (God's greater glory, or the false self), and thus their source (God or the "enemy of human nature"). Principles of discernment can be found in Catholic sources, such as Ignatius of Loyola and in Protestant ones, such as Jonathan Edwards and John Wesley.

Communal discernment builds on individual discernment and goes beyond it. As one very experienced author in this area recently wrote, communal spiritual discernment:

> is a continuous activity. Communities living this way of life are constantly going through a process that carries them through choices to decisions and actions. When discernment becomes a way of life for a community it embraces a communal process in the five phases discussed [above]. Members dispose themselves to find the movement of the Spirit in the group's *experience* (phase 1). They privately *reflect* (phase 2) on their experience and then they *articulate* (phase 3) the fruit of their prayer and meditation to the group. Together, members *interpret* (phase 4) the meaning of their experience in terms of their sense of themselves as members of Christ's body. Then the community moves confidently, prayerfully and with careful deliberation into consideration of their future by *deciding on action* (phase 5) that they can freely offer to God because they know it to be in harmony with God's ongoing work of creation.[4]

Communal discernment is a crucial bridge between individual spirituality and the spirituality of groups and institutions. When a group is able to articulate its own story, for example, in relation to the story of Jesus and the early church in Acts and recount its times of authentic spiritual consolation (i.e., those times when the group felt connected with the values of Jesus and the reign of God), that group has the capacity to listen to its own life as part of the data needed to discern the next steps to which God is calling it.[5]

IV. Bridging the World of Theological Education and Public Life: Spirituality and the Public Arena

The language of prayer and personal and communal discernment is language that is traditional and of the church. Yet theological educators, engaged as they are in the business of educating (and here formation and education are not to be distinguished) ministers for the church, need to ask themselves how they can help ministerial students learn ways of helping those Christians who are in positions of authority and leadership find a new language for their faith in the secular, public contexts of their work. Many of those folk find that their religious upbringing did not equip them to integrate their Christianity and public life.

As we have seen, there exists in Christian spiritual traditions a well-developed vocabulary for prayer, discernment of interior spirits, for movements of God in the individual person, for ways of seeking God's will in one's life. Not every Christian denomination is comfortable with this vocabulary of affection and choice found in an Ignatius of Loyola, a Teresa of Avila, a John Wesley, or a Jonathan Edwards, but developed vocabulary there is. What we still need to develop is a vocabulary for our institutional and public life that allows us to notice, stay with, and grow into the action of God that is at work in the human web of public power, authority, and leadership.

There is, as well, a vocabulary for interpersonal relationships, for friendship and intimacy and growth in this dimension of human life. And there is vocabulary for understanding our relationship with God in interpersonal terms. Not all theology professors or students of theology are comfortable with such talk, to be sure. But it is squarely in the tradition and "available" for employment by those who so desire.

But what resources can dedicated Christian laypeople find that will help support their efforts to incarnate the values of justice in their workplace? What can nourish their public courage, who can help them learn to partner in strategic ways not only with other people of similar fundamental values, but with God, who is laboring in every work situation to bring about true justice and honest, authentic peace, God's greater glory in human affairs. What learnings and skills are necessary for a late-twentieth-century Christian minister to serve such people? Here it is not a question of relating to them from some superior position, but as partners with them, partners who bring to the relationship theological and spiritual resources that help those laypeople in positions of authority and leadership stay in the fray for the long haul, not letting themselves get prematurely "bumped off," and learning to partner with God in the midst of the busyness, when they are taking the heat because you have frustrated some of the expectations of a constituency.

There are many people in professional schools in the greater Boston area who experience in themselves deep longings to serve the common good, to offer their intelligence and energy to the public world, and to develop not only strategic and tactical competencies and skills but who yearn for wisdom and spiritual grounding for their professional lives. These people are students, faculty, administration, and staff. In interaction with the Kennedy School of Government and the School of Education, I have begun to appreciate the depth of this longing. These are people actually exercising authority and leadership, or who are slated to exercise authority and leadership in the public sector, who want to partner not only with fellow professionals, but, more profoundly, with God. They want to notice God more in their lives, and respond to the initiatives of grace more faithfully. They view this invitation as not simply a matter of personal spirituality but as a matter of public life and service, but they are not interested in a narrow ideological use of religion. Rather, they want to share in something larger than themselves: God's project in the world, the fostering of God's reign, using language that is not traditional or overtly religious.

I would like to suggest some ways that ministers can help persons in public life develop a spiritual praxis in their exercise of authority and leadership. I want to offer three "cases" for reflection. For the sake of brevity, I will focus each time on a person who is called upon to exercise leadership from a position of formal authority.

First of all, I am assuming that one of the principal functions of authority — and here I mean primarily formal authority, a person who has been given a certain amount of formal authority in a group — is to help provide a holding environment, or container, or boundaries, for the activities of the group or organization. In her role as CEO of a medium-sized computer company, it could be very helpful for Mary Kay Perkins, a committed Christian, to become alert to the ways in which God provides boundaries, or a container for her and her activities as CEO, to learn more about how God acts in her life as source of ultimate holding environment.

Recently, Mary Kay's company has seen a big dip in profits as even newer firms have encroached on its market. The pressure from the board is strong, urging her to make some drastic decisions in order to recoup the losses, or at least control the damage. They are particularly concerned that the company has tried to connect with non-profits to make its software both usable and attractive to them. Some board members even accuse her of confusing business with charity.

Now in Mary Kay's life God offers a certain ultimate safety. As a Christian she is asked to let that conviction have influence in her life. But God in her life permits enormous room for unsafety, and she is never in a position to anticipate how much unsafety, but it is both of those things which God does in her life. God does not simply rescue her from unsafety, making all things safe, but there is some ultimate boundary that she is invited by God to believe is always going to be there, and she is being asked to stay connected with it.

This conviction offers some resources to a person like Mary Kay when, as the person in authority, she is having buttons pushed because the folks in the group want her as the authority figure to rescue it from its (necessary) discomfort and from the hard work that the members must do among themselves if they are to contribute to the adaptive work that needs to be done. That conviction of faith, and even better Mary Kay's noticing God offering that protective boundary, can act as a help for her to stay with that group in fidelity to its life and to its future. I am referring here to more than just a personal relationship between God and her, it is about something that is needed for the organization itself — as the temptation for the authority person is to simply land on one side of the discussion in order to bring it to closure, when the situation is a matter of adaptive challenge and is not ripe for closure. There are times when persons with formal authority — like CEO May Kay Perkins — have to invite the members of a group to move to a deeper level of work, when all they want, because of their fatigue and frustration, is for the authority person to do it charismatically for them.

A second "case": Tom Curtis has been feeling a good deal of inner distress recently as he has chaired his task force in the state attorney general's office. This particular group has been charged with the responsibility of coming up with proposals about plea bargaining in the court system. Dissident voices have emerged in the groups as members of the task force have exercised leadership from a position within the group. These members have instinctively recognized that the exercise of leadership — that is, the activity of defining and doing the work in the group, and of mobilizing in one way or another the resources of the group — can come from any subgroup or individual in the organization, even if they lack formal authority. The exercise of leadership is not identical with the exercise of the functions of authority. The dissident voices are pointing out that the chair has overlooked something, that there is data that needs to be attended to and has not, that there is a richer or tougher problem here than the group has up until now realized. They call the group, and its chair, to reframe the issues once again, or to admit this other element into the picture, one that Tom or some others on the task force may not want to touch with a ten-foot pole! Or perhaps the issue is simply one about which the group was not explicitly conscious.

Something about our own journeys with God have a bearing on this. Let me talk about Tom's journey with God a bit, at this point:

Tom has areas in his life that he wants to squelch. He wants them to simply go away or be quiescent, but they manage to show themselves again and again. Tom might be able to discover, if he pays attention to patterns in his life with God, that God provides room for those parts to enter again and again into his relationship with the divine Mystery. Tom may not have a theory about what God is going to do with those parts, he just knows that those dissident parts of himself (dissident in terms of his dominant self-image) are drawn in again and again. God is quite comfortable allowing those parts to be there because there is something about them that is supposed to become part of Tom's life. Tom can't see how this is going to happen; he is afraid that they will disrupt and tear him, or at least do that undesirable thing to his self-image if he really admits the stuff is there, but God seems to allow those dissident parts of Tom to come in the picture, and make, by God's grace, a contribution to the whole.

If Tom has learned something about this mysterious process in his experience of God, this can help him as someone exercising from a position of authority to listen to the dissident voice. There is a correlation possible between our personal, spiritual lives and the life of an organization. Perhaps what the task force needs is a drastic reframing of the point at issue, even though it means the group has to add more meetings to its schedule in order to let that new element come in. There is a time for bringing closure — I am not trying to speak for endless process here. That is not my presupposition or implication, but there is the question of what service is played by dissident voices when one is engaged in addressing adaptive challenges. We all have in class, if we are teachers, those dissident voices saying you never touched on this, or you make it seem like only men are affected by this, or let me tell you about my experience. Then, people have to be alert to a whole range of other experience. It can happen so many ways. But God models something in our concrete experience that also has to do with societal and organizational life, to encourage the person with authority to listen to the dissident voices, and even want to stir them up sometimes when there is too much easy agreement. We have had major disasters in American political life during the last thirty years because presidents wanted to have around their table only people who would say the same thing. That kind of "group think" is very tempting but it represents a false and premature unity while the dissident voice, disruptive as it may seem to be, may reframe the issue in a way that would make for a better adaptive change.

A third "case" has to do with "taking the heat." Pat recognizes, as she exercises her academic deanship in a large midwestern divinity school, that authority exists in function of expectations, either official expectations that make you someone with formal authority or the unofficial expectations. Faculty members in the school, for instance, have unofficial expectations of her (they did not appoint her to her position). Some of those expectations are conscious, many of them are unconscious. Perhaps some of the faculty members' expectations should not be met, if she is trying to reframe the description of the challenges facing the institution as the ordinary sources of both students and moneys are drying up. There is that back and forth going on between Pat and the faculty, which at times will entail taking the heat when people come to her and say this is enough and they want her to decide the way they want her to, in order to bring the matter (whatever it is) to conclusion.

"Assassinating" people in authority is an unconscious if not a conscious dynamic that occurs often enough in group life even among the nicest people. Sometimes niceness is a kind of assassination, psychologically speaking. There is a common psychological move Pat has learned to make when she functions in her position of authority, when she is taking the heat and her buttons are being pushed. The move involves disidentifying herself from the heat or from the stuff coming her way by recognizing that she is someone other than what's coming her way and not to take it personally. She has learned to "go to the balcony," to be in a position to notice that the group is playing out an aspect of its life as a group, namely, resistance. It helps her to remember that a big chunk of us is, at the best of times, ambivalent about life in a group. People are not always attracted and drawn in by something, and that ambivalence will show up somehow. Pat is learning the difficult art of not taking it personally. Indeed, she is learning to expect it to happen.

But isn't there another level besides that psychological move of not taking the resistance or attack personally because you recognize in group life that there has to be a playing out of resistance as well as attraction, just as in individual life? I think there is. How helpful it would be if Pat, when she finds herself taking the heat from some particularly forceful and articulate faculty member, could recognize, right at the point of the heat coming her way, from whence comes her identity at its deepest level. Who she truly is exists only here and now in the loving gaze of a God who is creating her right here and now. That is not simply psychology, it is an ultimate resource of our faith bearing on who Pat is as she tries to stay faithful to these people who are giving her a very rough ride now because she is not meeting their expectations. Who Pat is, is being created right now by a God whose whole being, as Sebastian Moore likes to say, consists in being-for-me (to the exclusion of no one else), and that's who I am.[6] Therefore, Pat would be helped to stay in the fray for the sake of the common good and take the heat if she learned to recognize that she is being defined into existence right now by an infinite act of love that allows her to not take everything personally, because ultimately who she is is being created in the gaze of this infinite lover. This is not just pious rhetoric. It is a balcony position about where our ultimate safety and our ultimate meaning come from. But so often this conviction lives in that part of our life that is our inner journey, but it is not allowed to help us stay in the public fray.

I cannot help thinking of church officials who have said things like, "You deeply pained His Excellency by what you did." I want to say, I take His Excellency and his office so seriously that I can't make central to my concerns the fact that he takes what was done personally. I think a church leader has a role to play in relation to a community that cannot be reduced to his or her expecting the community to help him or her feel good inside. I wish the individual would interpret his or her role more seriously than that. Yet if someone does not have spiritual resources upon which to draw, they will want the members of the group to have a unity among themselves that will make the authority figure feel really comfortable inside. I am afraid that feeling uncomfortable inside comes with the territory when you are in a position of authority. How easy it is to say these words, but how hard to live them out!

Recently, Weston School of Theology has been considering its future. Our conversations with Boston College made us realize that our presence in Cambridge is most important to us. We also recognized in a new way that there are possibilities of relating to professional schools in the area precisely in terms of theology and spirituality for the exercise of authority and leadership in professional life. Ethical decision-making calls for public courage, and public courage needs all the good partners that it can find. Theological and spiritual resources for persons in public service are a kind of formation for ministry that invites a school of theology to some significant adaptive work. Can we of the Boston Theological Institute help each other to provide this kind of resource?

Notes

1. Donald A. Schön, *The Reflective Practitioner: How Professionals Think in Action* (New York: Basic Books, 1983).
2. Ronald Heifetz, M.D., "Political Leadership: Managing the Public's Problem Solving," in Robert B. Reich, ed., *The Power of Public Ideas* (Cambridge: Harvard University Press, 1985), 179-203. I am very indebted to Dr. Heifetz for the views on authority and leadership presented here.
3. *The Spiritual Exercises of Saint Ignatius, A Translation and Commentary*, ed. George E. Ganss (St. Louis: Institute of Jesuit Sources, 1992).
4. John English, *Spiritual Intimacy and Community: An Ignatian View of the Small Faith Community* (New York and Mahwah: Paulist Press, 1992), 176.
5. See Thomas H. Groome, *Christian Religious Education: Sharing Our Story and Vision* (San Francisco: Harper and Row, 1980), chaps. 9 and 10.
6. Sebastian Moore, *The Inner Loneliness* (New York: Crossroad, 1982).

COMPETING PARADIGMS FOR THEOLOGICAL EDUCATION

Rodney L. Petersen

It has been the purpose of the prefaces in this volume to raise questions about the audience for theological education, its nature and content, and now, the question of how such education is to be done. Three competing paradigms for theological education are raised up in what follows by Eldin Villafañe, Kwok Pui-lan, and Robert C. Neville. Each position is symbolic of tendencies in society today. Each illustrates how seminaries and theological schools throughout the United States and Canada struggle with a central course of study grounded in the traditional disciplines of theology, history, biblical studies, and rhetoric (or homiletics and practical theology). Or, alternatively, how they wrestle with the extent to which such disciplines as comparative religion, sociology, psychology, and various ethnic or gender-oriented studies should enter into the curriculum. Indeed, in the history of university education many of these newer disciplines first emerged as problems to be dealt with in the preparation for ministry.[1]

Such educational questions are not restricted to any particular church's school or theological position. They are ones that challenge the entire membership of the Association of Theological Schools in the United States and Canada.[2] Historian George M. Marsden has alerted us to ways in which theological education has been shaped by religious debate that has flowed through the universities. Other contextual issues have also played their part in shaping theological education.[3] The currents and eddies of such controversy have contributed to the often-separated development of theological schools, schools at one time central to the identity and purpose of the educational enterprise in this country. The implications of such controversy around the control of biblical studies and extended theological reflection have had enormous implications for religious communities. This is particu-

larly true for Protestants with their "scriptural principle," as such has provided the foundation for the preparation and practice of Christian ministry.

Among the first graduate or professional schools in the United States,
seminaries, schools of theology, and university divinity schools have generally pursued a separate path of development from that of the colleges or
universities they founded or of which they had been privileged members.
As has been referred to in one of the previous introductions, this is partly
because of the rationalization of knowledge and development of professional education in this country. These schools were developed in order to
prepare persons for ministry, the making and forming of a Christian people for their own sake and that of the churches that stand within and
beyond society. Does the vision remain? What is to be the nature of the
educational program in these schools? How should it be done? Toward
what end is theological education in today's civil society?

Such questions assume a purpose. If there is a problem of vision in the
seminary, does this imply a problem with the schools or with our sense of
the church in the world? Seminary education is not simply a second degree in the liberal arts for those who did not get it the first time around. It
is not a degree in social work that is enhanced or diminished by a theological perspective. It does not simply foster another theory of society or
of the personality in society, one that antedates the development of the
social or psychological sciences. A seminary education assumes a content
that is both intellectual and moral, however self-critical it might be. It
assumes a vocation in society that is worthy of professional development
through its contribution to individual health and social well-being. It assumes a coherence and office that has a validity not limited by the perspectives of particular population groups in society.

These contributions are assumed in the following papers. In dealing
with such realities, Eldin Villafañe writes of "Elements for Effective
Seminary-Based Theological Education." He makes reference to the
"how" of theological education against a growing urban population characterized by increasingly complex multicultural dynamics.[4] Documented
recently for the city of Boston together with international implications,
this diverse population has been the basis for the ministry of the Center for
Urban Ministerial Education (CUME), the urban campus of Gordon-Conwell Theological Seminary.[5] To meet this challenge Villafañe outlines six
points. First, the nature of the constituencies faced by urban churches must
be recognized. Villafañe's own study of the Hispanic Pentecostal church
is an important contribution in methodology on this point.[6] The nature of
such constituencies determines how theological education is to be shaped.
Villafañe's second point is that of contextualization. He raises a number
of factors to be taken into consideration here, which he enters into more

specifically with respect to Hispanic Americans elsewhere. This contextualization determines his third point, that of curriculum. Given the nature of today's seminary and church communities, a curriculum needs to be constructed that forms, informs, and transforms a specific people in a given context. These contextual dynamics are worked out in relation to Villafañe's fourth factor, a local community.

With his own institutional connections in mind, Villafañe asks about the relationship of an urban education program to its host school. What kinds of attitudes are being fostered? What are the expectations in the two contexts of each other? Is there any integration between school and community leaders? Fifth, a seminary that recognizes the needs of today's urban population will be aware of patterns of coexistence between the community and the host school, its commitment to the development of an urban program, patterns of interaction between the host and urban programs. Finally, the above five points find their bottom line with issues of budgetary integration and the prioritizing of programs. Here seminary rhetoric and reality come together or diverge.

In addressing the needs of specific contexts, Villafañe's remarks bear some relation to the second paradigm reflected upon by Kwok Pui-lan of Episcopal Divinity School in "The Global Challenge." Her address sensitizes us to three challenges facing theological education posed by the need for a global conceptualization, a deeper identification with those who are marginalized in our society, and with contemporary feminist perspectives.[7] An awareness of this last point can be a means toward appreciating the former two as well, at least as argued by Elizabeth Bettenhausen.[8] The feminist perspective emphasizes the relationship of feminist experience, theory, and theology. Whatever else it may be, feminist theology is an effort to reunite body and soul.[9] If feminist theology can do this, it may not only heal a breach within the feminist movement itself,[10] but also open the way forward to that broadened theological perspective which counters all forms of illicit subjugation in the context of an integrated Christian vision.[11]

The nature of such an integrated vision is central to the perspective of Robert C. Neville, Dean of the Boston University School of Theology. In "The Classical Challenge," Neville scopes out the nature of theology and theological education against the collapse of those forms of Christianity which have embraced fully Enlightenment learning and modernization. The greatest intellectual challenge faced by seminaries today, Neville argues, is "to express the gospel with its spiritual power in terms of the best science, art, philosophy, and critical reflection of our time." The nature of this challenge is shaped by a gospel that has been on a continuum of translation since Paul. Neville's own task is confronting the fundamental issues that make up a comparative philosophy of religion so that we might better understand the ways in which Christian thinking relates to other theistic and non-theistic religions.[12] The perspectives of the Enlightenment and modernization as developed in the West are now spreading throughout the globe. In the development of this global culture it becomes all the more important to understand what represents a compromise with the prophetic dynamic of Christianity in relation to the modern world. Such thinking affects seminaries and schools of theology as they wrestle with academic and service-oriented ideals. It calls for not a reduced, but a deepened focus upon the classical fourfold curriculum in theological education against the widened contextual framework raised up by Eldin Villafañe and Kwok Pui-lan. The task is Herculean yet foundational for all theological ventures, whether radical, restorationist, or renewing in some further way.

Each of the three paradigms for refocusing theological education today underscores the difficulties that such education faces when dealing with persons seeking to be trained and those charged with the task of training, when facing questions concerning the content of theological education in a society that is both monolithic in its culture as well as characterized by deep social divisions. Cornel West reminds us that preparation for the ministry has never been easy.[13] His proposal for change begins with the self-image of seminary professors. He writes that their lives be fully in accord with the spirit of the content of their work. West goes on to argue that historians, as able cultural critics, be charged with greater responsibility for holding the seminary curriculum together. In this way he seeks to offer the model and the means for theological education. However, he admits that even this does little to alleviate the tensions involved with being a Christian minister in civil society today. Indeed, everything that has been said in the papers in this volume seems to support his contention. Ours is a society that accords a parabolic place to the church at best. The church is no longer a constitutional arm of government. It is seldom looked to as the mentor for social and psychological care. It can be, at best, only a model and one that competes with others for social envisioning and emulation in public life today.

In his closing chapter, "Coming to Our Senses," Robert Bellah writes about how such a model might appear. He lists three renunciations, those of violence, sovereignty, and abundance. Renouncing violence means affirming persons. It means renouncing destruction, defamation, and damnation. To be made in the image of God (Gen. 1:27), to be imitators of God (Col. 3:9-10) means to be those called to create, to name, and to bless one another. This means that theological education is about "mending severed connections."[14] It has to do with reconciliation. It is an education that is proactive of persons in their deepest identity and social relationships. The church has a "truth to tell" about this identity and society as we begin the twenty-first century.[15]

Renouncing sovereignty means affirming attentiveness. It means listening to nature and to neighbor. If we affirm that we, together with the natural order, are a part of a larger purpose, then close attention must be given to the intricacies of the cosmos and to the sensitivities of each other. The French philosopher of the Enlightenment, Etienne Condillac (1714-1789) referred to science as advanced language. It is not the thing, but enables us to map the territory. In its levels of abstraction language offers meaning as well as knowledge. Knowledge assumes cooperation, but language also makes conflict possible. Language provides for social cohesion, which can mean social control or meaningful liberation. Language is a gift or a curse that we give to one another. It is related to sovereignty and attentiveness. It is we who name things correctly or falsely in relation to the degree to which we let things speak for themselves. This is a shared gift or curse.[16] There is no understanding without some measure of community. There can be no community without giving attention to one another.[17] The most intimate community is the family. The largest community of which we are aware is the cosmos. Theological education makes us aware that if we affirm that God can speak to us, then apart from presumption, we must affirm that God can speak to others (James 1:19, 22). Theological education for public life assumes the need for such attentiveness.

Renouncing abundance means to be captive to the word and not to things. Attentiveness to the cosmos and to our neighbor is to listen to the word that calls all things into being. Words create worlds. To be captive to the word is to be a steward of the mysteries of this world (Col. 2:2-3). Such mysteries are twofold, those of society and those of nature. To be a steward, not a proprietor, is to nurture things to become what they are, not what we wish them to be. It is to affirm a depth of intent and sacramental being to things and persons. Theological education fosters such stewardship. With respect to the cosmos we can talk of "missionary earthkeeping."[18] In our day this means being attentive to the interplay of forces that contribute to environmental degradation with patterns of affluence, work, and population that are in keeping with biblical teachings on the care of the cosmos. Stewardship in society calls us to discern in our own history and that of others another mystery, one that, like the order of nature, is born, grows, enters into all that maturation involves, and dies, but ends in purpose, not death. Both mysteries call us to be a people in mission, the mission of nourishing things to be not merely what they are by nature or nurture, but also by grace. Theological education grows out of this mystery. Like the church, it finds its reason for being in that vision which calls us to move beyond Babel, the place of confusion and things, and to travel toward that which we are called to be. In this way theological education also gives shape to that call.[19]

The three renunciations cited by Bellah open up for the churches a way to move through resentment, a crisis in relationships both within the church[20] and as an increasing reality in advanced capitalist societies with their flashing images, consumer sensibilities, instant information — and inability to make good on their promises. In such contexts, if the church is to regain its credibility and then its public role, theological education must reintegrate its sense of being with its epistemology and ethics.[21] These are the factors that called the Boston Theological Institute into existence in the late twentieth century. This consortium, like others, offers the means and model toward recovering a public recognition of the sacred in civil society without giving way to the captivity of contemporary academic professionalism or a narrow and insular ecclesiastical denominational-ism.[22] Conscious recognition of these academic and social patterns is central to the church's public existence. They will help us to answer the questions, "What is to be the place of Christianity in civil society?" and, "What is or should be the nature of theological education in relation to public life?"

Notes

1. This can be seen in a reading of Marsden, *The Soul of the American University* (New York: Oxford University Press, 1994). The Christian missionary movement did much to heighten the awareness of wider contextual realities for Western scholarship; see Olav Guttorm Myklebust, *The Study of Missions in Theological Education*, 2 vols. (Oslo: Forlaget Land og Kirke, 1955).

2. See the areas for study blocked out in the articles appearing in *Theological Education*, vol. XXX, no. 2 (Spring 1994).

3. Marsden, *The Soul of the American University*; cf. Jaroslav Pelikan, *The Idea of the University: A Reexamination* (New Haven: Yale University Press, 1991) and Marsden's review of it, "Christian Schooling: Beyond the Multiversity," *Christian Century* (7 October 1992): 873-875. Such discussion is part of a similar debate surrounding education today; see Michael B. Katz, *Reconstructing American Education* (Cambridge: Harvard University Press, 1987).

4. One of the founding reasons for the BTI was to address this urban challenge. Indeed, such has been the purpose of many Christian ecumenical organizations, including one of the earliest of ecumenical organizations in the United States, the City Missionary Society of Boston (1816). See J. Leslie Dunstan, *A Light to the City: 150 Years of the City Missionary Society of Boston, 1816-1966* (Boston: Beacon Press, 1966); and compare Max L. Stackhouse, *Ethics and the Urban Ethos: An Essay in Social Theory and Theological Reconstruction* (Boston: Beacon Press, 1972).

5. Douglas Hall and Rudy Mitchell, *Christianity in Boston* (Boston: Emmanuel Gospel Center, 1993); and see Allan Figueroa Deck, S.J., *The Second Wave: Hispanic Ministry and the Evangelization of Cultures* (New York: Paulist Press, 1989).

6. Eldin Villafañe, *The Liberating Spirit: Toward an Hispanic American Pentecostal Social Ethic* (Grand Rapids: Eerdmans, 1993). See chapters one and two on the nature of Hispanic American culture.

7. These interests are particularized in the study by Kwok Pui-lan, *Chinese Women and Christianity: 1860-1927* (Atlanta: Scholars Press, 1992). Two sources for feminist perspective are Elaine Pagels, *Adam, Eve, and the Serpent* (New York: Vintage, 1988); Ann Belford Ulanov, *Receiving Woman: Studies in the Psychology and Theology of the Feminine* (Philadelphia: Westminster Press, 1981).

8. The Study/Action Program of the Women's Theological Center where Bettenhausen works is predicated upon this assumption (WTC, 140 Clarendon St., Boston, MA 02117).

9. Distinctions may be made among reform (Rosemary Radford Reuther, Letty Russell), rejectionist (Mary Daly), and evangelical (Letha Scanzoni, Nancy Hardesty) Christian feminists. See the review article by Julie Polter, "When Body Meets Soul," *Sojourners* (September-October 1994): 20-22. Susan Thistlethwaite alerts us to further differences in the experience of women in *Sex, Race, and God: Christian Feminism in Black and White* (New York: Crossroad, 1989).

10. Note the distinction between traditional and gender feminism in Jean Bethke Elshtain, "Sic Transit Gloria," *The New Republic* (17 July 1994): 32-36.

11. Miriam Therese Winter, Adair Lummis, and Allison Stokes, *Defecting in Place: Women Claiming Responsibility for Their Own Spiritual Lives* (New York: Crossroad, 1994).

12. See, for example, Robert Cummings Neville, *Behind the Masks of God* (Albany: State University of New York, 1991).

13. Cornel West, "The Crisis in Theological Education," in *Prophetic Fragments: Illuminations of the Crisis in American Culture and Religion* (Grand Rapids: Eerdmans, 1988), pp. 273-280.

14. Lynn Nell Rhodes and Nancy D. Richardson, eds., *Mending Severed Connections: Theological Education for Communal Transformation* (San Francisco: San Francisco Network Ministries, 1991).

15. Lesslie Newbigin, *Truth to Tell: The Gospel as Public Truth* (Geneva: WCC, 1991).

16. Much of contemporary linguistic and social analysis develops this point. See Pierre Bourdieu, *Language and Symbolic Power*, ed. by John B. Thompson (Cambridge: Harvard University Press, 1991), p. 8; and for social implications, Joe Holland and Peter Henriot, S.J., *Social Analysis: Linking Faith and Justice* (Maryknoll: Orbis Books, 1992).

17. Augustine, *On Christian Doctrine*, transl., by D. W. Robertson, Jr. (Indianapolis: Bobbs-Merrill, 1958), prologue, 4-9; pp. 4-7. See the dimensions of language surveyed by S. I. Hayakawa, *Language in Thought and Action* (New York: Harcourt Brace Jovanovich, 4th ed., 1978) and Roger Andersen, *The Power and the Word: Language, Power and Change* (London: Collins, 1988).

18. See the book of that title, *Missionary Earthkeeping*, ed. by Calvin B. DeWitt and Ghillean T. Prance (Macon: Mercer University Press, 1992).

19. Karl Barth, *Credo* (New York: Charles Scribner's Sons, 1962), p. 137.

Through its reflection upon the great motifs in scripture, *The City of God* by Augustine of Hippo remains a work that will continue to guide the reflective mind of the church into the twenty-first century.

20. *Metanoia — Towards the 21st Century: Challenges and Opportunities for Theological Education — Crisis and Challenge for the Ecumenical Movement: Integrity and Indivisibility.* A Statement of the Institute for Ecumenical Research, Strasbourg (Geneva: WCC, 1994).

21. See the study by Judo Poerwowidagdo, "Global Phenomena and the Local Imperatives," in *Towards the 21st Century: Challenges and Opportunities for Theological Education* (Geneva: WCC, 1993). Poerwowidagdo deals with the inception of the church and concomitantly theological education (p. 9). He argues that theological education is the responsibility of all of God's people. It is a part of the mission of the church. In this he draws upon Ross Kinsler, *Ministry by the People* (Geneva: WCC/Orbis Books, 1983), who argues that theological education is "to motivate, equip, and enable the people of God to develop their gifts and live their lives in meaningful service." It is the function of seminaries to enable the enablers to equip "the saints for the work of ministry, for the building up of the body of Christ until we all attain to the unity of the faith and the knowledge of the Son of God, to mature manhood, to the measure of the stature of the fullness of Christ" (Eph. 4:11-13).

22. Dieter Hessel, "Making a Difference after the Eclipse," in Hessel, ed., *The Church's Public Role* (Grand Rapids: Eerdmans, 1993), pp. 1-20.

7

Elements for Effective Seminary-Based Urban Theological Education

Eldin Villafañe

Our Cities — Our Nation

Our cities are not what they were fifty years ago, twenty-five years ago, or even ten years ago. Our cities are multiethnic, multicultural, and increasingly multilingual. They are increasingly divided between the "haves" and "have-nots" and between people of color and whites. While Marshall McLuhan spoke of a "global village" to highlight the critical communication and interdependency of contemporary life, we need to further qualify it to read an "*urban* global village." The apparent contradiction of urban/village underscores the reality of the global process of people/ethnic movements from village to major urban centers. This worldwide phenomenon is also (given our immigration patterns) the experience of large cities in the United States. Be it Boston, New York, Philadelphia, or Los Angeles, they also are experiencing this globalization process: a multiethnic and multicultural reality is increasingly defining its ethos.

Ben Wattenberg, author and demographer, speaks of our cities and our nation as experiencing "the dawning of the first universal nation." The notion of the United States as a "universal nation" is not new since historically the great American experiment has represented this very aspiration. It is important to note that this internal development is consistent with the

Eldin Villafañe is Professor of Christian Social Ethics and Associate Dean for Multicultural Affairs at Gordon-Conwell Seminary.

external "global mission" of America found in its cultural narratives — stories that shape American images of self and world.[1]

The implications both of demographic trends and American history for theological education are basic and simple. If we are to educate leaders for our urban scene effectively, the contextual reality — multicultural and socioeconomically poor — must inform all aspects of the theological enterprise. While urban ministry encompasses ministry to the middle-class and wealthy in our cities, too, the predominant focus in most seminary-based urban theological education programs (a correct one in my judgment) is for ministry to the "inner cities" of our great metropolis. The specificity of educating for ministry with the "poor" has biblical warrants as well as sociocultural relevancy.

Six Essential Elements

Six categories will be used to present essential elements for an effective seminary-based urban theological education program. These elements can be used as criteria or as a basis for evaluating existing and projected models. The six essential elements are: *constituency, contextualization, curriculum, community, coexistence with the host seminary,* and *cost.*

Constituency

A fundamental question seminaries must raise as they train urban leaders is *who* are we educating? There are several factors to this question of constituency. First is the issue of "clergy" vs. "people of God" paradigm.

We live in a complex urban world. Its diversity and numerical growth, the limitations and breakdown of present delivery systems of human, ecological, and socioeconomic resources,[2] call for *all* God's children to exercise their God-given gifts (1 Cor. 12:7) for the Shalom of the City. We must train *all* of God's people for ministry. The church as a whole must be educated, lay as well as clergy, to respond effectively and faithfully to the challenges of urban ministry. The whole gospel must be witnessed to in word and deed by the whole church. Given the times and the context in which we live, the burden is on those clergy-teaching models to justify, or should we say rationalize, their elitist-focused constituency.

Urban theological education should be structured to train both clergy and lay persons. While distinct tracks can be provided for each, the best programs will provide for interaction by way of a flexible curriculum. In other words, the curriculum will provide courses and projects where both the potential clergy and lay persons participate jointly. This principle applies equally in my judgment to those programs focusing on existing clergy. The dynamic and rich interaction of persons and issues found in a local class setting where the "people of God" model is present is critical for the life and mission of the church in the city. With an increasingly older, second-career, part-time, or bivocational student body, both good economic stewardship and sound pedagogical principles call for transcending the clergy model to a "people of God" model of seminary education.[3]

The second factor in the constituency equation is "monoethnic" vs. multiethnic focus. The demographic changes in America, as reported by the U.S. Census Bureau for 1990, are momentous. The census shows that the proportion of whites in the population continues to decline. In the past decade the number of Asian-Americans has more than doubled and the Hispanic population has grown by more than 50 percent. According to Carl Haub, a demographer at the Population Reference Bureau, "cultural diversity probably accelerated more in the 1980s than any other decade." The article in which this quote appeared states that, "Even compared with the period of high immigration early in this century, the 1980s will be seen as a period of remarkable ethnic change in this country."[4]

Our cities are the locus of this ethnic and cultural diversity. Our cities, already inhabited by the "traditional minorities" — African American, Hispanic, Asian, and Native American — are now receiving thousands upon thousands of new immigrants from Haiti, Brazil, the Caribbean, Central and South America, as well as from Asia and the Pacific Islands. The emerging churches in American cities increasingly reflect this reality. In Boston and in other major cities in America, "these immigrant and poor-black churches could dominate organized religion in the city."[5]

The seminary of the future, and the future of all seminaries, lies in how well they respond to this ethnic and cultural mosaic. Seminary-based urban theological education programs must be at the vanguard in providing creative and committed multiethnic and multicultural theological education. Programs must serve this diverse constituency as well as train whites and the traditional constituency to minister *with* and *in* this new reality.

A third constituency factor is gender. Seminaries are becoming more sensitive to the *needs* and *contribution* of women, but there is much room for improvement. In the case of urban theological education programs, the gender issue is paramount. Irrespective of the "ordination question" of women in many denominations, urban ministry in our cities would cease to exist if women were "left out." The role played by women in urban ministry is significant and historic. Be it Catherine Booth in London, Aimee MacPherson, "Mama Leo" or Nellie Yarborough, or your local church missionary, our cities have been greatly impacted by the sacrificial witness and ministry of women. Urban theological education programs must reflect at all levels the inclusion of women on a par with men. Administration, faculty, staff, and curriculum must reflect the gifts of the whole body of Christ. Space must be provided in our programs in which a spirit of "Lifting Voices — Praising Gifts" [6] can reign.

Let me briefly note a final factor in the constituency equation. Our cities reflect diversity at many levels, including religious diversity. As a Christian urban theological education program, it is important to emphasize and encourage an interdenominational presence. The many churches dotting our "barrios" from distinct Christian denominational confessions should find their students welcomed and affirmed in our programs.

Contextualization

Contextualization means many things to many people. The best image and clearest biblical insight into its meaning is the *Incarnation*. It is the "Holy Other" pitching God's tent among us in the person of Jesus Christ (John 1:14; Phil. 2:5-11). To contextualize our urban educational endeavors is to "pitch our tent," meaning the seminary resources — financial, intellectual, or personnel — in the context of urban ministry. It is to express humbly an "urban kenosis," emptying oneself for the service of others. For the seminary, church, or school, this is excellently summarized by Robert Pazmiño as he underscores the significant questions raised about contextualization by the Third Mandate Program of Theological Education Fund:

> What about *missiological contextualization*? Is the seminary or school focusing upon the urgent issues of renewal and reform in the church, and upon the vital issues of human development and justice in its particular situation? (A liberationist perspective would question the notion of reform and renewal in the face of injustice and would instead propose revolution and complete transformation.)
>
> What about *structural contextualization*? Is the church or school seeking to develop a form and structure appropriate to the specific needs of its culture in its peculiar social, economic, and political situation? (A liberationist perspective would require that the form or structure be liberating and transformational at points where the culture is oppressive.)
>
> What about *theological contextualization*? Is the church or seminary seeking to do theology in a way appropriate and authentic to its situation? Does it seek to relate the gospel more directly to urgent issues of ministry and service in the world? Does it move out of its own milieu in its expression of the gospel?
>
> Finally, what about *pedagogical contextualization*? Is the semi-

nary or school seeking to develop theological training that attempts to understand the educational processes as a liberating and creative effort? Does it attempt to overcome the besetting dangers of elitism and authoritarianism in both the method and goals of its program to release the potential of a servant ministry? Is it sensitive to the widespread gap between the academic and the practical?[7]

In a practical sense let me summarize some of the implications of contextualization for a seminary-based urban theological education program.

Contextualization implies that the urban program is *situated*, both administratively and programmatically, in the context of ministry, the inner city. One does not do effective urban ministry at a distance. It also implies a commitment to the Shalom of the City. The city, as context of training and ministry, is looked upon as a positive *locus* of God's redemptive activity. A holistic gospel is presented that emphasizes both evangelism and social justice in the seeking of Shalom of the City (Jer. 29: 7).[8]

Contextualization implies the application of the "homogeneous unit principle" in assuring that the directors, deans, or chief administrators of the urban program be representatives of the constituency served. Urban programs should be led by African-Americans, Hispanics, or others who have the credibility and legitimation of the inner-city churches served. There are a significant number of white directors of urban theological education programs. Given the multiethnic and multicultural reality of our inner cities, it would be wise to engage and develop indigenous leadership.

A significant number of the faculty should be indigenous. An urban program needs a "critical mass" in terms of African-American, Hispanic, and other multiethnic teachers. All efforts should be made to secure competent faculty members representative of the community served. This means that our seminaries must do more than they have done in recruiting and retaining minority faculty. Full faculty status and rank must be the goal of the seminary for its *core* urban faculty. The staff as well as members of advisory boards and other policy committees should also reflect as much as possible the community served.

Liberating forms and structures should be present in the educational delivery system. What this means is that the sociocultural reality and needs of the urban church and constituency informs the appropriate organizational and administrative style and ethos of the urban training program. For example, overly hierarchical organization and administrative structures should be lessened; bureaucratic and other "paper" formalities should be reduced; face-to-face and personal contact should be the norm; times of classes should reflect the times the constituency has at its disposal (evenings, late afternoons, weekends). Many church leaders and students must work (during the day) to support their families, in addition to their church ministries. And, when possible, it is wise to decentralize the operations of urban training programs; class locations can be distributed in existing church and parachurch facilities throughout the city. This is not only good stewardship of finances and facilities, but also permits the urban training program an opportunity "to impact more than one specific community, preferring instead to be 'salt and light' to the entire city."[9]

More will be said regarding theological and pedagogical contextualization when we address the other elements.

Curriculum

To speak about curriculum is to speak about *all* the factors in a school or program that contribute to the fulfilling of the objectives of theological education. Good theological education, urban or in general, focuses on the following triple objectives:

• To *form* pastors and teachers (and other leaders) among the people of God;

• To *inform* them about the scripture, tradition, reason, and experience in social, cultural, and concrete historical contexts; so that

• They may serve as agents of *transformation* in the churches, denominations, and social communities in which God has placed them.[10]

More specifically, urban theological education should develop an appreciation and understanding of the complexities and pluralities of the city and of the diverse ministries of the urban churches and parachurch organizations. It should also foster theological reflection and the integration of theological studies with the practice of ministry in urban contexts through supervised ministry and coursework while contributing to personal growth, spiritual development, and vocational identity.

The individual needs of differing constituencies should be met. Students with urban backgrounds should learn to integrate their experiences and to develop appropriate strategies for ministry. Students from nonurban backgrounds should gain urban experiences that can serve as a basis for learning and developing appropriate strategies. Education that meets the special concerns of racial and ethnic minority students should be provided.

Skills in ministering in a variety of settings in the urban situation — among the poor and disadvantaged, the city's diverse constituencies (Blacks, Hispanics, Asians, Haitians, Portuguese-speaking, and others), working-class groups, professionals and "high-risers" (gentrification), and among the various denominations and faith communities — should be developed.[11]

For urban church leaders already engaged in meaningful ministry, one can add the following: developing greater competence in ministry; developing greater self-understanding (identity) and sense of mission (vocation); developing coherence between explicit theology and implicit practice; and developing leadership potential in the church and the greater society.[12]

Robert Pazmiño reminds us, "Curriculum is the vehicle or medium through which educational vision takes root."[13] If we are to have an impact on our cities and educate competent and compassionate leaders, our curriculum must go beyond the "classical disciplines" to develop action-reflection approaches that are epistemologically sound and socially relevant.

In an action-reflection model of curriculum and teaching methodology, theory does not take the place of practice, nor practice the place of theory. There is a constant dialectic that permits courses to combine "field" experience — the whole city, churches, community, and other institutions — with classroom and library/research activities. A *pedagogical contextualization* is informed by the biblical paradigm of leadership education, an action-reflection approach (i.e., Samuel and the school of the prophets, Christ and the disciples, and Paul at the school of Tyrannus [Acts 19]).

In each of these biblical paradigms there is both action and reflection in the training process. Each phase informs the other, thus enriching the learning experience. We would do well in contemporary Christian educational circles to exhaust, exegetically or otherwise, the meaning and implications of these biblical models before we copy the "world" model of leadership education.

Excellence in an urban theological education program, especially its curriculum, is not defined by the university/seminary "guild" with its heavy emphasis on theoretical content mastery. Rather, excellence will be *contextually defined* by the quality — yes, rigorous demand — of integrating theory and practice in courses within the overall curriculum. Make no mistake, academic or theoretical knowledge (of the classical disciplines) is important. Yet sound educational philosophy and the biblical paradigms challenge us to go beyond to a holistic understanding of learning, leadership education, that gives serious weight to the dialectic of practice.[14]

It is important to note that an action-reflection approach in curriculum design also permits for the development of *theological contextualization*. Theology, as well as the other disciplines, is informed by the context of ministry. "Doing theology" becomes a normative experience for the student in this approach.

Justo González, in referring to several models utilizing the action-reflection approach, makes the following pertinent remarks:

> This is a model which believes that theological education must not only be grounded in the place where a Christian is already ministering, but should also make use of that ministry and that experience as

part of the raw material for theological reflection. While it believes
in academic rigor, it also believes that such rigor is not an end in
itself, but is rather to be placed at the service of education, and that
there are therefore other considerations that are just as important.[15]

Let me briefly note some specific programmatic elements that a sound
urban theological education curriculum should have: (1) curriculum divisions or tracks; (2) courses; (3) mentored ministry/colloquia program; and
(4) other program features.

(1) *Curriculum divisions or tracks* recognize the diversity of the student
body and their educational goals. As noted previously, it is good to have all
students in a class session, thus providing rich interaction and feedback.
Yet many students have distinct goals and many find themselves at different levels of "city experience" and academic accomplishments. Good curriculum design will provide courses and experiences for the "urban novice"
as well as for the mature city leader. Distinct educational achievement
tracks with proper recognition should be established. The curriculum
should provide for certificates, diplomas, or other such recognitions of
completion for those who may be interested in attending one or several
course sessions or series of seminars, as well as a more programmatic and
extended diploma track. By the same token, a more extensive track should
be developed for those interested in a seminary degree — M.A., M.Div.,
M.A. in C.E., and even D. Min. and Ph.D.

Given the reality of many urban church leaders, which includes many
pastors, alternative degree tracks should be developed. Individuals without
a college degree should be given the opportunity to do undergraduate
and/or graduate degree programs. Various creative programs providing
these services already exist.[16]

(2) *Courses* should cohere with the educational mission and objectives
of the urban theological education program. These can range from the basic
"classical traditions" (i.e., Bible, Theology) to more contextual ones (i.e.,
The City in the Bible, Urban Theology and Ministry, Inner City Ministry,
Urban Issues, History and Theology of the African-American Church,
Community Organizing and the Church, Hispanic Theology and Ministry,
Racism and the Church). When possible, a committee composed of students (who may be urban leaders), faculty, and administration should design the year-to-year curriculum. This will not only respond to the changes
and transformation occurring in the city — its churches, its people — but
will protect against "morphological fundamentalism." This term is used to
refer to "the fact that certain forms or structures may take on the character
of being sacred and, therefore, exempt from question or examination."[17]
Ministry in the city, given its oft-changing scenario, requires constant

evaluation and mid-course adjustments. Curriculum, to be relevant and effective, needs to be cognizant of this reality.

In view of the ever-increasing multilingual reality of our inner cities, it is important that urban programs reach out in *distinct languages* to the constituency in context. Given the large Hispanic reality in our cities, the question is not just of servicing them, but of doing so in their own language, Spanish. This can be also said, depending on the ethnic presence in a particular city, of courses taught in French (for Haitians) or Portuguese.

While one can suggest many courses to make up a good urban curriculum (as I noted some above), let me highlight three I think are critical: leadership in ministry; research and writing in urban theological studies; and the church and the community — urban structures and municipal delivery systems. These courses can be taught under whatever name seems proper for the program, but what is important is the emphasis on certain knowledge or competency.

"Leadership in Ministry" responds to the individual student's questions on personal identity and vocation. It deals with the substance and style of the urban church leader, while providing the knowledge and skill to develop other leaders in the students' church or ministry.

"Research and Writing in Urban Theological Studies" is an attempt not only to upgrade students' writing and research skills, but also to teach practical principles for lifelong learning.

"The Church and the Community: Urban Structures and Municipal Delivery Systems" seeks to introduce and develop a knowledge of city institutions and the church's role. It not only provides for development of referral files on specific municipal services, but also should give exposure to and knowledge of the complex city systems. This course provides the opportunity to emphasize the social responsibility of the church and the need to confront the injustices and systemic evil of contemporary society.

(3) *Mentored Ministry/Colloquia Program* acknowledges that classroom learning must be enhanced by an intentional and intense exposure to dialogue, counsel, and serious reflection on the student's personal identity and vocational development. Reflection groups that seek to integrate classroom content, church-ministry experience, and personal spiritual formation are one way of addressing this concern. Several schools and programs have found it necessary to structure a more formal program, variously called colloquia or mentored ministry, that throughout the student's seminary life seeks to be a bridge from classroom learning to the reality of ministry. The credit-bearing nature of these programs is important. It notes that this element of the curriculum is not peripheral but central to solid urban theological education.

(4) *Other program features* acknowledge that sound urban theological

education must creatively seek to respond to emerging needs and opportunities in the city with programmatic elements that may be of short or long duration. The development of church/ministry site for student assignments must be constantly updated and evaluated. Special short-term seminars or courses for particular churches or denominations, as well as seminar forums or guest lecture series, provide the opportunity to bring experts from distinct disciplines. Church-based economic leadership programs can be developed to respond to the pressing needs of the city. Citywide conferences and consultations, involving both local and national leaders, provide the opportunity for addressing specific church and urban issues (i.e., women's ministry, Christian development, urban theology and ministry). These conferences are not only an important source of *information*, but they also serve to *identify* and *inspire* urban leadership.

Community

No seminary-based urban theological education program will succeed without having the "blessing" or credibility of its host community. The leadership of the urban program, as well as its teachers, must be respected and trusted. It is imperative that the seminary establish a good relationship with key leadership of the constituency to be served before the urban program begins. This principle should also reign when introducing new program elements (i.e., new language tracks) to the urban program. As early as possible, urban leaders should be involved at all levels of program development.

While seminary-based urban theological education programs have their own legal boards, all efforts should be made to develop an urban advisory board composed of community leaders. The seminary should seek to have urban leaders represented on the school's legal board. The advisory board can serve in many ways to facilitate communication between the community-neighborhood, the urban theological education program, and the host seminary. Members can also help the urban program by serving on admissions, finance, and curriculum committees.

The sense of ownership of the urban program by the community is enhanced by the advisory board and committee membership of urban leaders. The leadership of the urban education program should not only live in the context of ministry, along with other program staff and teachers, but should also exercise its gifts in the churches and community. Strong community networks should develop between the urban program and the community. The resources of the urban program — facilities, intellect, personnel — should increasingly be placed at the disposal of the community, be it church, parachurch, or community social agency.

Ownership of the program by the community is a slow and sensitive process; no one formula will achieve it. Yet, the overall ethos of "servant-leadership" practice by the urban program leaders, staff, and teachers will go a long way. The "whole" of the elements discussed here (i.e., constituency, contextualization, curriculum, etc.), as a *Gestalt*, provides that vehicle which makes for the community having a sense of ownership.

It is important that a newsletter/bulletin be developed by the urban theological education program. It will provide an opportunity for better communication of urban educational events, as well as for communicating student-churches activities to the whole community.

The urban program should develop good relationships with other urban programs in the community. These other programs might include non-ATS (Association of Theological Schools in the U.S.A. and Canada) schools servicing Hispanic, African-American, or other constituencies in the city. Opportunities should be explored to interface, dialogue, or enter into joint projects with these schools, given the reality of their ministry in the same context, often the same constituency, and of course serving the same Lord. In many cases, these non-ATS schools can be "feeders" to the urban theological education program for students desiring further education. The urban program can often be, as the case in Boston (CUME), the advanced training ground for many Bible Institute teachers and directors.

The circle of "community relations" should be enlarged by the urban theological education program to include other national urban programs. Biblical stewardship and practical realities call for a sharing of educational, as well as resource (funding) leveraging "technologies and skills" among urban theological educational institutions.

Coexistence with Host Seminary

The distinct structures and interfacing/relationship patterns, roles, styles that develop between the host seminary and the urban theological education program are critical to the success of urban ministry. While there may be different organizational/structural ties (models) expressed as program, center, or campus, certain *guidelines* can be noted that apply across all of these and that are important for successful and faithful urban theological education ministry.

• Seminary involvement in urban theological education ministry must be clearly understood by all as part and parcel of the seminary's *mission* statement. The urban program is not peripheral to the life and mission of the seminary, but is a central part of its mission. Neither demographics, financial need, the "in-thing," nor expediency motivates involvement, but a clear call to service.

• Seminary involvement in urban theological education should be long range. Urban programs should not be viewed or planned as a three- or five-year pilot project. One does not "experiment" with urban ministry; rather, after prayerful (and yes, study as well) discernment, the seminary moves, as the Lord leads, into partnership with the urban church.

• Seminary involvement in urban theological education means a serious commitment and stewardship of resources — financial, intellectual, personnel, etc. It is important, though, that the urban church demonstrate its partnership by increasingly sharing its limited resources (2 Cor. 8: 2-5).

• The seminary's appointment of the *director* of the urban theological education program is one of the most critical elements toward the success of the urban program. Much prayer and dialogue with the urban church leadership should take place before such an appointment.

The director's academic credentials should be on a par with the parent seminary's requirements for faculty/administrator. Given the nature of seminary life, it is important that the director have full faculty status and rank and that he/she be perceived as a "peer" by the rest of the faculty. The director must also have credibility with the urban church constituency. As noted above, preferably that person will be an ethnic urban leader.

Among the qualifications the director needs is the ability to allow his/her colleagues to work as partners, enabling a strong sense of mutual ownership to develop. He/she must be able to evoke trust from among a widely diverse group of persons in terms of ethnicity, denominational, and theological backgrounds; be versatile, able to feel at home and function comfortably in a wide variety of religious communities; take authority lightly and yet know where the buck stops; be concerned for the personal growth and nurture of all staff members; and be stimulated by living on the frontier of theological education, willing to run the risk of new ventures, and able to respond to new options and ideas.[18]

• The seminary must not *marginalize* the urban theological education program by keeping it at a distance from the normal calendar of activities. In other words, without compromising its urban integrity, the urban program will be *institutionalized* as much as possible to the host seminary through the following:

The director, as part of the faculty, will serve the host seminary, *as time permits*, on committees, speak in chapel, and fulfill other functions that encourage his or her full acceptance by faculty, administration, staff, and students.

The seminary will provide space and promote urban chapel services, seminars, urban guest speakers, and other functions that "in-house" the urban vision to the whole seminary community. The seminary will also provide office space for the urban program on its campus. This will provide visibility for the program as well as a practical location for interact with campus students and faculty.

The seminary will keep its "community-at-large" (trustees, administration, faculty, staff, students, alumni, donors, friends) informed through normal communication channels of the "events" of the urban program. From time to time special communications highlighting the urban program will be made.

The seminary will treat the urban theological education program budget as a central piece of the overall school budget, not just a peripheral project (more will be said in the next section on cost).

The seminary will *encourage* qualified faculty to teach in the urban program; this will fulfill part of the normal teaching load for faculty. There will be an effort to monitor other seminary teaching programs (i.e., Continuing Ed.) so that they do not compete with faculty serving the urban program.

The seminary, by word and deed, will encourage all its departments and units to be open and disposed to provide services to the urban program.

The director of the urban theological education program should be a member of the president's "administrative council" or a similar high-level seminary-wide administrative committee.

• The urban program, and by implication the director, should be under the supervision of the seminary's academic vice-president or dean. Given the nature and complexity of the urban scene and the need for sensitive and timely handling of many issues, it is critical that organizationally the urban program be "housed" at the highest rung of authority. It should not be subsumed under second- or third-level authority structures (i.e., director of continued education or extension education, associate dean, etc.)

• The seminary's academic dean and urban program director will schedule systematic meetings throughout the academic year. Communication lines should be open and flexible. The staff meeting minutes of the urban program should be sent to the academic dean, as well as to other pertinent seminary administrators or committees. A semester progress report and a final academic year report by the director should be submitted to the dean of the seminary.

• The president, academic dean, and other key administrators of the seminary need to make their presence felt in the urban program. Besides attending graduation functions and other special events in the city, it would be good if during the year official meetings would be scheduled with the urban director and staff on site.

• The seminary's trustees should not only be kept informed of the urban theological education program through normal communication channels, but every effort should be made by the president to "bring them down" to the city. This is very important, particularly for those trustees not familiar with urban life. A two- or three-year plan should be instituted that will see to it that *all* trustees have an opportunity to visit the city — participating in the urban theological education program at one level or another.

• The seminary will welcome and encourage the urban program's advisory board, urban church leaders, and students to visit and participate in seminary functions and events.

Cost

A sure indication of a seminary's commitment to urban ministry is *financial* investment. Long-range urban theological education programs can be costly. It is imperative that the seminary be financially committed for the long haul. The urban budget should be a central part of the host seminary's overall budget allocations. All means should be explored to place the urban ministry budget on a solid financial base — it should not be supported by "soft moneys." Endowments, long-range foundational support commitments, and trustee prioritization should be sought.

At the beginning of the urban theological education program, the seminary should demonstrate its financial commitment by presenting a three- to five-year funding program. This financial plan will show the seminary's obligation to fund the urban program at a level that does not *depend* on "outside" funding sources for it to get off the ground and succeed. Relative to the seminary, this "dependency factor" from outside sources — urban churches, foundation giving, etc. — can range up to 50 percent of total cost. Subsequent years a scale-down of seminary investment in urban program can be planned. This is contingent on a serious financial development program instituted for the urban program that will see increased revenues. As part of the urban program, a development officer or portfolio (director's job description, perhaps?) should be in place. Whether responsibility lies with the director, another staff member, or other seminary official, the funding officer should work closely with urban program staff in all facets of proposal and/or funding program development.

A word about personnel salaries is perhaps appropriate here. If we want excellence in our urban theological education program, we must "pay" excellent salaries. Often salaries of urban program staff are so meager that "turnover" is frequent. Retention requires a just salary scale, one that reflects the professional qualifications of staff and the real expenses of city living.

In view of the socioeconomic status of the inner-city churches, it must be understood that they will not be able to carry the major financial burden of urban theological education programs. As previously noted, though, all means must be explored for the constituency served to exercise their biblical stewardship by supporting the urban program (2 Cor. 8: 2-5). Besides tuition and fees, other cost recovery and financial development projects can be developed by the urban churches. Among the activities that can be included are: a special Urban Theological Education Day at each of the school's participating urban churches; a special banquet for scholarship and programmatic support; inclusion of urban theological education program in urban churches' list of *missionary* giving; from time to time a special request letter for gifts by the churches; a special committee of "friends" of the urban program that includes community-wide representation of business persons and others committed to giving and developing financial support for the program; and the development by urban program students, with support of staff if possible, of "creative entrepreneurship projects" — from school T-shirts and buttons to gospel music concerts, etc.

The seminary must earnestly seek a *true partnership* with the urban churches, foundations, and the Lord's people everywhere in developing sound fiscal responsibility for its urban theological education program.

Concluding Remarks

As we approach the twenty-first century, the challenges of urban living and ministry will increase exponentially. The church of the Lord Jesus Christ must prepare a leadership *willing* and *able* to confront the challenge.

The conditions of our cities, the call of our Lord, and the commitment of the Lord's people all point to a greater challenge for urban theological education programs to contribute to the Shalom of the City. This challenge is a challenge to excellence and faithfulness, one that needs biblical wisdom and Spirit guidance.

> Seek the Peace of the City . . .
> Pray unto the Lord for it:
> For in the Peace thereof shall
> Ye have Peace
> — Jeremiah 29: 7

Notes

1. Roger G. Bentworth, *Social Ethics: An Examination of American Moral Traditions* (Louisville: W/JK Press, 1990), 107-137; see also "Toward the First Universal Nation," *The Boston Globe* (16 March 1991), p. 22.

2. See J. John Palen, *The Urban World*, 3rd ed. (New York: McGraw-Hill, 1987); Clarence N. Stone, Robert K. Whelan, and William J. Murin, *Urban Policy and Politics in a Bureaucratic Age*, 2nd ed. (Englewood Cliffs: Prentice-Hall, 1986).

3. Edward Farley, *Theologia* (Philadelphia: Fortress Press, 1983).

4. Barbara Vobejda, "Board Growth Is Found in U.S. Hispanic, Asian Population," *The Boston Globe* (11 March 1991), p. 4.

5. Maureen Dezell, "The Third Coming," *The Boston Phoenix* (22-28 June 1990), p. 6.

6. March 1990 and March 1991 Center for Urban Ministerial Education (CUME) Women's Conference theme.

7. Robert W. Pazmiño, *Foundational Issues in Christian Education: An Introduction in Evangelical Perspective* (Grand Rapids: Baker House, 1988), 158-59.

8. Eldin Villafañe, "The Jeremiah Paradigm for the City," *Christianity and Crisis*, 52 (16 November 1992).

9. Bruce Jackson, "The Center for Urban Ministerial Education (CUME): Impact on Boston," unpublished report, Boston, 1990.

10. "New Alternatives for Theological Education," *Fraternidad Teológica Latinoamericana*, Quito, Ecuador, 1985, mimeographed, p. 9.

11. "Purpose Subcommittee Report: Theological Education in and for an Urban Global Village," unpublished report in The Center for Urban Ministerial Education: Evaluation and Long-Range Planning Project, Boston, 1987.

12. Ibid.

13. Robert Pazmiño, *op. cit.*, p. 207.

14. See among others, Donald Schön, *The Reflective Practioner: How Professionals Think in Action* (New York: Basic Books, 1983); Don S. Browning, *A Fundamental Practical Theology* (Minneapolis: Fortress Press, 1991); and Paulo Freire, *The Pedagogy of the Oppressed* (New York: Seabury Press, 1970).

15. Justo L. González, *The Theological Education of Hispanics* (New York: The Fund for Theological Education, 1988), 102.

16. For distinct and creative models see those provided by New York Theological Seminary, the Center for Urban Theological Studies, Fuller Theological Seminary, and Gordon-Conwell Theological Seminary's Center for Urban Ministerial Education (CUME).

17. Robert Pazmiño, *op. cit.*, p. 216.

18. George and Helen Webber, *The Center for Urban Ministerial Education — An Evaluation 1986-87: Contextualized Urban Theological Education* (Boston: Gordon-Conwell Theological Seminary, 1987).

8

The Global Challenge

Kwok Pui-lan

In the summer of 1992, Professor Derrick Bell, the first African-American professor tenured at Harvard University, was dismissed from his position as Weld Professor of Law for refusing to end his two-year leave of protest against the absence of tenured minority women on the Harvard Law School faculty. About the same time, I arrived at Cambridge to begin teaching in one of the member schools of the Boston Theological Institute. As one of the few women of color teaching among some two hundred full-time faculty in the Boston Theological Institute, I think Professor Bell's protest has significant implications for our discussion of competing paradigms for theological education.

Professor Bell's protest has raised many issues, such as the diversity of faculty, the control of the hiring processes, the standards of academic excellence, the competing "regimes of truth," the foundations of knowledge, the responsibilities of intellectuals to their communities, and the definition and structure of professional education. These crucial issues are relevant not only to the legal profession, but also to theological education. A number of theologians have expressed similar concerns.[1] For example, Fumitaka Matsuoka poignantly describes the crisis of theological institutions as follows:

> The relatively homogeneous makeup of our institutions — ethnically, culturally, and its gender and class makeup, particularly of their faculty and administration — makes it very difficult to find an opportunity for the emergence of a counterparadigm to go beyond

Kwok Pui-lan is Associate Professor of Theology at Episcopal Divinity School.

the impasse. Homogeneity breeds intellectual and political myopia, and perpetuates an existing educational and symbolic ordering of the dominant culture.[2]

In the past decade, the nature, purpose, structure, and pedagogy of theological education have been under serious scrutiny by theological educators such as Edward Farley, Barbara G. Wheeler, Joseph C. Hough, Jr., John B. Cobb, Jr., Charles M. Wood, Elisabeth Schüssler Fiorenza, and Rebecca S. Chopp.[3] Their books and articles on theological education have fundamentally challenged the established paradigm of "what and how are we learning." As we begin to search for new paradigms, I would like to offer my contribution as an Asian woman who has been active in the ecumenical movement and who is a member of the Ecumenical Association of Third World Theologians. I think theological education in the 1990s should take into consideration three important challenges: (1) the faces at the bottom of the well; (2) the religious sensibilities of the marginalized; and (3) the feminist model of knowing and learning.

1. The Challenge of the Faces at the Bottom of the Well

Derrick Bell, in his most recent book, *Faces at the Bottom of the Well*, admonishes us to "listen carefully to those who have been most subordinated."[4] The challenge to theological education is whether it can deepen our commitment to listen to the marginalized and the oppressed, to search for alternative orderings of the world, and to envision a common future so that all God's children can flourish.

Any discussion of theological education in the 1990s must take into account the rapid transformation of the world in the past several years: the Tiananmen massacre, the crumbling of the Berlin Wall, the crisis of Eastern European socialism, the defeat of the Sandinista government, the Gulf War, the disintegration of the Soviet Union, and the end of the Cold War era. These breathtaking sociopolitical changes have prompted divergent theological analyses of complex world situations. For some, these recent happenings mean we are living in an era of the collapse of socialism and the end of history. The final triumph of capitalism would ensure that Pax Americana will soon be realized on the earth and the liberation theologies of the Third World would be a thing of the past.

Meeting in Nairobi in January 1992, participants of the third assembly of the Ecumenical Association of Third World Theologians devoted much time to discerning the signs of the time, the present moment in world history. Its final statement says:

The disappearance of cold war and the break-up of the socialist system in Europe have left us in a situation where world politics tends to be under the increasing control of a single power maintained by aggressive militarism targeted primarily at the Third World. In the new military and political configurations the poor in the Third World are expendable. It is this reality that compels us to believe that the emerging new world order is antipeople and antilife. Meeting in 1992, the year that marks the 500th anniversary of the colonial conquest, we are painfully aware that the tentacles of power are still colonial in one form or another.[5]

For theologians in the Third World, the widespread poverty and oppression that prompted the development of liberation theology have not gone away, but are likely to worsen in the years to come. The 1990s will be a time of realignment of world powers according to their geoeconomic interests. The globalization of market economy controlled by the financial institutions of the powerful countries will mean a "new world order" dictated by the market logic without either accountability to the democratic process or significant participation of people of all races and classes.

The great majority of the people of the southern hemisphere would become even more marginalized in these restructuring processes. With the development of new technology and industries, the First World will be less and less dependent on the raw materials and labor provided by the Third World. The huge foreign debt accumulated in the past decade results in the increasing control of the economies of developing countries. While the poor will become poorer, women and children will suffer most. Describing the dire world situation, Latin American theologian Pablo Richard writes: "The great majority of the South is in total abandonment. It can no longer be called dependent, but is simply nonexistent. We have moved from dependency to dispensability; today being dependent even seems to be a privilege."[6]

From a global perspective, today's poor do not exist only in the southern hemisphere, but in the rich countries of the northern hemisphere as well. At the present moment, the economy in the United States is facing tremendous difficulties for many reasons: the huge federal deficit, the loss of technological competitiveness and productivity, the deterioration of public infrastructures, the heavy burden of military expense, and the emergence of competing regional markets. We see similar patterns of abandonment of the weak and the poor especially in the inner cities, the permanence of racism and sexism, and the perpetuation of the under class. The struggles of the poor and oppressed in the United States are tied to the struggles of people around the globe because similar power dynamics are at work here as elsewhere.

The globalization of the world market challenges us to reflect on the meaning and relevance of the globalization of theological education in the North American context. On the one hand, the observation Don S. Browning made some years ago is even truer today: "The context of theological education can no longer be simply the local congregation, the local community, a particular region, state, or nation. The context of theological education must be the entire world, the entire global village that influences our lives in multitudes of direct and indirect ways."[7] On the other hand, globalization must go further than the four meanings Browning suggested: evangelization of the world, ecumenical cooperation, interfaith dialogue, and mission of the church in solidarity with the poor and oppressed.

First, globalization in the 1990s must shift from an ecclesiocentric paradigm to a people-centered paradigm. The crisis of the 1990s is not just a crisis for people of faith, but a crisis for the whole of humanity, a crisis of civilization. Korean *minjung* theologian Kim Yong Bock argues that the traditional understanding of the mission of the church is too limiting because "the typical church was too tied to the ecclesial concern of church order and confessional formula to be an incarnating community in the life of the people."[8] Instead Kim emphasizes the notion of the mission of God, which provides a wider orientation and a theological basis for ecumenical involvement among the peoples. This people-centered understanding of globalization challenges us to think about theological education in radically new ways. Christopher Duraisingh, convener of the Unit on Education, Mission and Witness of the World Council of Churches, envisages theological education to be "an invitation and an initiation of persons into a life process of visioning, with passion, the *missio Dei* in concrete historical struggles of people. It is a process of faith reflection upon the context and developing a lifestyle of being partners with God in personal and social transformation."[9]

Second, globalization means the collective search for new alternatives for the ordering of the world. Since the so-called "collapse of socialism," theologians in the Third World have engaged in the critical reexamination of the relationship between faith and ideology, and in the creative process of rethinking their faith in the new historical reality.[10] Pablo Richard writes: "With the crisis of Marxism, there has been an effort to repress our theoretical capacity, to close the theoretical space necessary to resist and continue struggling, to destroy the possibility of formulating alternatives and at the same time crush our hope."[11] At the third assembly at Nairobi, Third World theologians committed themselves to the search for new alternatives for society and affirmed several fundamental principles: the participation of women and men in the decision-making process at all levels, sustainable economic growths that meet human needs without exploitation of persons and nature, space for ethnic and cultural identity and spiritual development, and an international relationship of mutuality and solidarity.[12] The challenge for theological institutions in North America is whether collaborative efforts can be developed so that we can participate meaningfully in the common search for an alternative ordering of the world.

Third, globalization challenges us to envision new forms of communities in which there will be inclusivity, mutuality, and solidarity. Theological educators have articulated different images and visions of such a community. For Rebecca S. Chopp, such a community would respect differences, welcome heterogeneous discourses, and encourage the marginalized "others" to speak. Chopp calls upon the church to model such community in and for the world. For her, theological education would serve the church and world "by preparing persons to live in and signify to the world the possibility of such community."[13] According to John S. Pobee, doing theology with a global consciousness implies a process of building a community of communities. While each community should have its own identity and integrity, a vision of a community of communities enables us to work together to form the fully constituted body of Christ.[14] If theological institutions do not model and practice a new form of community, they will not have credibility when speaking to the world.

2. The Challenge of the Religious Sensibilities of the Marginalized

Since the seventh assembly of the World Council of Churches held in Canberra in 1991, the worldwide church has continued to discuss the controversial keynote address by Professor Chung Hyun Kyung of Korea. Accompanied by music, slides, dance, drums, and rituals, Professor Chung employed religious symbols and cultural concepts from her Korean culture to address the assembly theme "Come Holy Spirit, Renew the Whole Creation."[15] Her provocative presentation raised the questions of interreligious dialogue, religious pluralism, inclusiveness, and the discernment of the limits of diversity, issues that theological educators in North America have often discussed.

In the ecumenical discussion following the Canberra assembly, the issue of the relationship between the Christian gospel and culture is brought to the forefront. This is not just an issue that concerns the younger churches, but the church as a whole. In the past, the process of inculturation, indigenization, and contextualization of the gospel has often been discussed in a *missiological* context. The question has been how to "translate" the gospel into the cultural settings historically not shaped by the biblical faith. But since the Canberra assembly, the discussion assumes a more *theological* nature with implications for contextual theology, hermeneutics, biblical exegesis, and mutual communication in the ecumenical movement. The question has become how can different theologies, each seeking to incarnate in the life situation of particular peoples and communities, continue to challenge each other without breaking ecumenical fellowship.[16]

The debate has gone beyond the usual parameters of interfaith dialogue wherein people of different faith traditions meet and dialogue with one another. Living in a multireligious world, many Asian theologians have argued that they embody the different traditions of shamanism, Buddhism, Hinduism, Confucianism, and Christianity simultaneously.[17] If they do not want to compartmentalize their various identities and heritages, they have to bring them to bear in their theological reflection. The presentation of Professor Chung highlights the complexities of articulating theology from such a context, which can be more adequately called an intrafaith dialogue. In her book *Struggle to Be the Sun Again*, Chung has urged her colleagues to "move away from the doctrinal purity of Christian theology and risk *the survival-liberation centered syncretism.*"[18]

It is also noteworthy that the discussion among the theologians in the Third World has focused not so much on syncretism, but on the cultural and religious expression of the oppressed. In response to Professor Chung's presentation, K. C. Abraham of India has said:

> The important debate of our times is not between capitalism and socialism (both are found to be oppressive and destructive), but between an alternative vision of life in the marginal cultures and the oppressive systems of technological society . . . in the present situation, where the dominant culture is oppressive and dehumanizing, we need to take seriously the cultural sensibilities of the marginalized. This is the most timely emphasis of Chung's presentation, and we need to pay heed to it.[19]

In the past several years, theologians in the Third World have seriously reexamined the religiocultural dynamics inherent in struggles for liberation. The theme of the African continental theological conference in 1991 was "Culture, Religion and Liberation." African theologians gathered to discuss how African culture and religion have been used as instruments of domination or as resources of resistance. Women theologians seriously critiqued African patriarchal rituals and religious practices.[20] At the same time, theologians have examined how their indigenous religious traditions offer new ways of looking at the world and anthropology, and some theologians such as Simon S. Maimela of South Africa have begun to discern the salvific role of African traditional religions.[21]

Similarly in Latin America, theologians who in the past have focused more on socioeconomic analysis and political-military liberation have paid more attention to cultural struggles in the ethical and spiritual arenas. The crisis of Marxism has challenged them to find new concepts based on the experiences and languages of marginalized peoples to interpret their new historical situation. There is an emphasis on the understanding of popular religiosity of the masses, women's culture and movements, and the holistic and ecological dimensions of the spirituality of indigenous people.[22]

The current ecumenical discussion challenges us to think about the implications for theological education in North America. First, a theological curriculum that does not include an appreciation of different religious ways of being in the world does not prepare students to live in a religiously pluralistic world. Moreover, it ill-equips students to understand and participate in the current ecumenical discussion. Paul F. Knitter is insightful when he suggests that:

> Theology can no longer do its job mono-religiously. If it is going to perform its task effectively of preparing Christians to continue interpreting and reconstructing Christian belief and praxis, it will have to do so multireligiously; that is, through a close relationship with other traditions and other believers.[23]

This would mean that courses on the study of religion and on other religious traditions should feature more significantly in theological curricula. Furthermore, the focus of these courses should not be just on the high culture or literate culture of various religious traditions, but also on the popular experiences of the masses.

Second, the ways that interfaith dialogue is being conducted in the academy and in the religious hierarchies should be reexamined. It is not enough to provide opportunities for dialogue among the scholars, who are usually male educated elites, leaving out the majority of the women in the different traditions. In Asia, there is an ongoing project to facilitate interfaith consultation of Asian women representing the traditions of shamanism, Buddhism, Confucianism, Hinduism, Islam, and Christianity.[24] In Africa, women theologians critically reappropriate their ancient customs and rituals.[25] Dialogue among women living in the different religious cultures provides a new lens to look at various traditions from the perspective of the marginalized. Moreover, it raises methodological questions about the neutrality and responsibility of religious scholarship because dialogue among women often goes beyond the academic exercise of seeking to understand the identifying points of solidarity in the common struggle to transform oppressive situations.

Third, the ecumenical debate also challenges us to pay more attention to the complex cultural and religious dynamics in our study of the Bible and Christian tradition. The biblical tradition emerged from multicultural, multireligious, and multiracial contexts. The historical encounter between people of different cultures, the politics of racial relations, and the hidden voices of women in the biblical account must be made more explicit in our critical analysis. Similarly, the religious and cultural assumptions of theological formulations in the Christian tradition need to be carefully examined. The Western paradigm of doing theology should not be transposed to other parts of the world as if it is normative.

3. The Challenge of the Feminist Model of Knowing and Learning

The broader understanding of globalization and the ecumenical discussion on gospel and culture requires us to reexamine the praxis of theological education. The challenge to do theology in a global context and to listen to radical theological voices from the Third World calls into question our Eurocentric assumptions of knowledge and learning. I find the feminist model of knowing and learning a helpful guide to look at some of the problems of our theological institutions.

Feminists believe that the knower is shaped by his or her own environment and cultural context. There is no objective and value-free scholarship not colored by our own presuppositions and biases. Feminists have unmasked and debunked the bias of white, male, middle-class elites when they claim their viewpoints as objective and universal. They have also pointed out how scholarship of the dominant ruling group has rendered invisible the experiences of women, the poor, and all "others," and have questioned the androcentric canon of knowledge and reappropriated the texts.

In theological education, a large part of the curriculum has been the study of the lives and thought of white, male, Euro-American theologians, to the exclusion of many other voices.[26] More importantly, the theologies done by these people are considered normative, which set the standards and parameters of what "theology" should be. Commenting on this lopsided situation, Mercy Amba Oduyoye writes:

There was a time when the only acceptable adjective to append to the word *theology* was the word *German*. In those days before the

turbulent 1960s, Asian theology, black theology, water-buffalo theology, and so on, did not exist as recognizable bodies of distinctive
Christian thought. Indeed, they could not have existed, for "Christian" theology was considered an all-inclusive entity.[27]

The problem today is that these different theologies do exist, but the
theological curriculum of many schools is so biased or outdated that it
does not take serious consideration of these theologies. Some theologians
actively resist curricular changes that would incorporate feminist and multicultural paradigms.

By recognizing the limitation of one's own horizon, feminists urge us
to pay attention to the question of *with whom* one is learning. Our own
limitations and blind spots will be more easily pointed out by someone
with a different social and historical location. The voices of women of
color are particularly important. Because they are living under multiple
jeopardy, they have developed multiple consciousness, which enables
them to see the linkage of different forms of oppression.[28] African American theorist Patricia Hill Collins characterizes the standpoint of black
women as the "outsider-within," because they are forced to live within a
society defined by the dominant white culture, and yet they exist as out-
siders. This "outsider-within" position creates a new angle of vision to
look at both the white and black community.[29]

Two books on feminism and theological education, *Your Daughters
Shall Prophesy* and *God's Fierce Whimsy*, written by two women's
groups, both emphasize the significance of learning across racial and cultural lines.[30] The Mud Flower Collective emphatically states:

Insofar as anyone, or any group, theologizes solely on the basis of its
own experiences of reality — and takes no care to listen to anyone
else — its theology ought to lack credibility. We who are white have
been guilty at times of this approach. We are well advised by our
racial/ethnic sisters to open our lives and theologies to serious engagement with the lives and theologies of our racial/ethnic sisters.[31]

The Cornwall Collective, likewise, emphasizes the importance of race-
consciousness in the structure, power dynamics and decision-making in
theological education.[32]

Since feminists believe that each person participates in the construction
of knowledge, the politics of learning and acquiring knowledge must be
addressed. Feminists criticize the "banking" model because it is a "trickle-
down" pedagogy that assumes the teacher has all the knowledge to be
given to the students. Instead, feminist scholars emphasize the contribu-

tion of students and their sharing of perspectives. Feminist pedagogy, as Elisabeth Schüssler Fiorenza says, "seeks to support and strengthen democratic modes of reasoning by recognizing the importance of experience, plural voices, emotions, and values in education." [33]

Theological education, therefore, should be a process of *mutual empowerment*. In critical feminist thought, power is not a property *possessed* by somebody to be given or handed down to someone else. Rather, power is *exercised* in specific context and empowerment means the exercise of power in an attempt to help others exercise power.[34] The process of mutual empowerment leads to the production of new knowledge: knowledge about oneself, about others and about the world we live in. The Cornwall Collective describes the process of empowerment in this eloquent way:

> To be empowered is to experience the value of oneself, to take the self seriously in the totality of one's reality — body, mind, history, vision, and dreams. To be empowered is to feel oneself expanding, getting in touch with one's own needs and goals, developing powers of decision, acquiring new skills, becoming able to do things formerly feared or viewed as impossible.[35]

Finally, feminist scholars debunk the myth of dispassionate investigation and propose a more holistic learning process of integrating the intellect with emotion, knowing with feeling. In her classical study of the scientific discovery of Barbara McClintock, Evelyn Fox Keller shows how McClintock's feeling and empathy for individual kernels of corn led her to account for these differences.[36] In other situations, women experiencing their powerful emotions of resentment, anger, and outrage are often led to new insights and perspectives. Alison M. Jaggar has discussed how "our emotional responses to the world change as we conceptualize it differently and how our changing emotional responses then stimulate us to new insights."[37]

In theological education, a disinterested, "objective," and dispassionate study of God and other people's theology has often led to inaction because it fails to stir our souls and touch our emotion. Instead of "objectivity," feminist scholars have used the term "intersubjectivity" to describe the interacting relationship between the knower and the known. The study of theology should entail entering into others' experiences of God and trying to feel with others their passion for God. In this way, doing theology in a global context will increase our capacity for compassion, understanding, empathy, and acceptance, and deepen our commitment for action and solidarity.

I would like to conclude by quoting from Derrick Bell. When asked what it is that gives him courage and vision, he said:

I and other minority teachers are encouraged, even inspired in our scholarly pioneering by the Old Testament's reminder that neither the challenge we face nor its difficulty are new. Indeed, no fewer than three psalms begin by urging "O sing unto the Lord a new song"; as does Isaiah, who admonishes: "Sing to the Lord a new song, his praise from the end of the earth!" [38]

Notes

1. Rebecca S. Chopp, "Situating the Structure: Prophetic Feminism and Theological Education," in *Shifting Boundaries: Contextual Approaches to the Structure of Theological Education*, ed. Barbara G. Wheeler and Edward Farley (Louisville: W/JK Press, 1991), 71; and Robert M. Franklin's contribution to "Political Correctness, the Reformed Tradition, and Pluralism: Implications for Theological Education," *Theological Education* 29:2 (Spring 1992): 83.

2. Fumitaka Matsuoka, "Pluralism at Home: Globalization within North America," *Theological Education* 26 Supplement (Spring 1990): 37.

3. Edward Farley, *Theologia: The Fragmentation and Unity of Theological Education* (Philadelphia: Fortress, 1983); Barbara G. Wheeler and Edward Farley, eds., *Shifting Boundaries*; Joseph C. Hough, Jr., and John B. Cobb, Jr., *Christian Identity and Theological Education* (Chico, CA: Scholars Press, 1985); Charles M. Wood, *Vision and Discernment* (Atlanta: Scholars, 1985); articles by Elisabeth Schüssler Fiorenza and Rebecca S. Chopp can be found in Don S. Browning, David Polk, and Ian S. Evison, eds., *The Education of the Practical Theologian* (Atlanta: Scholars, 1989).

4. Derrick Bell, *Faces at the Bottom of the Well: The Permanence of Racism* (New York: Basic Books, 1992), 198.

5. "A Cry for Life: The Spirituality of the Third World. A Statement from the Third General Assembly of the Ecumenical Association of Third World Theologians, January 5-16, 1992, Nairobi, Africa," *Voices of the Third World* 15:1 (June 1992): 112.

6. Pablo Richard, "Liberation Theology Today: Crisis or Challenge?" *Envío* 11:133 (August 1992): 26.

7. Don S. Browning, "Globalization and the Task of Theological Education in North America," *Theological Education* 23:1 (Autumn 1986): 44.

8. Kim Yong-Bock, "The Mission of God in the Context of the Suffering and Struggling Peoples of Asia," in *Peoples of Asia, Peoples of God: A Report of the Asia Mission Conference, 1989*, ed. Christian Conference of Asia (Osaka: Christian Conference of Asia, 1990), 7.

9. Christopher Duraisingh, "Ministerial Formation for Mission: Implications for Theological Education," *International Review of Mission* 81:321 (January 1992): 42.

10. See for example Marta Benavides, "Spirituality for the Twenty-First Century: Women, Mission, and the 'New World Order,'" *International Review of Mission* 81:322 (April 1992): 213-26; Julio de Santa Ana, "Spirit of Truth — Set Us Free," *The Ecumenical Review* 43:3 (July 1991): 364-71; and Leonardo Boff, "The Poor as the Center of a Possible World Politics," in *Third World Theologies in Dialogue: Essays*

in Memory of D. S. Amalorpavadass, ed. J. Russell Chandran (Bangalore: Ecumenical Association of Third World Theologians, 1991), 120-31.

11. Richard, "Liberation Theology Today," 26.

12. See the statement from the third assembly at Nairobi.

13. Rebecca S. Chopp, "Emerging Issues and Theological Education," *Theological Education* 26:2 (Spring 1990): 118.

14. John S. Pobee's lecture on "Doing Theology in a Global Context," on 29 September 1992 at the Episcopal Divinity School, Cambridge, MA.

15. Chung Hyun Kyung, "Come Holy Spirit — Renew the Whole Creation," in *Signs of the Spirit: Official Report, Seventh Assembly*, ed. Michael Kinnamon (Geneva: WCC, 1991), 37-47.

16. See Konrad Raiser, "Beyond Tradition and Context: In Search of an Ecumenical Framework of Hermeneutics," *International Review of Missions* 80:319-320 (July/October 1991): 340.

17. See Virginia Fabella, Peter K. H. Lee, and David Kwang-sun Suk, eds., *Asian Christian Spirituality: Reclaiming Traditions* (Maryknoll: Orbis, 1990), 113.

18. Chung Hyun Kyung, *Struggle to Be the Sun Again: Introducing Asian Women's Theology* (Maryknoll: Orbis, 1990), 113.

19. K. C. Abraham, "Syncretism Is Not the Issue: A Response to Professor Chung Hyun Kyung," *International Review of Missions* 80:319-20 (July/October 1991): 340.

20. Anna Nasimiyu-Wasike, "Liberation of Coopted and Oppressive Culture and Religion," in *Culture, Religion and Liberation: Africa Continental Conferences 6-11 January 1991* (Harare, Zimbabwe: EATWOT African Offices, 1991), 127-39.

21. Simon S. Maimela, "A Christian Encounter with African Traditional Religions," in *Third World Theologies in Dialogue*, 170-85.

22. Richard, "Liberation Theology Today," 28; Sergio Torres González, "The Inculturation of the Gospel in the Latin American Continent," in *Third World Theologies in Dialogue*, 19-28.

23. Paul F. Knitter, "Beyond a Mono-religious Theological Education," in *Shifting Boundaries*, 171.

24. The first interfaith consultation took place in Malaysia in 1989. See Dulcie Abraham, Sun Ai Lee Park, and Yvonne Dahlin, eds., *Faith Renewed: A Report on the First Asian Women's Consultation on Interfaith Dialogue* (Hong Kong: Asian Women's Resource Center for Culture and Theology, n.d.). The second consultation was held in Sri Lanka in 1991.

25. See Mercy Amba Oduyoye and Musimbi R. A. Kanyoro, eds., *The Will to Arise: Women, Tradition, and the Church in Africa* (Maryknoll: Orbis, 1992).

26. See Mark K. Taylor, "Celebrating Difference, Resisting Domination: The Need for Synchronic Strategies in Theological Education," in *Shifting Boundaries*, 265-68.

27. Mercy Amba Oduyoye, *Hearing and Knowing: Theological Reflections on Christianity in Africa* (Maryknoll: Orbis, 1986): 1.

28. Deborah King, "Multiple Jeopardy, Multiple Consciousness: The Content of a Black Feminist Ideology," *Signs* 14:1 (1988): 42-72.

29. Patricia Hill Collins, *Black Feminist Thought: Knowledge, Consciousness, and the Politics of Empowerment* (London: HarperCollins Academic, 1990), 11.

30. The Cornwall Collective, *Your Daughters Shall Prophesy: Feminist Alternatives in Theological Education* (New York: Pilgrim Press, 1980); and The Mud Flower

Collective, *God's Fierce Whimsy: Christian Feminism and Theological Education* (New York: Pilgrim Press, 1985).

31. The Mud Flower Collective, *God's Fierce Whimsy*, 25-26.

32. The Cornwall Collective, *Your Daughters Shall Prophesy*, 38-48.

33. Elisabeth Schüssler Fiorenza, *But She Said: Feminist Practices of Biblical Interpretation* (Boston: Beacon, 1992), 191.

34. Jennifer Gore, "What We Can Do for You! What *Can* 'We' Do for 'You'? Struggling over Empowerment in Critical and Feminist Pedagogy," in *Feminisms and Critical Pedagogy*, ed. Carmen Like and Jennifer Gore (New York: Routledge, 1992), 54-73.

35. The Cornwall Collective, *Your Daughters Shall Prophesy*, 80.

36. Evelyn Fox Keller, *A Feeling for the Organism: The Life and Work of Barbara McClintock* (New York: Freeman, 1983).

37. Alison M. Jaggar, "Love and Knowledge: Emotion in Feminist Epistemology," in *Gender/Body/Knowledge: Feminist Reconstructions of Being and Knowing*, ed. Alison M. Jaggar and Susan R. Bordo (New Brunswick: Rutgers University Press, 1989), 164.

38. Bell, *Faces at the Bottom of the Well*, 145-46.

9

The Classical Challenge

Robert Cummings Neville

I

Robert Bellah neatly framed the question for theological education in the opening chapter by asking "how to understand the Church in an individualistic society." He then answered his question by analyzing, criticizing, and appropriating parts of three contemporary approaches to ecclesiology: Enlightenment individualism (Habermas), immanent critique (Taylor), and a pure Christian culture of resident aliens (Hauerwas). The most striking element of his judicious analysis, however, is that his own approach is ecclesiological. He deals with Habermas, Taylor, and Hauerwas from within the interest structures of the Christian movement, and hence takes up a posture of defense.

Paradoxically, a more general *theological* approach is both more neutral with regard to theological education and more particularistic in supporting the culture-building aspects of Christian discipline than Bellah's ecclesiological stance. By theology, of course, I mean something broader than what Bellah means, or than is meant by most of my colleagues in this book. Theology has, I shall argue, three different, related, and equally necessary genres. One is church theology —theology in, by, and for a religious tradition or community. This is what most of my colleagues mean and it is the most important kind for theological education where that means training leaders for the church. The other two genres, equal in

Robert Cummings Neville is Dean and Professor of Philosophy, Religion, and Theology at Boston University School of Theology.

dignity and necessity, are philosophical theology and comparative theology.[1] I shall begin with the last two and return to church theology.

Philosophical theology is the philosophical examination of the meaning and truth of theological assumptions and claims, and the attempt to solve certain intellectual problems related to these. By "theological" I mean the study of God and divine matters and, in religions and cultures that do not employ the Western theistic idea of God or a close analogue, those assumptions and claims that exclude or substitute for "God and divine matters." Thus philosophical theology would deal not only with the positive assertions of theism but with their negations, as for instance in the writings of Sartre; where Buddhism and Hinduism have altogether too many gods to be serious theisms, philosophical theology would deal with questions of unconditionedness, emptiness, the Buddha-nature, the One, Brahman, and so forth; where enlightenment secularism would reject all "transcendent" theological references, philosophical theology would examine the grounds for and validity of that denial. In addition, there are fundamental issues — such as the problem of the one and the many, being, nothingness, time, immortality, finite-infinite relations, and eternity — long associated with the divine, that can be approached by philosophical theology in at least some of their dimensions. The nature of theological thinking in all its genres is also a topic of philosophical theology.

Philosophical theology is wholly public discourse into which anyone can enter irrespective of initial theological position or confessional commitment. Its purpose is to ascertain the truth in divine matters and also the helpfulness of certain terms that might be used in other genres of theological reflection. Philosophical theology, invented by Plato or his immediate predecessors, has a rich history in the West as practiced by Jewish, Christian, and Muslim theologians.

Comparative theology recognizes the fact that religious terms, even abstract metaphysical ones, arise within particular traditions. With the sophistication of hermeneutics in our time, it has become apparent that philosophical theology has often too glibly assumed similarities or contradictions across religious traditions. Precisely because of the historical character of all thinking, the explicit problematizing of comparative questions is extremely important.

Yet our practice of comparative theology is not half so sophisticated as our understanding of hermeneutics. There is a vast need for detailed comparative studies, both empirical and dialectical. What deceits lurk in that list of "alternatives to God" above: unconditionedness, emptiness, Buddha-nature, One, Brahman? We simply do not know, and comparative theology has a great contemporary urgency because philosophical theology depends on comparative theological sophistication. What can a Western philosophical theologian's response be when an East Asian Mahayana Buddhist says "the proofs for God are blinded by (the limited) assumptions of theistic cultures"? Philosophical theology is impossible in a serious way until comparative theology creates a common language for discourse and the uncovering of assumptions. But then, comparative theology was impossible until philosophical theology in its hermeneutical work made some progress on the nature of comparison.

Church theology is reflection on divine matters with the aim of appropriating the historical life of a faith community for the present time by recovering, understanding, and perhaps reconstructing the scriptures, liturgies, songs, symbols, and practices of the tradition, including previous theologies. Without being committed to the specifics of Tillich's "method of correlation," its dual focus is present in any church theology. On the one hand, the church theology must recover the tradition and its revelations; on the other hand it must present these as viable for a contemporary way of life, understanding the times. For this, church theology needs both philosophical theology and comparative theology, the former to be able to assert theological claims as true, the latter to know what difference they make relative to alternatives.

Although many scholars of religion now believe that philosophical and comparative genres of theology can be pursued without church theologies, that belief is dubious. Comparative theology is hermeneutically blunted if it does not get on the inside of the church theologies being compared. Philosophical theologies too now recognize that they do not begin from a neutral starting point but from some theological assumptions and practices embodied in language and the formulation of problems. Each genre of theology needs the others if it is to do its own work.

Another way of looking at Habermas, Taylor, and Hauerwas is to see them as practicing one of the three genres of theology respectively. Habermas is the philosophical theologian, indeed a transcendental philosophical theologian carrying out the project of Kant's theology. Taylor is not a practicing comparativist but approaches the theological topics from the liberal expansive dialectic that is acutely conscious of historical limitations; his critiques are not only immanent but they require examination of religions from the outside as well as inside. Hauerwas is a church theologian thinking apologetically for the Christian community in a hostile world. Not much is to be inferred from this quick comparison. But I suspect that each thinker would be far more public to the others if he were to engage explicitly in the genre of theology in which the others are centered. Given his particular philosophical theology (enlightenment transcendentalism), Habermas is likely to be closed to church theology. Given his particular purist, narrative, and conservative church theology, Hauerwas is likely to be closed to philosophical theology. Taylor has the most mediating approach of the three but is so close to his roots in analytic philosophy as to be uncomfortable with the speculative side of philosophical theology and unenthusiastic about the concrete life of church theology.

Where does this leave us with regard to theological education? Theological education in the senses discussed in this volume means the training of church leaders. Surely theological education ought to include church theology of the Christian sort, and also philosophical and comparative theology for the reasons just given. But the more important point is that we can see theological education in the sense discussed here as part of the life of the Christian community.

The Boston Theological Institute is an extremely interesting part of the Christian movement, uniting several Christian traditions that have had reason to be disunited in the past. We share theological resources in libraries, faculties, and students. We in the Boston Theological Institute need to befriend and come to know persons in religious communities outside the Christian movement; but we do not need to confuse our theological education with what would be theological education for them. We need to relate to our secular neighbors, indeed to the secular dimensions of ourselves, but not accommodate to them in our theological education except where that would contribute to the reflective cultivation of leadership in the Christian life. Rather, we in the Boston Theological Institute should attend to the classical contours of Christian theological education and make them relevant to the missions of the church in our time. The next section attempts to spell out some of these classical contours for one large context of theological education.

II

Theological education takes place in many settings, not all of them institutional. The free church tradition abounds in pastors who are successful by many standards with little or no formal education. The Holy Spirit works in many ways. Among the educational institutions for "learned ministry," as the Methodists call it, there are many variations, several of which are represented in the Boston Theological Institute: university-based religion departments, university-based denominational seminaries, university-based nondenominational seminaries, free-standing denominational seminaries, free-standing nondenominational seminaries, and free-standing interdenominational seminaries representing two or more churches. Denominations themselves differ in the people and areas they represent. Seminaries also differ in geographical location, location in cities, suburbs, or rural areas, in size, in wealth, and in means of securing wealth such as through endowment, denominational support, local-church support, tuition, gifts, and grants.

These and other variations legitimately affect what theological education should mean in our time for different institutions. It would be foolish for any theological school to attempt to be everything for everyone. The position I shall develop here is aimed to be appropriate for an American seminary with a worldwide constituency, as biased toward the strengths and needs of a university-based denominational seminary such as the Boston University School of Theology.

The first principle that guides this conception of theological education is that the purpose of an educated ministry is to guide the extension of Jesus' ministry from Galilee in his time across the earth down to our time in the various places in which we can minister. At the heart of Jesus' ministry is the proclamation by word and deed of God's love, mercy, and quickening Spirit, with the consequence that our salvation comes from God and that we are therefore free and obligated to work for the reconstruction of the original covenant between God and creation in those parts of our neighborhood we might affect. Included in the obligations of the covenant are the pursuits of justice, health, well-being, beauty, and respect for nature — all undertaken in thanks for salvation without any expectation that our success or failure is ultimately important: salvation itself comes from God.

A relatively small band of disciples of Jesus through history, Christians tailor their ministry to the needs of their time and place, nurturing both those of their own number who find their salvation to be worked out in Christian service and also those of other flocks. Christians are the leaven in the vaster loaf of the world and need make no claim that everyone has to become yeast.

The first condition guiding this conception of theological education is that in point of fact ours is one of the greatest times of the growth of Christianity in history. Hardly apparent in New England, the growth is taking place in those areas of the world not much affected by the institutions of Christendom. Although in some places this growth might be fueled by mercenary ambitions, overall it has focused and galvanized a sense of the spirit of the gospel. Our students from Africa and Asia come asking what implications Christianity might have for their societies, not how to sustain tired Christian institutions. They come from families where Christ has brought the sword separating parents from children. We need to touch, feed, and grow from the spirit of Christ that again produces martyrs at the same time that we bring our international students to sophistication, and then to supersophistication so that they can again be simple for their people.

The second condition for contemporary theological education is that by and large the spiritual center has collapsed or become enfeebled in those forms of Christianity which have embraced Enlightenment learning and modernization. This spiritual impoverishment has attempted to disguise itself by renewed commitment to several natural and necessary outgrowths of the Christian gospel, especially the devotion to social justice, to psychotherapy, and to the arts. Commitment to these pursuits is indeed a natural and necessary consequence of embracing the salvation of God. No contemporary theological education can neglect them, especially because they have developed new instruments of effectiveness in our time. But they are in fact the realms of politics, clinical psychology, and the arts and can be pursued with integrity without any religious connection at all. In fact, the disciplines appropriate to them are different professional developments from those provided easily in theological education. Because they are so necessary to religious practice, they are easily confused with spiritual reality itself and can deflect attention from the essential and central matters of theological education having to do with the proclamation of God's salvation and the direction of life to personal and social holiness. Furthermore, by appearing to be the heart of ministry, they attract into the profession persons concerned more with aesthetics than religion, with healing their own psychological wounds, and with expressing the political anger of the oppressed or the guilts of the accused. These people often have extra hurdles to overcome in order to address the central elements of theological education, as if the understanding of the gospel were not hard enough.

A consequence of these two conditions is that one of the major orienting tasks of theological education today is the expression of the spiritual power of the gospel now in terms that address the intellectual rigors of the modern world. The greatest challenge to theological education in America, I believe, is intellectual: to express the gospel with its spiritual power in terms of the best science, art, philosophy, and critical reflection of our time. Several objections, however, can be raised to this point.

First, it can be objected that the gospel already has its final form and does not need reexpression. On the contrary, the gospel has been in translation since the beginning, starting with St. Paul's attempt to say what the life of Jesus the Galilean meant for the Hellenistic world. Not to address the suppositions of our own time, those suppositions most critical and vulnerable to correction, is simply to fail to preach.

Second, it can be objected that the intellectual focus is too academic and that seminaries should focus more on service. On the contrary, seminaries are academies, places of learning where informed, disciplined, and self-critical thought are concentrated. Churches look to seminaries for learning. Other institutions in the church are focused on more specific forms of service. The service of theological education is to provide educated Christians.

Third, it can be objected that an intellectual focus is merely the agenda of the First World, the elite society whose Christianity has become effete; the flight to intellect, it can be objected with irony, is just like the flight to justice, psychotherapy, or the arts. On the contrary, although perhaps only the First World seminaries have leisure for the intellectual work now, modernization and Enlightenment learning are coming to all portions of the globe. The great Christian missions in Africa, Asia, and Latin America will quickly turn out to be nothing but more Western economic imperialism if we do not discover effective ways to express the center of the gospel in terms that hold their own with contemporary science, philosophy, and the critical arts. The best in all cultures, not merely that of the West, needs to be addressed. If we do discover an expression of the gospel that leads rather then follows contemporary intellectual life, then the new Christian communities can remain Christian after they have become part of the modern world.

Fourth, it can be objected that the intellectual focus in seminaries settles too easily for the outlook of the modern world to which Christianity is supposed to bring prophetic witness. On the contrary, Christianity can only bring the gospel in true Spirit to the modern world when it understands and works through and around contemporary categories. The gospel grows in expression when it must confront, think through, and criticize a new dimension of experience or culture it has not encountered before. That is as true for a Christian critique of contemporary situations across the globe as it was for St. Paul's commentary on life in Corinth.

III

In consequence of these considerations, I recommend theological education of the following sort for the M.Div. degree. For trinitarian simplicity, there are three grids of three factors. The first grid expresses the motive of including three dimensions in each course in the curriculum: the historical, systematic, and evangelical dimensions.

The historical dimension reflects the fact that each topic studied in a course should be treated according to its place in the historical evolution of Christianity from the first century (or from its Hebrew roots) down to the present time. This dimension is expressed most naturally in explicitly historical courses; but it can also be expressed in other topics such as philosophy, theology, ethics, pastoral care and counseling, liturgy, preaching, and religious education. The purpose of honoring this dimension universally is to guarantee that all students understand how their ministry is continuous with, perhaps critical of, and a fulfillment of the central mission of the church of Jesus Christ in its contemporary local setting.

The systematic dimension has to do with how the topic under study relates to the overall practice of ministry. Most obvious in systematic theology courses, which should provide the motifs and themes of systematic integration, every topic whose inclusion in the curriculum is justified has a connection to ministry as a whole. System in this large sense also includes a systematic integration of how we should approach all the various periods and parts of Christian history, for better or worse.

The evangelical dimension has to do with how the gospel is confronting some culture, part of culture, or aspect of experience that it has not confronted before, learning the vocabulary of the new realm and determining creatively how the gospel is to address that realm. Included in the evangelical dimension today are feminist and liberationist concerns, the concerns of indigenization, and the concerns of dialogue among world religions. Some of these topics have been addressed in other chapters of this book. In every course, it should be possible to show how the topic is on the growing edge of the gospel, adding to the gospel's culture while providing a Christian orientation in the new realm.

The three dimensions need each other. Without the evangelical dimension, the historical dimension becomes antiquarian; without the systematic dimension it loses its normative thrust. Without the historical dimension, the systematic dimension becomes a captive of the language of its time; without the evangelical dimension it loses in relevance and power. Without the historical dimension, the evangelical dimension defines itself in terms of the self-perception of its new realm of discourse and loses the normative Christian edge; without the systematic dimension, the evangelical becomes captive to party interests. Together they check and balance one another.

In the study of liberation theologies, seminaries must be careful not to overstep the legitimate contributions of academic thinking by prescribing to those theologies on the basis of theory; even liberationist theories become ideological and mischievous too quickly when applied to situations that need to develop their own intrinsic understanding. The contributions of the academy to liberation theology are mainly Christian historical thinking, systematic theology, and cultural analysis, as well as leisure to think of these in connection with the situation to be liberated.

The second trio of considerations is topical. Theological students need a series of courses in the tradition, beginning with the Bible and including the developments of the tradition in all parts of the world. They need a second series of courses in philosophy, theology, and ethics. A third necessary series of courses is required in the arts of church life, including preaching, worship and liturgy, Christian education, church administration, and pastoral care and counseling. The topics speak for themselves. The courses should be in series so that they build upon one another, with only the first courses being of an introductory nature. Theological students, for matters of self-respect as well as real competence, need to know they have mastered a subject matter at the graduate level. The mastery should be of such a degree that students can continue lifelong learning on their own.

The third trio of considerations consists of aspects of professional formation; they include spiritual development, pastoral training, and involvement in mission. Personal spiritual formation and development does not lend itself to the medium of courses because the only relevant Grader is to be approached eschatologically. But seminaries need to provide a variety of experiences of spiritual direction, of small support groups concerned with spiritual formation, and of personal and corporate worship in order to initiate and reinforce habits of spiritual growth sufficient to sustain a person through the vicissitudes of ministry.

Along with this, students need to be introduced to the actual practice of ministry. Field education is the most common vehicle for this. Its limitations must be realized: one cannot learn what it is like to be a pastor in charge until the responsibility is upon oneself. But no newly installed pastor ought to discover funerals, house calls, or church finances for the first time.

Finally, students need the opportunity to relate their growing ministerial education to the world the church serves. To this end, it is important for seminaries to have close relations with churches and mission projects in the neighborhood. A program of congregational life, for instance, can provide opportunities for students to participate in the congregations' mission to the world and also for the members of the congregation to make use of the intellectual and other facilities of the seminary. For all the importance of its intellectual life, the seminary is obligated to help students think for the mission of the church.

In sum, theological education ought to be the institution for thinking well, with a pure commitment to truth, about the matters pertaining to salvation and holiness, both personal and corporate. It should be the mind of the church as the extension of the ministry of Jesus, especially insofar as this is strengthened by the learning of the academy.

IV

The context in which I have tried to put this "classical" challenge to theological education is the full publicity of theology. Theology aims to be true, however fallible we know its hypotheses to be. Theology aims to catch and give appreciable expressions to the deepest revelations, however clumsy and historically particular we know its language to be. Therefore no ground whatsoever exists for a particular faith's theologians to draw back from critical dialogue and say, simply, "this is what we believe." "This is what we believe" is a sociological statement about a group, not a theological claim about the truth of divine matters. The reflective needs of practicing religious communities do not rest with sociology but press the question of truth, to which theology must answer.

Religious communities have long argued what in Christianity is called the position of "faith seeking understanding." The apologetic bite of this is that only those practicing members of the community deep in the faith can begin to understand the important religious issues. In India this position is associated with yoga: only after years of discipline and moral life can one gain the experience necessary to recognize truths that are ubiquitous but opaque to the unready. Under the impact of hermeneutics in our own time the buzz word has become "participant observation." Surely the degree to which one must be committed and schooled in the "cult" of Jesus Christ is itself a matter of theological discussion. The Christian epigraph "I believe — help my unbelief" guarantees that the degree of faith cannot be 100 percent. The theological quest for truth, on the part of our students and the future leaders of the church, must move through both faith and unfaith.

When liberation theologies become advocacy theologies, they cease to be theologies in the sense of knowing God and the truth about divine matters and become instead sociological expressions of what some people believe and want others to believe. Most Christian liberation theologies are indeed true and powerful moral statements. The church has great need of moral invigoration and leadership. But the validity of liberation theologies depends on and requires continuous dialogue with the critical, vulnerable, open-ended theologies of the church in systematic reflection, of the comparative enterprise, and of philosophy. When liberation theologies assume that only those who already share their assumptions, perspectives, or living experience can hold a valid opinion or make a valid argument, they become ideological programs. The classical challenge to theological education today is to insist that theology make truth claims about God and divine matters and not merely about what some people think or want.

The classical approach to theological education surely cannot mean repeating a curriculum that was good for another era. If conditions have changed significantly, graduates of an old curriculum would be miseducated for our time. But the classical approach does not mean that the texts, songs, symbols, liturgies, and theological ideas that in the past have quickened people with the revealing and transforming Spirit of God need to be reassessed and reconstructed so that the revelation and transformation occur today. Theological education gains nothing by retreating to a socio-logical repristinization of how "we" do and think things. The gain comes from being vulnerable to criticism and learning from it to do better. I salute our students who have the erudition to rest easy in a critical appro-priation of their faith!

Notes

1. These three genres of theology stand in some contrast with the trio made popu-lar by David Tracy in his excellent study, *The Analogical Imagination: Christian Theology and the Culture of Pluralism* (New York: Crossroad, 1981), chapter 1. Closely corresponding to philosophical theology is what he calls fundamental theol-ogy. Closely corresponding to church theology is what he calls systematic theology; church theology also ought to include biblical and liturgical studies as well as the systematic study of doctrine. He distinguishes practical or liberation theologies, the-ologies of advocacy, from his other two, and I would include those within church theology. He does not recognize comparative theology as distinct. In my own work, *A Theology Primer* (Albany: State University of New York Press, 1991) is part of church theology, *Behind the Masks of God* (Albany: State University of New York Press, 1991) is comparative theology, and *God the Creator* (new edition; Albany: State University of New York Press, 1992) is philosophical theology; the introductory material in each of these discusses the distinction.

An Afterword

"Coming to Our Senses"

Robert N. Bellah

The contributions gathered in this volume are impressive, particularly in the various ways that they call upon us to reassess where we are in theological education and consider new directions, particularly with respect to the role of Christianity in civil society. Inevitably anyone who thinks about Christianity and the present state of our world must worry about the tendencies that modernity has unleashed, and the stance that Christians take toward modern society. In my opening talk I took note of what we can learn from the Enlightenment and what in its assumptions we must call in question, pointing out that the Enlightenment has brought valid criticisms to bear on all traditional institutions, including the church, but has proven unable to provide viable substitutes.

As we move into the post-Westphalian world, it is our task to recover and renew what is valid in our faith, not through the denial of criticism, but through and beyond that criticism. One of the few real prophets who can help us with that task today in my opinion is Vaclav Havel, in spite of his ambiguous stance toward religion. Havel, the former president of Czechoslovakia and the present president of the Czech Republic, published in 1991 his *Summer Meditations*, one of the most remarkable testaments that any chief of state has ever left to his nation and world. In it he writes:

> All my observations and all my experience have, with remarkable consistency, convinced me that, if today's planetary civilization has any hope of survival, that hope lies chiefly in what we understand as the human spirit. If we don't wish to destroy ourselves in national, religious, or political discord; if we don't wish to find our world with twice its current population, half of it dying of hunger; if we don't wish to kill ourselves with ballistic missiles armed with atomic

warheads or eliminate ourselves with bacteria specially cultivated
for the purpose; if we don't wish to see some people go desperately
hungry while others throw tons of wheat into the ocean; if we don't
wish to suffocate in the global green house we are heating up for
ourselves or to be burned by radiation leaking through holes we
have made in the ozone; if we don't wish to exhaust the non-renew-
able, mineral resources of this planet, without which we cannot survive; if, in short, we don't wish any of this to happen, then we must
— as humanity, as people, as conscious beings with spirit, mind and
a sense of responsibility — somehow come to our senses.

I once called this coming to our senses an existential revolution. I
meant a kind of general mobilization of human consciousness, of the
human mind and spirit, human responsibility, human reason.[1]

What exactly Havel means by "coming to our senses" or undergoing an
"existential revolution" would require an exegesis of all his writings,
which, even though I have read everything translated in English, I am not
prepared to undertake here. But I want to pursue one of his constant
themes just a bit further. There is in Havel a concern for Being (with a
capital B), as he sometimes puts it "something higher," and as he occa-
sionally but very infrequently puts it "God." He believes that without an
ultimate value and purpose, modern life becomes increasingly destructive.

Havel is very cautious in the way he speaks. I was able to speak to him
briefly at a conference in Prague in the fall of 1991. I asked him if his
moral and spiritual concerns were as central as they had been earlier,
when he was in opposition to the Communist regime, particularly in his
prison writings. He said they were stronger than ever (which is certainly
confirmed by *Summer Meditations*, which he had already written but
which did not appear in English for another year). I then asked him
whether the church could be of help in these concerns. He said yes, but
you must remember the history of the church in this country. And indeed
the history of religion in Bohemia and Moravia since before the Reformation, since the time of Jan Huss in the fifteenth century, has been one of
almost unending persecution.

Havel is a profound critic of the Enlightenment and of many of its
assumptions, although he also in some ways, for example in his admira-
tion for Immanuel Kant, stands within it. By calling us to "come to our
senses" he is asking us to undergo a conversion, to open ourselves to a
religious transformation, to turn away from many of the assumptions of
modern life. Indeed, he feels that without such a conversion, the future is
bleak.

Yet he cannot identify with any of the existing churches, even though he allows himself once in a while to use the name of God. He finds his strength in the Czech tradition of humanistic democracy, the tradition of Tomas Masaryk and Jan Patocka. He locates himself in a strong narrative that gives him solidarity with others past and present. Yet for those of us who are Christians, Havel is both inspiring and chastening, calling us to our better selves and reminding us of how far we have often come short of being what we ought to be. But he is also exemplary of what we need today: voices who can speak to each other respectfully but urgently, calling on strong narratives to help us face the dangers that surround us. Only through that vigorous conversation between and among the cultures that are now inextricably linked in our complex world can we begin to formulate solutions to our problems, the first step toward building a more human and more viable world.

As my final contribution to this symposium I would like to specify some of the things that "coming to our senses" might mean. What Havel is asking, as I interpret him, is no easy thing. What is needed makes more demands on us human beings than in any previous period of history. It is perhaps not too much to say that we stand under the millennial pressure of the approaching year 2000, and that judgment of God is indeed near.

I would like to sum up those demands in terms of three necessary renunciations. I am sure there are many other things we are called to do, but for now I will concentrate on these three.

First, what is required is the renunciation of violence. It has been stated that war between any of the advanced industrial nations today has become unthinkable: the consequences for the whole world would be simply too devastating. Already in the 1930s Walter Lippmann argued that any war between the great powers would be a civil war and that everyone on the planet would suffer from it.[2] I believe history has borne out that argument. But we are fast approaching the time, if we have not already reached it, when the consequences of "small" wars between or within "minor" powers are simply unacceptable. A post-Westphalian world requires the formation of an effective international peace-keeping force that can stop not only aggression between nations but gross violation of civil rights within nations. The movement of the world community in this direction has been uncertain at best, but pressure for such a step continues to build.

We cannot imagine that the demand for the renunciation of violence excludes the United States. We are at the moment the chief arms supplier to the world. President Bush's election campaign offer to sell fighter planes to Saudi Arabia and Taiwan was only the most visible evidence of our massive involvement in arms sales to Third-World nations, the consequences of which have been catastrophic in Africa, the Middle East, and other parts of the world. While we are talking about the renunciation of violence we might consider that we are the only advanced nation in the world that allows junior high school children to own machine guns. As Amitai Etzioni has said, we need domestic disarmament in the United States.

Taking a longer historical view, asking the United States to renounce violence is a rather astounding demand. In 1992, during the commemoration of the five hundredth anniversary of Columbus's arrival in the new world, we were frequently reminded that we took this land by violence from its native inhabitants, a large proportion of whom met their death in the process. We then brought slaves from Africa by violence to work the land. We have, as de Tocqueville warned with respect to democracies, fought our wars with ferocious violence. Those who sat through a whole week of Ken Burn's documentary on the Civil War know how horrible that war was, one of the two most destructive wars of the nineteenth century after the Napoleonic wars, only rivaled by the Taiping rebellion in China. Since I am frequently in Japan, it is often on my mind that we have never apologized for our atrocities in the Second World War. We entered that war condemning the axis powers for the indiscrimning bombing of civilians and then we proceeded to undertake the carpet bombing of Leipzig and Tokyo, and, one of the greatest horrors of the twentieth century, the atomic bombing of Hiroshima and Nagasaki, rivaled only by the actions of Hitler and Stalin. Unfortunately the story does not end there. If there were time I would have to talk about Vietnam, and indeed about the Gulf War. I am not so foolish as to imagine that this nation will easily renounce violence. I am simply saying that that is what is required of us.

The second renunciation is also no easy matter anywhere, and again particularly in the United States, namely, the renunciation of sovereignty. The whole implication of what I have been calling, following Bryan Hehir, the post-Westphalian era requires that we renounce sovereignty in the near absolute sense in which modern nation-states have interpreted it. We have reached the point in the world, as Daniel Bell has put it, where "the nation-state is becoming too small for the big problems of life, and too big for the small problems of life."[3] The big problems will require international arrangements that will curtail sovereignty in major respects. The first step is the recognition that we are no longer a super-power in a world where super-powers are obsolete. We are only one of many "normal nations." Once we recognize that, then we may be ready to face the second and much harder step, the renunciation of sovereignty.

The third renunciation is no easier but also no less necessary than the first two. That is the renunciation of abundance, that dream of the Enlightenment. Material prosperity was to introduce such a benign social atmosphere that moral problems would take care of themselves. We are now